GW00370842

THE SECRET CODE OF CREATION

The power of the word

About the Author

Donald Tyson is a Canadian from Halifax, Nova Scotia. Early in life he was drawn to science by an intense fascination with astronomy, building a telescope by hand when he was eight. He began university seeking a science degree, but became disillusioned with the aridity and futility of a mechanistic view of the universe and shifted his major to English. After graduating with honors he has pursued a writing career.

Now he devotes his life to the attainment of a complete gnosis of the art of magic in theory and practice. His purpose is to formulate an accessible system of personal training composed of East and West, past and present, that will help the individual discover the reason for one's existence and a way to fulfill it.

To Write to the Author

If you would like to contact the author or would like more information about this book, please write to him in care of Llewellyn Worldwide. We cannot guarantee every letter will be answered, but all will be forwarded. Please write to:

Donald Tyson
c/o Llewellyn Worldwide
P.O, Box 64383
Dept. 0-7387-0528-4
St. Paul, MN 55164-0383, U.S.A

Please enclose a self-addressed, stamped envelope for reply or $1.00 to cover costs.
If outside the U.S.A., enclose international postal reply coupon.

THE SECRET CODE OF CREATION

DONALD TYSON

2004
Llewellyn Publications
St. Paul, MN 55164-0383, U.S.A.

The Power of the Word. Copyright © 1995 by Donald Tyson. All rights reserved. Printed in the United States of America. No part of this book may be used or reproduced in any manner whatsoever, including Internet usage, without written permission from Llewellyn Publications except in the case of brief quotations embodied in critical articles and reviews.

FIRST EDITION
Fourth Printing, 2004
(formerly titled *Tetragrammaton*, three printings, 1998)

Cover design by Kevin R. Brown
Cover illustration © John Hunt
Cover background and fire images © Photodisc
Editing, design and layout by David Godwin and Darwin Holmstrom

ISBN: 0-7387-0528-4
(Library of Congress Cataloging in Publication Data under former title)

Library of Congress Cataloging in Publication Data

Tyson, Donald. 1954–
    Tetragrammaton : the secret to evoking angelic powers and the key to the Apocalypse / Donald Tyson. -- 1st ed.
      p.   cm. -- (Llewellyn's high magick series)
    Includes bibliographical references and index.
    ISBN 1–56718–744–7 (pbk.)
    1. Tetragrammaton. 2. Angels. 3. Cabala. 4. Magic. 5. Bible.
N. T. Revelation--Criticism, interpretation, etc. I. Title.
II. Series.
BF1623.T47T87 1995
135' .4--dc20

                                    95–31174
                                        CIP

Llewellyn Publications
A Division of Llewellyn Worldwide, Ltd.
P.O. Box 64383, St. Paul, MN 55164-0383
www.llewellyn.com

Printed in the United States of America.

Other Books by Donald Tyson

The New Magus, 1988
Rune Magic, 1988
The Truth About Ritual Magic, 1989
The Truth About Runes, 1989
How to Make and Use a Magic Mirror, 1990
Ritual Magic, 1991
The Messenger, 1993
New Millennium Magic, 1996
 Extensively revised and updated version of *The New Magus*
The Tortuous Serpent (fiction), 1997
Enochian Magic for Beginners, 1997
Scrying for Beginners, 1997
Sexual Alchemy, 2000
The Magician's Workbook, 2001
Familiar Spirits, 2004

Editor and Annotator

Three Books of Occult Philosophy
 Written by Henry Cornelius Agrippa of Nettesheim, 1993

Cards and Kits

Rune Magic Deck, 1988
Power of the Runes Kit, 1989
Rune Dice Divination Kit, 1997

Acknowledgments

The author wishes to express sincere thanks to the following authors and publishers for permission to quote from these works:

The Bahir. Translated by Aryeh Kaplan. Copyright © 1979 by Aryeh Kaplan. Reprinted by permission of Samuel Weiser, Inc.

The Hieroglyphic Monad by John Dee. Translated by J. W. Hamilton-Jones. Copyright © 1975 by Samuel Weiser, Inc. Reprinted by permission of Samuel Weiser, Inc.

The Tree of Life by Israel Regardie. Copyright © 1969 by Samuel Weiser, Inc. Reprinted by permission of Samuel Weiser, Inc.

The Ladder of Lights by William G. Gray. Copyright © 1968 by Samuel Weiser, Inc. Reprinted by permission of Samuel Weiser, Inc.

The Kabbalah by Gershom Scholem. Copyright © 1974 by Keter Publishing House Jerusalem Ltd. Reprinted by permission of Keter Publishing House.

Ritual Magic by E. M. Butler. Reprinted by permission of Cambridge University Press.

The Book of Tokens: Tarot Meditations by Paul Foster Case. Copyright © 1934 by Paul Foster Case; Copyright © 1960, 1968, 1989 by Builders of the Adytum. Reprinted by permission of Builders of the Adytum, Ltd.

The Tarot: A Key to the Wisdom of the Ages by Paul Foster Case. Copyright © 1947 by Paul Foster Case; copyright renewed 1975; Copyright © 1990 by Builders of the Adytum. Reprinted by permission of Builders of the Adytum, Ltd.

Grateful acknowledgment is made to Builders of the Adytum, Ltd., 5101–05 North Figueroa St., Los Angeles, California, 90024, for permission to use excerpts from *The Book of Tokens* and *The Tarot*. The permission granted for the use of its materials by Builders of the Adytum, Ltd. in no way endorses anyone's interpretation thereof.

Contents

Introduction xiii

CHAPTER I
History of the Name 1

CHAPTER II
Traditional Meanings 7

CHAPTER III
Correspondences 13

CHAPTER IV
Understanding the Name 19

CHAPTER V
Invoking the Name 31

CHAPTER VI
Vibrating the Name 37

CHAPTER VII
Pentagrammaton 47

CHAPTER VIII
The Hieroglyphic Monad 55

CHAPTER IX
The Twelve Stones 67

CHAPTER X
The Breastplate of Aaron 77

CHAPTER XI
The Ring of Solomon 87

CHAPTER XII
Banner Rings 97

CHAPTER XIII
Empowering the Rings 105

CHAPTER XIV
Form and Function of the Wings 119

CHAPTER XV
Assuming the Christ-Form 147

CHAPTER XVI
The Watchtowers and the Keys 163

APPENDIX A
    The Keys 189
        First Key 190
        Second Key 191
        Third Key 193
        Fourth Key 197
        Fifth Key 199
        Sixth Key 201
        Seventh Key 202
        Eighth Key 204
        Ninth Key 207
        Tenth Key 211
        Eleventh Key 216
        Twelfth Key 218
        Thirteenth Key 219
        Fourteenth Key 221
        Fifteenth Key 225
        Sixteenth Key 227
        Seventeenth Key 228
        Eighteenth Key 229
        Key of the Thirty Aethers 230

APPENDIX B
    Commentaries on Tetragrammaton 239

APPENDIX C
    The Hours of the Wings 257

APPENDIX D
    The Stones on the Breastplate 259

APPENDIX E
    Table of the Banners 261

APPENDIX F
    The Banners According to Agrippa 265

APPENDIX G
    The Twelve Apostles 267

APPENDIX H
    Numerical Breakdown of the Banners 269

APPENDIX I
    Table of the Hebrew Alphabet 273

APPENDIX J
    Table of the Enochian Alphabet 275

GENERAL INDEX 277

INTRODUCTION

Of all the words of power employed in magic since the dawn of time, none is more mysterious and profound than the Ineffable Name of God with four Hebrew letters, IHVH (יהוה), called by the Greeks Tetragrammaton. By uttering it, God created the world and breathed life into the first man. Moses called upon its authority to bring down the ten plagues on Egypt. Solomon used it to compel the spirits of the earth to build the first temple at Jerusalem, then turned it upon them and sealed them beneath the sea in a prison of brass. Prophets and exorcists used its fabled might to restore the dead to life, to rule storms and calm the seas, to turn back the course of the sun, and to drive demons out of those possessed.

So revered was the Name by the ancient Jewish priests that they forbade anyone to speak it. After the fall of Herod's Temple to the Romans in A.D. 70, its true pronunciation was lost to the general Jewish population, but esoteric sects and solitary magicians continued to rely upon its potency as the foundation of all their works. In the Middle Ages, *Ba'alai Shem*, or Masters of the Name, employed Tetragrammaton to heal the sick and banish evil spirits.

One such *Ba'al Shem* was the great Jewish magician Rabbi Loew of Prague, who breathed life into lifeless clay by means of the power of the IHVH and with it created the dreaded Golem. During the Renaissance,

Johannes Reuchlin and other Christian kabbalists transformed Tetragrammaton into the esoteric fivefold Name of Jesus and proclaimed it the key to all the mysteries. Alchemists employed it prominently in their emblems, as did visionary mystics such as Robert Fludd and Jacob Boehme.

Almost all the great figures in occultism over the past two centuries have recorded observations and speculations about the Name. The nineteenth-century French magician Gerard Encausse, better known by his pen name Papus, devoted most of his influential work, *The Tarot of the Bohemians,* to unraveling its secrets. His countryman Alphonse Louis Constant, who wrote under the name Eliphas Levi, spent entire chapters of his popular books on magic wrestling with the meaning of Tetragrammaton. The speculations of these and many other occult writers have been collected together for the first time in Appendix B. It is fascinating to compare the words of Levi with those of Papus; of S.L. MacGregor Mathers, the leader of the Golden Dawn, with those of Aleister Crowley, his former student and the self-proclaimed Great Beast of the Apocalypse; of Helena P. Blavatsky, the leader of the Theosophists, with Paul Foster Case, the founder of Builders of the Adytum; of P.D. Ouspensky, the disillusioned former pupil of the mystic Gurdjieff, with Frater Achad, a rebellious student of Crowley.

Even in modern times, Tetragrammaton continues to exert a powerful fascination over magicians working in the Western tradition of ceremonial magic. Contemporary kabbalists and occultists discover in the arrangement of the four letters of the Ineffable Name the essential pattern of the entire universe. The many magical correspondences of its Hebrew letters with the elements, the tarot, the magical instruments, the compass points, the winds, the *sephiroth* of the kabbalah, the planets and the signs of the zodiac, are examined in detail in Chapter III, where the vital role of Tetragrammaton at the very heart of the Western magical tradition is established beyond dispute.

Yet this book gives more than just the fascinating ancient history and modern magical use of the Name. It examines the symbolic relationship of the letters from a numerical and a graphic perspective. The significance of the dual threefold and fourfold composition of the Name, which is so vital to its true understanding, is treated in depth. From this analysis, a bridge is constructed linking the four elements, the seven planets, and the twelve signs of the zodiac. Tetragrammaton is shown to be the primeval binary code that forms the basis for the genetic pattern of DNA and the language of modern computers and digital storage systems. It is also the foundation for two ancient methods of divination—the sixty-four hexagrams of the I Ching of China and the sixteen geomantic figures of medieval Europe.

Presented here is a totally original technique for invoking and banishing
the Banners of the Name (twenty-four forms, twelve overt and twelve occult,
that result from the permutation of the four letters), with a new symbol that
I have christened the tetragram. It is used in much the same way as the
pentagram is employed in ceremonial magic for invoking and banishing the
four elements. This technique will prove of immense value to occultists, both
in their ritual work and as a mnemonic for the forms and associations of the
Banners. As I will demonstrate, it also provides a graphic explanation of the
underlying relationship between the Banners and the zodiac signs.

The fivefold names of Jesus, IHShVH and IHVShH, which were created
by the Christian kabbalists of the Renaissance to supplant IHVH, are examined in both a theoretical and practical way, and their vital role in *The
Hieroglyphic Monad* of John Dee is revealed. Clues provided by Dee in his
Monad and in his Enochian Keys lead to the extraction, by traditional kabbalistic methods, of a previously unsuspected order of twenty-four angels,
which I have named the Wings of the Wind, from the biblical book of the
Revelation of St. John the Divine. These angels will be of extreme interest
to kabbalists and Enochian magicians alike. Not only are they of great practical value in ritual magic, but they support the theory of an underlying connection between Dee's hieroglyphic monad, his Enochian diaries, and the
biblical book of Revelation.

In addition to all this, methods are provided for vibrating upon the
breath the twenty-four Banners of Tetragrammaton; for using a new technique called the commanding voice to implant instructions directly into the
subconscious of others, bypassing their conscious control; for creating a set
of powerful Banner rings and ritually charging them with the Wings of the
Winds; for resurrecting the lost ancient Hebrew divination by Urim and
Thummim; and for assuming the god-form of the warrior Christ of Revelation to command the Enochian and Banner angels.

The complex structure of Tetragrammaton and its various permutations
is expressed by two very important symbolic forms: the throne of God,
described by St. John in Revelation 4; and the cosmic clock, which appears
throughout the Enochian diaries of John Dee, but particularly in the third
and fourteenth Enochian Keys. As I will demonstrate in this work, it is possible to prove that the throne and the cosmic clock are at root the same symbol, both designed to express the structure and parts of IHVH. The throne of
God and the cosmic clock illustrate the strong link that exists between the
vision of St. John, Dee's *Hieroglyphic Monad*, and the Enochian diaries, and
unlock many of the secrets in these works. Because the throne and clock are
so important in understanding Tetragrammaton, I have examined the system of Enochian magic in considerable detail in Chapter XVI.

Appendix A contains the corrected English text of all eighteen Enochian Keys and the Key of the Thirty Aethers, with an accompanying analysis of the symbolism in the Keys. This study shows the angels of the Keys to possess the same apocalyptic nature as those described by St. John the Divine in his biblical book of Revelation.

I have put forward the theory, which will undoubtedly arouse controversy, that the Watchtowers and Enochian Keys are parts of a great ritual of ceremonial magic designed to trigger the chaotic final destruction of our universe. In my opinion it was the desire, perhaps the necessity, of the Enochian angels that this destruction of the world be initiated by humanity itself through the instrument of the forty-eight Keys, which open the protective guardian gates of the four Watchtowers and allow the entry into our time-space of the forces of Coronzon, the great dragon.

The gates of the Watchtowers cannot be forced open from the outside. They open inward. We must ourselves unlock them with the Keys and initiate our own annihilation. This is the terrible legacy of human free will—we are free to choose our own destruction. It was to set the stage for this potential apocalypse (which will not happen unless we make it happen) that the angels gave the patterns of the Watchtowers and the Keys to Dee, who never grasped their true purpose during his lifetime.

Many of the occult correspondences found in this book differ from those in the widely used Golden Dawn system of magic. Although I have a high respect for the magical ability and knowledge of the founders of the Hermetic Order of the Golden Dawn, it is time modern occultists recognized that they were not infallible. They worked from a limited number of flawed sources, and sometimes they made mistakes. Rather than slavishly follow the rules laid down by them nearly a century ago, I have preferred to analyze my sources independently, and where I disagree with the Golden Dawn, I have not hesitated to make changes in the occult correspondences. These departures from the Golden Dawn system have been pointed out to avoid confusion.

Much of the work I am doing is completely new, and I sometimes make mistakes myself. In my book *The New Magus**, where I presented the correct order of the twelve Banners of Tetragrammaton for the first time, I applied each elemental trine of Banners to its corresponding elemental trine of signs counterclockwise around the zodiac, in the order cardinal, fixed, mutable, because this is the usual order of the signs and I saw no reason to depart from it. However, in developing the invoking and banishing sigils of the Banners presented in the present work, I became aware that each elemental trine of Banners should have been applied to its elemental trine of signs *clockwise,* in the order cardinal, mutable, fixed.

This important change is necessitated by the inherent, underlying graphic structure of the Banners, which was only revealed when I applied

---

*New Millennium Magic, an updated and expanded version of *The New Magus*, will be available in May 1996 from Llewellyn Worldwide, Ltd.

the Banners to the tetragram in the course of generating the Banner sigils. Since I had not developed the sigils when I wrote *The New Magus,* I was unable to take advantage of this new information, which is completely set forth in Chapter V.

This book offers the most complete treatment of the Name, both in theory and practice, that has ever been presented. The sections on the sigils of the tetragram, the hieroglyphic monad of John Dee, the angels known as the Wings of the Winds, the Banner rings, the divination by Urim and Thummim, the twelve stones of the tribes of Israel, the breastplate of Aaron, the ring of Solomon, and the Enochian Watchtowers and Keys, all represent groundbreaking work in magic. It is my sincere hope that some of the innovations presented here will find their place in the day-to-day practices of kabbalists, ritual magicians, and astrologers over the years to come.

LVX
DONALD TYSON

March 21, 1994
Bedford, Nova Scotia

I

˒˒˒˒˒˒˒˒˒˒˒˒˒˒˒˒˒˒˒˒˒˒˒˒

HISTORY OF THE NAME

etragrammaton, from the Greek *tetra* (four) *gramma* (letter), is the word used by early Jewish authors writing in the Greek language to signify the most sacred and powerful name of God composed of four Hebrew letters. It appears in the works of Philo Judaeus, an Alexandrian of the first century, and Flavius Josephus, a native of Jerusalem who lived during the same period.

The pronunciation of the Name was forbidden except to priests of the Temple during the benediction of the people (Num. 6:22–7) and on the Day of Atonement, when the high priest spoke it ten times before the assembled worshippers (Lev. 16:30). Because unpointed Hebrew is composed entirely of consonants, it was possible to write the name in the books of the Torah and yet still conceal its pronunciation. It appears as יהוה, which is transliterated into the Latin characters IHVH (sometimes YHWH or JHWH). But the name could not be written in Greek without revealing the way of saying it. Josephus was a priest and knew the correct pronunciation of the Name, but states in his *Antiquities* (II, 12, 4) that religion forbids him to divulge it. Philo calls the Name ineffable and says that it is lawful only for those whose ears and tongues are purified by wisdom to hear and utter it in a holy place—in other words, for priests in the Temple.

In their own language the Jews referred to the Name as Shem ha-Mephoresh (שֵׁם הַמְפוֹרָשׁ), "the distinctive excellent name." This designation

1

is often assigned by occultists to the seventy-two names of three letters extracted by kabbalistic methods from three verses in Exodus, but it more properly belongs to Tetragrammaton itself.

In biblical times, the Name was known to the common people and was used in a form of greeting not unlike "God be with you." As early as the fourth century before Christ, its use was suppressed. The reason for the restriction of the Name is not known. Possibly it was to avoid profanation of the Name by heathen lips, or to prevent its abuse in vulgar magic. I tend to believe it was connected with a growing social gulf between the priest class and the people. The priests reserved the name exclusively as the supreme emblem of their authority, in very much the same way that the Catholic Church of the Middle Ages bitterly resisted the translation of the Bible into the common tongues of Europe. Knowledge is power.

Several generations before the fall of Jerusalem to the Romans in A.D. 70, the priests had ceased to speak the Name openly even within the confines of the Temple. Under the veil of holiness, they adopted the duplicitous device of whispering it in so low a voice that it was drowned out amid the chants and other sounds of ritual. With the seizing of the temple, the public use of the Name in religious ceremonies ceased altogether, but it continued to be preserved in the schools of the rabbis, who according to one tradition (*Qiddushin* 71a) communicated the true pronunciation of the name to their disciples "mouth to ear" once every seven years.

It was the most serious blasphemy for a layman to speak the Name. Philo says the penalty was death. It shocked and enraged the rabbis that for some time after its use was forbidden, the sect of the Samaritans continued to employ the Name in their judicial oaths. A Jew reading aloud the Scriptures who encountered the letters IHVH was directed to speak the name "Adonai," which means Lord. If the names IHVH and Adonai occurred together on the page, "Elohim," translated the Omnipotent, was voiced in place of the ineffable Name to avoid the awkward Adonai-Adonai. This continues to be the practice today.

With such fanatical secrecy, it was inevitable that the true pronunciation of the Name would be lost, but this did not take place overnight. As late as the fourth century, perhaps much later, it was known in Babylonia, and the Jewish magicians, who styled themselves *Ba'alei Shem* (Masters of the Name) used it widely in driving demons out of the possessed and healing the sick. Among the kabbalists of the Middle Ages, it was handed down from master to disciple. Much of the ire of the rabbis against these mystics may have been incited by the fear that they would misuse the Name in secular magic and thus profane it.

Biblical tradition has it that the Name was first revealed to Moses when he went up upon Horeb, the mountain of God, and saw the burning bush

(Exod. 3:14–5), and it is explicitly stated that prior to this revelation to Moses the Name was not known among the Hebrews: "And I appeared unto Abraham, unto Isaac, and unto Jacob, by the name of God Almighty (Shaddai); but by my name Jehovah (IHVH) was I not known to them" (Exod. 6:3).

This has led to speculation that the Name originally belonged to the resident deity of the holy mountain who was worshipped by the tribes that dwelt in the region south of Palestine. In receiving the Name, Moses also took on the authority of the god of the mountain and conveyed its power to his people. That is why he married a daughter of the priest of Midian (Exod. 3:1)—the tribe of Midian grazed their flocks in the land of the sacred mountain and worshipped its god with sacrifices. That is why he led the Israelites to this mountain after their deliverance from Egypt and taught them how to worship IHVH. He wished them to have the continuing protection and blessing of this most potent god who had secured their freedom through his miracles.

The meaning of the Name is not known with certainty. It is often stated that while the numerous other names of God are merely descriptive of divine attributes (see the comments of Moses Maimonides in Appendix B), the ineffable Name means supreme deity completely and exclusively and cannot be referred to any lesser function.

The derivation of the word is obscure, but it may have descended from the Hebrew verb *hayah* (to be), as is implied by the words of God to Moses on Horeb. Thus the meaning of the Name may be "He who is always the same," or "He who is truly existent," or even "He who is sufficient unto Himself." If a more active sense is sought, it might be "He who causes things to be," or "He who calls events into existence." Another speculation, from the root *hawah* (sink down, fall) yields the meanings "He who causes to fall," or "He who strikes down." The name has also been connected by some scholars with the Arab *hawa* (the void between heaven and earth), leading to the interpretation "He who rides the wind," or "He who makes the winds to blow."

Earlier speculations that there is a connection between Tetragrammaton and the Greek god of thunderbolts (Jehovah = Jove), or with the Gnostic deity IAO, are generally discounted (although Gershom Scholem finds a connection between IAO and the truncated Name IHV used in *Sepher Yetzirah* to seal the six directions of space—see Scholem, *Kabbalah,* p. 27). So are wilder claims that the Name can be traced back to ancient China, Egypt, or Babylonia. All these propositions have been put forth at different times, but there is little hard evidence to support them.

The pronunciation Jehovah, which occurs in many English Bibles, including the King James, is the result of an error that arose due to a lack of familiarity with Hebrew scribal practices on the part of European scholars of the fourteenth century. In Hebrew, all the letters are consonants, and the vowels sounded with them are indicated by putting small marks or "points" near the letters. The consonants IHVH were pointed with the vowels for Adonai in Hebrew Bibles to indicate that when IHVH was encountered it should be read as Adonai. Ordinarily, when such a substitution is made, the consonants of the substituted word are written in the margin to avoid confusion, but since the use of Adonai for IHVH was so well known to Jewish readers, this was deemed unnecessary. European scholars, unaware of this practice, read the consonants IHVH and the vowel sounds for Adonai together, and the result was the impossible hybrid "Jehovah."

The correct pronunciation is thought to be Yahveh or Yahweh, with the accent falling on the second syllable. Writing in Greek around the end of the second century, Clement of Alexandria states that the pronunciation is Ιαουε, IAOVE. Variants in the manuscripts are IA OVE, IA OVAI and IAOV. Epiphanius, who was born and lived for a considerable period in Palestine, reports around the end of the fourth century that the true pronunciation is Ιαβε, IABE, or in another manuscript IAVE. Theodoret, who was born at Antioch, says that the Samaritans used the pronunciation IABE, or in another passage, IABAI.

In magical manuscripts, where the Name was used as a word of power, the form Ιαβε, IABE, occurs frequently, and the form Ιαβα, IABA, is also common. In a magical manuscript from Ethiopia that lists the occult names of Jesus, *Yawe* is found.

Even though the manner of speaking the Tetragrammaton may be said to have been lost officially, there are many in modern times who have claimed, and continue to claim, possession of the single, true esoteric pronunciation. Early in the present century, it was recorded (Montgomery, *Journal of Biblical Literature* XXV [1906], pp. 49–51) that the modern Samaritan priests use the form *Yahweh* or *Yahwa*. Kabbalists have always maintained a knowledge of the Name that has been handed down from master to disciple through the centuries. The higher degrees of Freemasonry purport to possess it. There are many occultists of the present day who are convinced that they, and they alone, preserve the true way of speaking it, which is the only way to release the awesome power of the Word. Samuel L. MacGregor Mathers, the head of the Hermetic Order of the Golden Dawn, boasted: "I myself know some score of different mystical pronunciations of it" (*The Kabbalah Unveiled* [London: Routledge and Kegan Paul, 1962], p. 30).

It is the custom in modern magic to pronounce the Name by sounding out each of its Hebrew letters fully: *yod-he-vau-he* (pronounced "yod-hay-vav-hay") in order to more accurately express its compound esoteric meaning and also to acknowledge that the true Name is unspeakable.

No scholar or mystic of modern times, regardless of depth of learning or profundity of intuition, can be sure that a particular way of sounding the four consonants IHVH is identical to the way used by the high priest in the

Temple at Jerusalem before the Roman conquest. It is equally impossible to be certain that the pronunciation of the Jewish priests, though historically accurate, was the correct mystical manner of vibrating the Name. Merely because it was spoken a certain way for centuries does not necessarily mean that it was spoken rightly. It is much easier to carry on an error than to preserve the truth. Presumably Moses knew the Name, having received it directly from God, but after him doubt must creep in.

II

TRADITIONAL MEANINGS

The correct pronunciation of the Tetragrammaton may seem a trivial matter to those who view a name merely as a label, to be exchanged for another, different label as casually as we might change hats. In magic, a name is far more significant. It embodies the identity, the very being, of what it signifies. When a name is rightly vibrated by the tongue and lips upon the air, it comes alive. A resonance is established between the living name and the thing itself. By manipulating the name, the potential of the named thing is released upon the world. To articulate IHVH is to harness the power of Supreme Deity, both to create and destroy, for human ends.

According to the esoteric doctrine of the Jewish mystic-magicians known as kabbalists, the structure of Tetragrammaton forms the blueprint upon which the entire universe of space and time, matter and energy, good and evil, humans and angels, is based. The Name does not merely reflect the makeup of the world—it *is* the world. In the most ancient book of the kabbalah, *Sepher Yetzirah* (The Book of Formation), it is written: "He selected three letters from among the simple ones and sealed them and formed them into a Great Name, I H V, and with this He sealed the universe in six directions. He looked above, and sealed the Height with I H V. He looked below and sealed the Depth with I V H. He looked forward, and sealed the East with H I V. He looked backward, and sealed the West with H V I. He looked to the right, and sealed the South with V I H. He looked to the left, and sealed the North with V H I" (*Sepher Yetzirah*, Westcott translation [New York: Weiser, 1980], p. 17).

The very substance of space itself is composed of the letters of IHVH. Only three letters of the Name are employed, not all four, because it is possible to permute three letters in six different ways, and in three-dimensional space there are six fundamental directions—up, down; before, behind; left, right. This is sufficient, because there are only three different letters in the Name, the H being repeated.

In the later kabbalistic theory of the *Zohar,* which was written centuries after the *Sepher Yetzirah,* the relationship between Tetragrammaton and the creation of the world became more complex and specific. To understand this relationship, it is necessary to say a few words about the doctrine of emanations. Kabbalists hold that creation, all forms of creation of being from nothingness, occurred and continues to occur through the mediation of ten spheres of living sacred fire called *sephiroth.* These spheres are connected by pathways that allow a progression from one to another either downward from Deity to matter or upward from matter to Deity. They form a ladder of lights connecting earth to heaven that can never be broken without the utter annihilation of the universe.

Each *sephirah* is in its most basic nature a name for one of the attributes of God. The kabbalah calls these "the ten names which must not be erased." In addition to these divine names, the *sephiroth* have descriptive names of their own, resident archangels, angelic choirs, and heavenly spheres. Late in their evolution, from the fourteenth century onward, they were ordered into a graphic pattern of connecting channels that is known as the sephirothic tree of the kabbalah.

From highest to lowest these *sephiroth* are:

1. Kether—The Crown
2. Chokmah—Wisdom, the Supernal Father (ABBA)
3. Binah—Understanding, the Supernal Mother (AIMA)
4. Chesed—Mercy
5. Geburah—Severity
6. Tiphareth—Beauty, the Son (Messiah)
7. Netzach—Victory
8. Hod—Splendor
9. Yesod—Foundation
10. Malkuth—The Kingdom, the Daughter

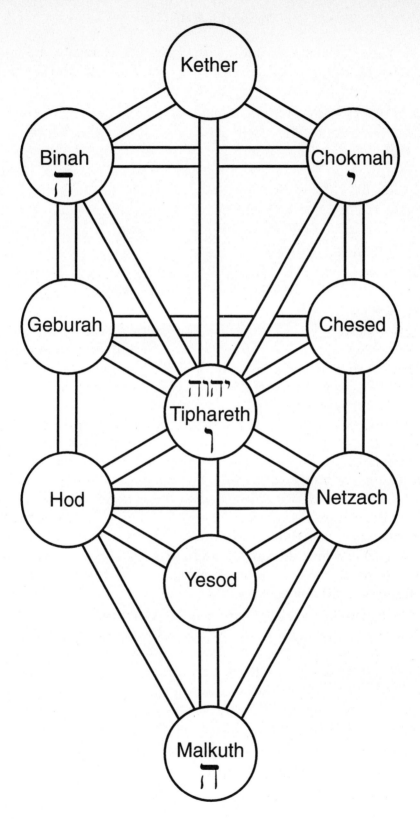

Tree of the Sephiroth

The holy name IHVH is specifically assigned to *Tiphareth,* the heart of the sephirothic tree. In a sense, the sixth *sephirah* is in itself the active process of creation. The three highest spheres, called the Supernals, are considered to be so exalted that a gulf separates them from the lower seven, while *Malkuth* has no active force of its own but only receives the impression of the nine higher *sephiroth.*

Recognizing that no single *sephirah* can adequately express Tetragrammaton, kabbalists also assign the most holy Name to the entire tree. The point at the top of the *yod* (') represents the Nothingness (*ain*) that manifests itself first through *Kether,* the Primordial Point. The *yod* itself, seed of God the Father, they assign to *Chokmah.* The first *he* (ה), feminine and fertile, is given to *Binah,* the Great Mother. The *vau* (ו), male offspring of the union of the first two letters, kabbalists give to *Tiphareth,* and by virtue of its numerical value, six, to the six *sephiroth* that lie between the three Supernals and *Malkuth.* The final *he* they assign to *Malkuth* on the theory that, since the lowest sphere of emanation is passive and has no independent power, it cannot receive its own unique letter but must be given the second *he,* which has already acted in the higher process of creation as the first *he* and now manifests itself in the fulfillment of *Malkuth.* As the first *he* was the Mother, so the second *he* is the product of the Mother, and is her earthly reflection, the Daughter.

The complete Tetragrammaton also plays an essential part in the process of *zimzum* (contraction) that takes place before the first emanation from the limitless void of non-being. Before the *sephiroth* were projected within the Primordial Point of *Kether,* which in fact forms the boundary of the universe, there was only the featureless, unending essence of God. For something else to come into being, it was necessary for God to turn in upon Himself and thereby create a point of vacuum where He was not present, or was present in a different degree. This involved the bringing about of an imbalance through the power of *Din* (critical judgement).

The movement within the *ain soph* (Limitless Void) was accomplished through the primordial Torah, the archetypal world of ideas that was woven into its very substance. This Torah is called a garment *(malbush)* that is not distinct from but is still a part of the substance of the Divine, "like the grasshopper whose clothing is part of itself." The length of the garment is the twenty-two Hebrew letters, which form 231 gates, the total number of possible combinations of two letters (AB, AG, AD, etc.). The breadth of the garment, measured by its hem, is composed of four extended forms of Tetragrammaton. It is possible to write out each of the letters of IHVH in four different ways, each of which has a different numerical value:

Tetragrammaton in the form of the human body

45 (אה, ואו, הא, יוד) IVD, HA, VAV, HA
52 (הה, וו, הה, יוד) IVD, HH, VV, HH
72 (הי, ריו, הי, יוד) IVD, HI, VIV, HI
63 (הי, ואו, הי, יוד) IVD, HI, VAV, HI

This garment is said to be twice the area necessary to cover the entire universe. After it was woven, it was folded in half back upon itself. The names of forty-five and fifty-two fell behind and were shadowed by the names of seventy-two and sixty-three, and as a consequence the final *yod* in the name of sixty-three was left without a partner. By the contraction of the garment, a void was created in the *ain soph* that was not the same as the *ain soph* itself. The single remaining letter of the Tetragrammaton, the *yod*, served as the instrument through which was transferred the infinite holy radiance of the *ain soph* into the shadow that lay beneath the folded garment of the primordial Torah. This light became the fiery spheres or vessels of the *sephiroth* that exist within the Primordial Point, *Kether. Kether* is no more than an infinitesimal speck in the endless expanse of Deity, yet that speck is large enough to comprehend all things.

Medieval kabbalists believed in a set of cosmic cycles called *shemittah* that were connected with the seven lower *sephiroth* that emanate from the Great Mother, *Binah.* Each cycle is active for a period of six thousand years corresponding to the six days of creation, followed by a period of a thousand years of chaos corresponding to the day of rest, during which the universe is torn down and rebuilt in the pattern of the succeeding *sephirah.* Presently we are living in the *shemittah* of *Geburah,* the age of strict judgement and severity, which accounts for our unceasing wars. The previous age was that of *Chesed,* a period of happiness and love that is dimly echoed in the Greek myth of a Golden Age of heroes. The next *shemittah* will be that of *Tiphareth,* characterized by beauty and harmony.

At the end of the seven cycles of 49,000 years there is a grand jubilee of a millennium when all the lower worlds together and the seven *sephiroth* that support them are reabsorbed into *Binah,* and the universe begins to repeat itself. Each of these *shemittah* is said to experience a unique revelation of the Torah, which is the complete articulation of Tetragrammaton. However, the combination of letters of the Name varies from age to age. Therefore the divine wisdom is interpreted differently in each cycle, in the context of the *sephirah* that rules it. The present interpretation is one of law and prohibition ("Thou shalt not...") because this is the *shemittah* of *Geburah.* Some kabbalists believed that old souls who had lived in the previous age of *Chesed* were reincarnated in the present cycle.

The microcosm, represented by its physical sheath, the human body, is the exact miniature of the macrocosm, the universe. It is not surprising, therefore, that kabbalists assigned the *sephiroth,* along with their divine names and letters of Tetragrammaton, to the human form. The three Supernals, *Kether, Chokmah,* and *Binah,* they gave to the three lobes of the human brain. *Chesed* was placed in the right arm that dispenses blessing. *Geburah* was the left arm that admonishes. *Tiphareth,* the center of the sephirothic tree, goes with the heart, the center of the body. *Netzach* is linked to the right leg and *Hod* to the left leg. *Yesod* falls on the organ of generation. *Malkuth* is given to the feet.

There is another more simple pattern that shows the letters of Tetragrammaton arranged one above the other in the crude shape of the human body. *Yod* is the head of this figure, the first *he* its arms and shoulders, *vau* its breathing torso, and the second *he* its pelvis and legs.

The esoteric message inherent in this seemingly childish stick man is extremely significant. Not only is the IHVH the living pattern of the Creator whereby the power of God may be released and harnessed, and the structure of the universe through which the world may be subdued, but it is also the shape and foundation of humanity. Its proper use permits a human being to rule, not only other human beings, but more importantly his or her own nature. By Tetragrammaton it is possible to separate out and refine the gold of our higher being and purge it of dross vices and other impurities.

III

ʾ ʾ ʾ ʾ ʾ ʾ ʾ ʾ ʾ ʾ ʾ ʾ ʾ ʾ ʾ ʾ ʾ ʾ ʾ

CORRESPONDENCES

Before the Name can be used as an instrument of power for bringing about willed purposes, it is necessary to know the correspondences of its individual letters to various ideas, symbols, and tools in modern magic. These relationships must be grasped below the level of mere intellect if the letters of the Name are to actually become the things they represent during ritual acts. A nominal understanding of the link between letter and symbol is never enough. In magic a thing is not made true because we say it is so; it is true because we *know* below the level of thought that it actually *is* so.

The most fundamental correspondence with the Name is the number four, because the name is made up of four letters. Four is the number of manifest being. All the universe as we know it exists on the fourth level of creation, *Assiah*. Existence itself is *Assiah*. Therefore IHVH is the power word for the realization of purpose, a quality that makes it highly useful in practical magic.

The quaternary is visually embodied in two dimensions by the square, which is a flat representation of the three-dimensional cube, mathematically the square squared, the most material of all symbols. Square and cube often occur coupled with Tetragrammaton in Jewish and occult practice. The holiest of holy places in the Temple of Jerusalem built by King Solomon, where God communicated his purposes to the high priest, was twenty cubits

13

in all dimensions (1 Kings 6:20); the altar itself was square (2 Chron. 4:1), as was the breastplate of Aaron (Exod. 28:16); holy Jerusalem described in the vision of St. John the Divine is in the shape of a cube (Rev. 21:16). All these are places where the power of IHVH is manifested.

There is a numerological paradox in the structure of Tetragrammaton. Although it has four letters, two of those letters are the same. In the most straightforward sense, it is a name of four letters, but in another sense it is a name of three letters. It embodies and conveys the essences of both three and four simultaneously. This is a great mystery that extends far beyond the bounds of Jewish mysticism. The relationship between three and four is the dynamic upon which the world is constructed. It is one of the most arcane secrets of both religion and magic.

The Greek sage Pythagoras graphically captured this eternal marriage of three and four in his famous *tetractys,* a triangle formed out of ten dots, with four dots at its base. For centuries occultists have used the Hebrew letters of IHVH in place of the dots, which lends the *tetractys* a much more intricate and organic aspect:

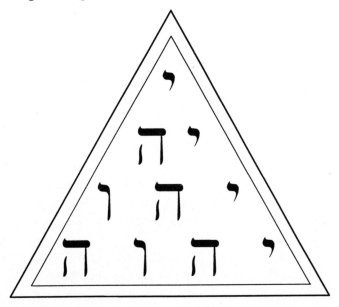

Three is divine and heavenly; four is mundane and earthly. In Christianity, there are the three persons in God, namely the Father, Son, and Holy Ghost, and the four evangelists, Matthew, Mark, Luke, and John, who make manifest or establish the law of heaven upon the Earth. Three is perfect and sacred; four is flawed and profane. Carpenters know this from experience. The triangle is the strongest geometric shape in construction

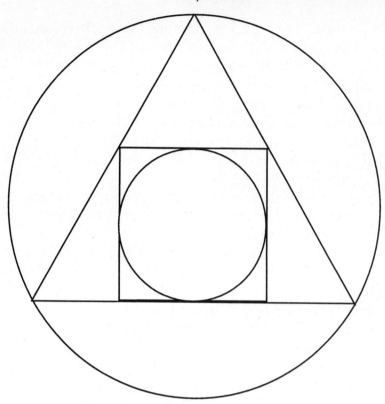

Squaring the Circle

because it will not deform under stress. The square, on the other hand, will collapse. To keep a structure "square," triangular braces are needed.

The perfection of three is further illustrated by the three-legged stool. No matter how uneven the floor, a stool with three legs sits firm and will not rock. The addition of a fourth leg makes the stool less perfect, because it introduces the third dimension of space into its pattern, the dimension of matter. The tips of three legs always lie in a single plane—the fourth may or may not occupy that plane. Into the divine realm of certainty, the fourth factor introduces doubt, thereby contaminating it and rendering it profane. Yet it is precisely this element of uncertainty that permits choice and human free will. Four is the number of the real world of human misery, and human potential, into which the human race fell when it was cast forth from Paradise.

The dynamic interrelationship of three and four was a central puzzle of medieval alchemy. One of the foremost authorities on this subject, the psychiatrist Carl Jung, writes: "The number three is not a natural expression of wholeness, since four represents the minimum number of determinants in a whole judgement. It must nevertheless be stressed that side by side with the distinct leanings of alchemy (and of the unconscious) towards quaternity there is always a vacillation between three and four which comes out over and over again" (*Psychology and Alchemy* [Princeton University Press, 1980], p. 26). Jung saw the shifting of focus back and forth between systems based on three and four as a wavering between a spiritual and a physical emphasis.

Alchemists captured this dynamic relationship in the symbol of the squared circle. Along with the making of the Philosopher's Stone and the discovery of the Water of Life, the squaring of the circle was the prime achievement of alchemy. It was represented geometrically by a circle within which was a triangle, within which was a square, within which was a circle. From the unity of the circle arises trinity, and trinity gives birth to quaternity, which in the highest mystery returns to unity once again. The center and perimeter meet and are the same.

The same shifting of emphasis between three and four that occupied the minds of alchemists and Christian theologians is evident in Buddhist symbolism as well. As Jung points out (*Psychology and Alchemy,* p. 96), all Lamaistic mandalas are based on a quaternary system, yet the great symbol of the World Wheel is based on a ternary system.

The four occult elements naturally fall under the letters of IHVH. Masculine and creative fire is given to the *yod;* feminine and receptive water is given to the first *he;* active intellectual air is placed under the *vau;* and heavy material earth is put with the second *he.* This quaternary of manifest elements that compose the substance of existence is separate and different from the ternary of ethereal elements that occur in the Hebrew alphabet, where the Mother letters *aleph* (א), *mem* (מ), and *shin* (ש) stand for, respectively, air, water, and fire. There is no Hebrew letter for earth, indicating that the three elements represented in the alphabet are heavenly rather than earthly.

From the solid foundation of the four elements, other occult associations branch forth. The most important of these is the four suits of the tarot, a set of seventy-eight picture cards widely used in modern magic. The symbols of the suits are related to the elements, and through them to the letters of the Name. There is some disagreement over the correct relationship, as indeed there is for many of the secondary occult associations of the letters, but in the Golden Dawn arrangement, which is the most widely accepted, the suit of Wands stands for fire, and thus the *yod* of the Name. The suit of Cups is water and the first *he.* The suit of Swords is air and the *vau.* The suit of Pentacles is earth and the second *he.*

Within each suit of the tarot are four face cards, and these are subdivided into elements. Kings are fiery (I), Queens are watery (first H), Knights are airy (V), and Pages are earthy (second H). In this way it is possible to characterize the nature of the sixteen royal cards of the Lesser, or Minor, Arcana of the tarot variously as water of fire (Queen of Wands), air of earth

(Knight of Pentacles), earth of earth (Page of Pentacles), and so on (see Crowley's *Book of Thoth,* p. 23).

Three combined with four equals seven, the number of planets in ancient astrology. The planets are compounded out of combinations of three pure principles, which may conveniently be called sun, moon, and earth. Four of the planets are based on pairs of these principles: Venus (sun-earth), Mars (earth-sun); Jupiter (moon-earth), and Saturn (earth-moon). Mercury is formed of all three, moon-sun-earth. It is highly instructive to compare the structure of the planets with the structure of Tetragrammaton. The sun corresponds with the initial *yod.* The moon is the first *he.* Mercury is the threefold aspect of the Name, IHV, out of which the six directions of space are formed in *Sepher Yetzirah.* There are six possible permutations of the glyph for Mercury. The paired planets Venus-Mars and Jupiter-Saturn may be related to the fourfold IHVH itself, because these four planets have in them the principle of earth, yet are not complete individually, but only when considered as a set.

These three principles, under the names cardinal, fixed, and mutable, together with the four occult elements fire, water, air, and earth, combine in pairs to form the twelve signs of the zodiac. Not surprisingly, there are twelve possible permutations of the letters of the Name, and these make up distinct names in their own right (were it not for the repetition of the letter H, twenty-four permutations would be possible). The twelve overt Banners of Tetragrammaton are individually assigned to the signs of the zodiac, which they rule through the authority of highest divinity. To evoke the particular potential of a sign, or summon its resident spirits, the Banner ruling that sign is physically drawn and vibrated upon the air with the tongue and lips.

The usefulness of Tetragrammaton in dealing with the powers of the zodiac can scarcely be overstressed. A new technique for graphically projecting the twelve Banners is presented in Chapter V.

In traditional magic, the ordering of the twelve forms of the Name is incorrect, as I have demonstrated in my book, *The New Magus,* * from the underlying numerical pattern of the Banners. Very likely the true arrangement was known but was concealed from the vulgar to prevent its misuse. The key to the correct arrangement lies in the letters that begin each Banner. The letters of IHVH are linked to the four elements: I = fire, H = water, V = air, and the second H = earth. Each letter begins three Banners. Similarly, each element is related to three signs of the zodiac. Clearly a parallel relationship may be established between these triplets, and it is logical to begin such a series with IHVH, the base form of Tetragrammaton from which the others are derived, by linking it to Aries, a fire sign and traditionally the first sign of the zodiac.

New Millennium Magic, an updated and expanded version of *The New Magus*, will be available in May 1996 from Llewellyn Worldwide, Ltd.

The corrected sequence of the twelve Banners, and their corresponding signs, is as follows:

IHV**H**	Aries	Fire-Cardinal
IH**H**V	Sagittarius	Fire-Mutable
IV**H**H	Leo	Fire-Fixed
HVHI	Cancer	Water-Cardinal
HVIH	Pisces	Water-Mutable
HHIV	Scorpio	Water-Fixed
V**H**IH	Libra	Air-Cardinal
V**H**HI	Gemini	Air-Mutable
VI**H**H	Aquarius	Air-Fixed
HIHV	Capricorn	Earth-Cardinal
HIVH	Virgo	Earth-Mutable
HHVI	Taurus	Earth-Fixed

The boldface type in the permutations of the Name indicates the position of the second H in each Banner. This relationship between the Banners and the zodiac signs originates in my own work and is not the common practice. It is usual among occultists to ignore the elemental associations of the initial letters in the names and simply assign them to the zodiac in order, counterclockwise, beginning with IHVH-Aries, IHHV-Taurus, IVHH-Gemini, and so on. All too often, those who attempt to use the Banners have an imperfect idea of their structure, and ignorance makes error inevitable.

The term *Banner* has here been loosely applied to all permutations of Tetragrammaton, because this is the usual practice in Western magic. However, I should point out that it is more correct to refer to each group of three forms that begin with the same letter as a Banner, and to call each individual permutation a Seal. Thus, in proper kabbalistic terminology, the three Seals IHVH, IHHV, and IVHH jointly compose the first of the four Banners (see Gikatilla, *Gates of Light*, Harper Collins, 1994, p. 233). Because the focus of this work is magical, I have chosen to follow the occult practice and call each permutation a Banner.

IV

UNDERSTANDING THE NAME

The letters of Tetragrammaton designate the four essential principles that form the foundation of the universe and constitute the mechanism of both creation and destruction. These principles are the bare backbone of the world. Any symbols might be used to signify them—shapes, numbers, or letters of other alphabets than the Hebrew. Pythagoras used simple dots in his *tetractys*. In attempting to understand the essence of cosmos, we are eventually faced with four boxes into which we must put everything that is manifest. Each box is different, yet its difference is not absolute but dependent upon its relationship with the other boxes. Somehow we must reduce the infinite number of different things into four categories (see the comments of P.D. Ouspensky in Appendix B).

At first thought, it would be natural to assume that the process of bringing ideas forth and sustaining them in manifestation would be supported by four completely different factors. This would need to be symbolically represented by a name composed of four different letters. However, creation is not a closed circle but a double helix, represented in two dimensions by the standing wave (see illustration on next page).

In the illustration, I (י) and V (ו) are a polarity of forces and exchange their charges or potentials as they pass through H (ה), which acts very much as a kind of switch. The result is a continuous flowing forth into being with no obvious sign that this polarity-switching is taking place. A useful physical model of this archetypal process is the electric motor. The axis of a motor turns smoothly in one direction even though the polarity of the electromagnets around that axis is being very rapidly switched back and forth from positive to negative.

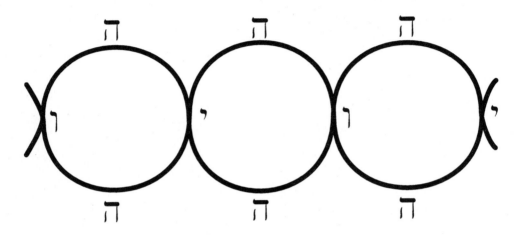

Standing Wave of IHVH

The creation-destruction double helix of the Name resembles closely the serpent staff of Hermes (see illustration on opposite page).

The mystical staff with its two united and intertwined snakes coiling around it has from ancient times represented life, the bringing forth of being from nothingness. It used to be believed that snakes entwined in this intimate manner were mating (actually, they were fighting). The staff of Hermes is a two-dimensional physical representation of a transcendent intellectual action that flows forth unceasingly from the mind of the Creator.

It would be closer to the fundamental reality if the model were made in three dimensions. Then it would consist of two helical paths twining up an invisible central axis, and in fact would look very much like the molecular models of DNA. It is no coincidence that the building blocks, or "bases," of DNA—adenine, cytosine, guanine, and thymine—are four in number. This correspondence is inevitable because the basic patterns of being replicate themselves endlessly on all levels of manifestation, both mental and physical. The Hermetic maxim of the Emerald Tablet testifies to this replication: "What is below is like that which is above, and what is above is like that which is below: to accomplish the miracle of the One Thing." In the same way that the molecular pattern of a crystal is revealed by its gross shape, so is the mental pattern of the creating Mind of the universe exhibited in the structure of the genetic coding of life.

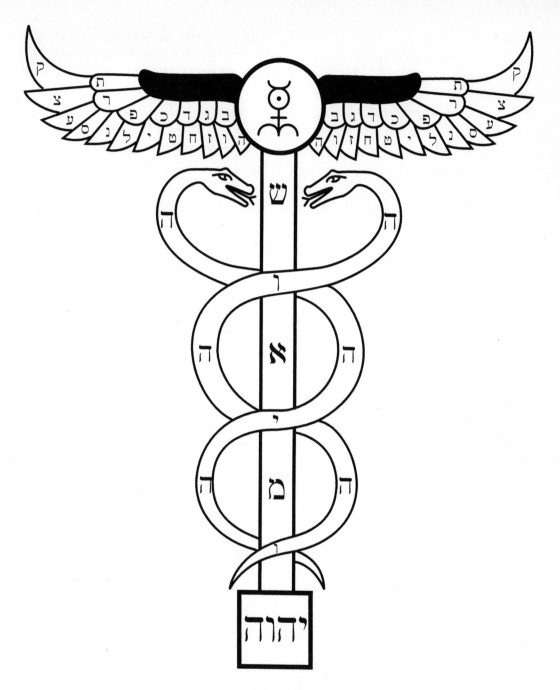

Serpent Staff of Hermes

On this three-dimensional staff of Hermes, no point on either helix is closer to the ideal axis, which the path of each helix defines, than any of the limitless number of other points, and at no point do the two balanced helixes touch. Like the side rails of the DNA-ladder, they remain always at the same separation. Any single point on either helix is identical, considered by itself, to any other point. Differentiation occurs through the relationship of one point to another, considered from a specific (and arbitrary) external point of view. Shift the point of view and these essential qualities change. An I can become an H, and an H can become a V. For example, if the illustration of the double helix of the Name were rotated around on its axis ninety degrees, the points designated H would seem to touch, and become alternately I and V, and the I and V would separate and become H.

It is easy to misinterpret occult symbols by failing to recognize that the way they appear on the page, or carved into clay or stone, is not their true form but only a flat rendering of a three-dimensional relationship. Just as a blueprint of a ship will not convey all the information it is capable of conveying to the shipbuilder unless the shipbuilder realizes that it is a flat image of a three-dimensional object, so ancient symbols such as the staff of Hermes cannot be understood unless we recognize that they are only images of mental models that possess depth as well as height and breadth.

An excellent example of this error is the spiral. This fundamental occult symbol cannot be wholly grasped in two dimensions. A spiral is really the flat image of a helix, a line winding in a regular way around the side of an infinitely long invisible cylinder. As we look at a spiral on the flat page, we are regarding this cylinder through the open end, and naturally its perspective lines converge at the center—the infinitely distant end of the cylinder—as they do when we look at a straight railroad bed and seem to see the gleaming steel rails come together and meet on the horizon.

When we see a photograph of a railroad track from this one-point perspective, we understand it because we are familiar with the physical three-dimensional reality. But when we look at a Stone Age petroglyph of a spiral, we do not understand it because it represents the three-dimensional model of an ideal form, not some common and familiar object. Nevertheless, the ancient shaman who carved it into the rock intended that it be considered in three dimensions. So did Greek philosophers who represented the occult symbol of the Hermes staff intend that its mystery be interpreted in three dimensions. And when we make a model or image representing IHVH, we must make it with length, breadth, and height if it is to possess a useful meaning.

Needless to say, any mystical three-dimensional symbol is only a jumping-off place for grasping an awareness of a higher truth that transcends the physical limitations of space. It is necessary first to recognize the fullness of flat symbols and hold them unfolded in the mind, and then attempt a further unfolding into a higher dimension which transcends our inner visual sense. Since we are incapable of holding a four-dimensional (or higher) image in the mind we must seek an intuitive perception of the mentally examined symbol, a wordless and pictureless apprehension of its fundamental identity. Only in this manner can the true Ineffable Name be approached. Words and mental images are useful signposts along the way but, if we cling to them, they quickly become barriers to a higher awareness of Tetragrammaton.

Besides the staff of Hermes, which is the pre-eminent symbol for understanding the Name, intuitive awareness may be approached through the symbol of the cross. Each arm of the cross is assigned one of the letters. The vertical arm receives the masculine I and V, while the horizontal arm is given the feminine first and second H:

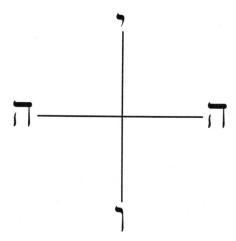

It should come as no surprise after what has just been revealed that the cross must also be considered in three dimensions before it makes any useful sense esoterically. Meaning can be derived from the flat cross on the page, but a higher meaning is possible from the expanded three-dimensional cross. The expanded cross is the geometric figure known as the tetrahedron (see figure on following page).

The tetrahedron is the simplest regular solid body. It has four planes, each of which is defined by an equilateral triangle, and four points where these planes intersect. A letter of IHVH is assigned to each point. If we examine the

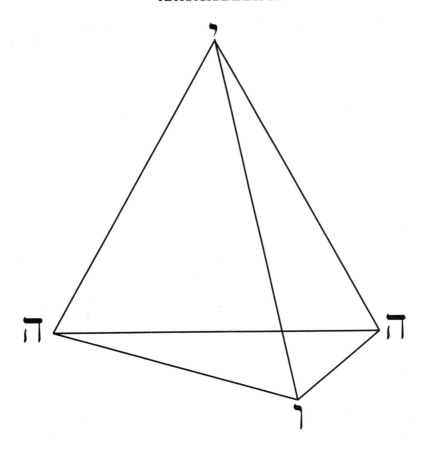

Tetrahedron of IHVH

tetrahedron mentally, or actually construct a skeletal model out of toothpicks or wire, it is readily seen that, when considered perpendicularly to any of its edges, it appears to form a cross of equal arms surrounded by a square (See the figure on page 29).

If we look at the two planes of the tetrahedron that intersect and define the axis I-V, we see that each plane has the family of letters I-H-V at its three points. The second or final H is not on the same plane, but is linked to each of the former letters by a line segment. Thus there is something special or distinctive about the final H that transcends the plane of the other three letters. The distinction is not inherent in the point of the second H itself but derives from its position relative to the other three points.

It is equally possible to mentally isolate the planes that intersect on the H-H axis. Then we get the family I-H-H with V on a higher level, or the family V-H-H with I on a higher lever. What does this tell us? That I and V are capable of inverting roles, depending on their circumstances, even though they are not outwardly identical, as are the two feminine Hs.

The magician Aleister Crowley had something important to say on this very matter. In addition to the Tetragrammaton, he used the four royal cards of the tarot to illustrate his views:

> The relations between these Four Elements of the Name are extraordinarily complex, quite beyond the limits of any ordinary treatise to discuss; they change with every application of thought to their meaning.
>
> For instance, no sooner has the Princess [second H] made her appearance than the Prince [V] wins her in marriage, and she is set upon the throne of her Mother [first H]. She thus awakens the Eld of the original old King; who thereupon becomes a young Knight [I], and so renews the cycle. The Princess is not only the perfect Maiden, but, owing to the death of the Prince, the forsaken and lamenting Widow. All this occurs in the legends characteristic of the Aeon of Osiris. It is hardly possible definitely to disentangle these complications, but for the student it is sufficient if he will be content to work with one legend at a time. (*The Book of Thoth* [New York: Weiser, 1974], pp. 150–1)

The square brackets in the above quotation are mine. Crowley viewed the dynamic of the Name as a series of family trines in which the father and mother (I and first H) alternately generate the son (V) and daughter (second H). The generative unit is complete in the trinity, but this trinity endlessly alternates its polarity, male-female-male giving way to male-female-female, and vice versa. The V elevates his twin sister, the second H, to the throne of the now barren mother, the first H, whom she replaces. Her mature beauty arouses the creative lust of the V, who ascends to the throne of his father, the I. By this ascent he is transformed and his old identity "dies" or passes from existence. The renewed and fertile male-female pair in turn produce the next generation.

It is interesting to note that in ancient Egypt it was the custom for the young Prince to replace the dying King, his father, on the throne and marry his own sister, the Princess, who became Queen and took over the post of her mother. In this way, the King was forever renewed in his own blood and might be said symbolically to be deathless. This Egyptian custom is an imitation on the human level of the creative process of Tetragrammaton. On this question see also the remarks of Crowley in Appendix B.

In order to understand the essential differences between the letters of the Name, it is necessary to reduce them to binary symbolism. This is the same symbolic system of logic that runs the modern computer. The binary system is composed of only two characters, which are usually represented by the digits 0 and 1. They might just as accurately be represented by On-Off, or Yes-No, or indeed any set of opposites.

By arranging these two symbols in multiple patterns, it is possible to express not only any numerical calculation but also any idea conveyed by alphabetical text. Even romantic poetry and classical music can be translated into binary symbols. In fact, binary is the basis of the modern digital recording method used on compact disks.

The binaries in computer coding that make up the yes-no switches are not abstractions, but represent the basic duality of the natural world. They are related to Tetragrammaton in this way:

$$1 - 1 = I$$
$$0 - 0 = H$$
$$1 - 0 = V$$
$$0 - 1 = H$$

Although binary language seems like a modern innovation, it has been used to convey subtle philosophical concepts for many centuries. The quintessential binary symbol is the yin-yang of ancient China (see figure below). This is nothing more than a circle representing totality or wholeness, half of which is white and the other half black. In the black half is a white dot, and in the white half a black dot, to signify that these opposites are relative rather than absolute, that black under other circumstances appears white and white under other conditions looks black. The division between the sides is S-shaped to give the appearance of turning movement in the circle, indicating that this primal duality is not static but in constant flux.

The Yin-Yang Symbol

This binary pair of opposites is represented in Oriental philosophy by the more basic symbolism of a solid line and a broken line. The solid line is masculine and the broken line feminine. These basic signs can be used to represent all opposite pairs such as hot-cold, up-down, dark-light, long-short, good-evil, and so on.

In themselves these simple signs are of limited usefulness, but the number of different things that can be represented by them increases exponentially as they are combined. Simply by placing the two signs one over the other, we arrive at four possible combinations that graphically reveal the essential distinctions between the four letters of Tetragrammaton:

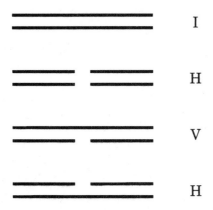

These four symbols are the second of the six stages of what is called the "Shao Yung Sequence," which graphically illustrates how the sixty-four hexagrams of the I Ching are evolved from a solid and a broken line (see Hellmut Wilhelm, *Change* [Pantheon Books, 1960], figure 1).

It will be observed that the binary symbol of I, who is Abba, the primal masculine principle, and that of the first H, who is Aima, the primal feminine principle, are completely distinct. When they combine sexually, half of their binary coding is passed into each of their offspring, just as a human child receives half of its genetic code in the sperm of its father and the other half in the egg of its mother. The binary symbols for V and the second H both contain a solid line and a broken line, the solid line from the father and the broken line from the mother.

This is the reason Crowley describes the second H as the "twin sister" of V—they are made up of the same parts, but in an inverted order. In the case of

V, the masculine solid line is dominant, whereas in the second H it is the broken feminine line that determines gender. When in turn the V and second H combine to generate offspring, the seed of the V is purely masculine, composed only of the solid line in the binary code, and the egg of the second H is purely feminine, composed only of the broken line. In this sense, when brother and sister mature and come together to reproduce new life, they assume the pure gender identities of their parents. As immature children, they are both male and female in one, but as sexually mature adults they are of single gender.

It may be more useful to think of the I and the first H not as complete male and female human figures, but as sperm and egg. With this in mind, it is easier to grasp how the V can be distinct from the I and yet at the same time embody the I within himself; and how the second H can be both the product of the first H and also hold the first H latent within herself.

This binary system was not entirely unfamiliar to the Western world in ancient times. It appears in the symbols of geomantic divination, which was known to the Romans and early Europeans. In the geomantic figures, two dots stand for the feminine and one dot for the opposite masculine. Using this system, the letters of Tetragrammaton would be represented in the following manner:

I   H   V   H

•   • •   •   • •
•   • •   • •   •

Each geomantic symbol is composed of one of these letter sets in combination either with itself or with one of the other three sets. There are thus sixteen distinct geomantic figures. Expressed in the form of solid and broken lines rather than dots, these same sixteen figures form the fourth stage of the Shao Yung Sequence. Each, esoterically speaking, is based upon two letters of Tetragrammaton.

For example, the geomantic figure known as Via (the Way) is composed of *yod* plus *yod:*

•
•   Via
•   (the Way)
•

This is an inherently active and willful symbol, because it is based upon two fiery *yod*s. Its traditional meaning reflects this forcefulness—Via means street or road and, by extension, travel or a journey. It is neither a good nor an evil figure, since travel can bring either good or evil.

Where the traditional meanings of the geomantic figures are in disagreement with their symbolic meanings, as based upon the letters of Tetragrammaton that compose them, the symbolic meanings must take precedence and supplant the traditional meanings, because these symbolic meanings represent the actual make-up of the figures.

From these examples, it is clear why the kabbalists regarded Tetragrammaton not merely as a blueprint of the world, but as the basic fabric of reality. It is this fundamental nature of the Name that gives it so much power in modern ritual magic.

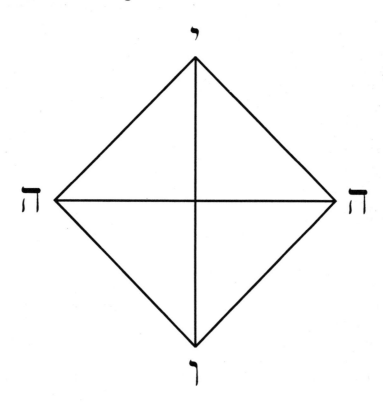

The Tetragram

V

ʼ ʼ

INVOKING THE NAME

To use the twelve overt Banners of Tetragrammaton easily during rituals, they must be converted into a set of sigils. A sigil is a graphic representation of a significant word, usually a name, that may be projected onto the air, or inscribed upon a physical surface, for the purpose of calling forth or commanding the spiritual intelligence of that name, or controlling the lesser spirits ruled by the intelligence of the name.

The system of sigils presented here for the permutations of Tetragrammaton is completely new, but its usefulness has been verified many times in ritual workings. It allows each form of the Name to be quickly and easily projected, both for invoking and banishing, and also acts as a mnemonic, making it impossible to forget the correct spelling and order of the Banners.

The structure of the sigils is based upon the two-dimensional representation of the tetrahedron, the meaning of which was examined in the previous chapter. As was pointed out, when we look directly down upon one of the edges of a transparent tetrahedron, its outline traces a cross with equal arms enclosed in a square. To each point of this figure is ascribed a letter of Tetragrammaton. The result is the tetragram, from which the sigils of the twelve Banners are extracted (see figure on preceding page).

The invoking sigil of any Banner is formed by tracing its lines on the tetragram from letter to letter, beginning with the first letter in the Banner. The banishing sigil is formed by mentally inverting the two Hs in the

Banner, then tracing the lines from letter to letter as before. This inversion of the first and second H causes the banishing sigil to be the exact mirror opposite of the invoking sigil.

In fact, the twelve banishing sigils are based upon the set of twelve hidden, or occult, permutations of the Name that result if the Hs in each Banner are inverted. Since there is no way to distinguish the first H in a Banner from the second H, unless one is marked, inversion does not change the spelling of the Banners. The banishing sigil for the overt form of a Banner is actually the invoking sigil for its opposite, occult form; conversely, the invoking sigil for the overt form of a Banner is the banishing sigil for its opposite, occult form.

This sounds confusing, but it is simple in practice. When we inscribe the invoking sigil for a Banner upon the air during a ritual, we are simultaneously suppressing its opposite occult polarity—the form of the Banner that occurs when its first and second H switch position. Later, when we banish the spirit or power of that overt Banner by inscribing its banishing sigil upon the air, we are actually invoking its opposite, occult form, which *cancels out* the already present overt form the way a negative electrical charge cancels a positive. If we were to inscribe the banishing form first, it would *invoke* the occult form of the Banner. To banish this occult form, we would have to inscribe the invoking sigil, which would summon the power of the overt form of the Banner, neutralizing or cancelling out its opposite, occult form.

So, in actuality, all twenty-four sigils invoke the Banners they represent. But once a Banner has been invoked, whether it is an overt or an occult form, the invocation of its mirror opposite twin neutralizes it and dissolves its power to nothingness, in effect sending it away. The overt and occult forms of each Banner are like matter and antimatter—they cannot coexist. However, for the sake of convenience, the invoking sigils of the overt Banners are called Invoking, and the invoking sigils of the occult Banners are called Banishing—because they banish the overt forms of the Name.

When projecting the sigils upon the air, they are distinguished by the motion of their formation. When writing or inscribing them upon the magic circle, or upon amulets or talismans, this motion of formation is indicated by marking the beginning of the sigil with a small cross and the termination with an arrowhead.

Each group of three Banners beginning with the same letter is related to the element of that letter. For example, the Banners IHVH, IHHV, and IVHH are all Banners of elemental fire. The three Banners in each elemental group have very distinct forms that are based upon their cardinal, mutable, and fixed energies. The tracing of a cardinal sigil creates a circular, or spiraling, energy flow. The tracing of a mutable sigil creates a linear zig-zag like a lightning bolt. The tracing of a fixed sigil creates a crossing pattern, as shown in the illustration on page 34.

Invoking	Banishing		Invoking	Banishing

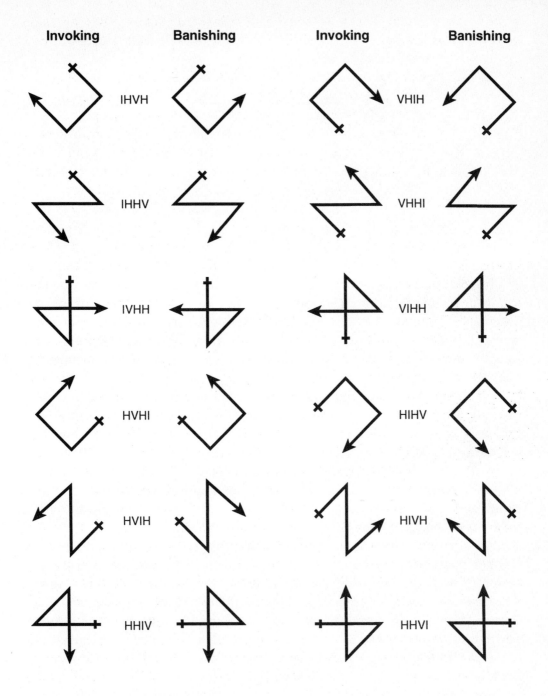

IHVH

IHHV

IVHH

HVHI

HVIH

HHIV

VHIH

VHHI

VIHH

HIHV

HIVH

HHVI

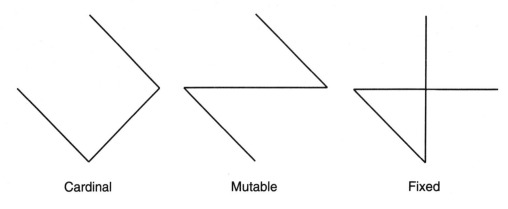

| Cardinal | Mutable | Fixed |

The Three Sigil Forms

It is useful to remember that the initial turning motion in all invoking sigils for the overt Banners is clockwise. Even in the case of the mutable sigils, the first diagonal line is traced clockwise to invoke. Contrarily, when using the sigils to banish the intelligence of a particular overt Banner, or the spirits ruled by that Banner, the first movement around the tetragram is counterclockwise.

Once this underlying pattern is understood, it becomes impossible to forget any of the Banners, or misspell them, or forget which *he* is first and which is second in a name—something difficult to remember without the tetragram. It becomes an easy matter, without consulting any written notes and without ever memorizing the permutations, to invoke all twelve overt Banners in order, merely by remembering the graphic structure of the tetragram and the correct order of the three sigil forms. It requires only a moment of thought to mentally select a particular sigil.

For example, suppose we wish to draw the invoking sigil for the overt Banner of the Name that rules the sign of Capricorn, but we do not recall which form of the Name this is, or the shape of its sigil. By knowing the tetragram, we know that the sigil begins at the left corner, because Capricorn is an earth sign, and the second *he,* on the left corner, is the letter of Tetragrammaton related to elemental earth. Also, we know Capricorn is one of the cardinal signs—therefore the sigil of its Banner will be of the circular kind, its initial movement in a clockwise direction because we wish to invoke an overt form. Remembering the tetragram and the position of the letters at its corners, and knowing the cardinal sigil form, we mentally trace around the edge of the tetragram clockwise from the second he of earth, which gives us the correct Banner of Capricorn, HIHV.

The uses for these sigils of Tetragrammaton are endless and scarcely need to be enumerated to the working ritualist. They are especially potent in commanding the spirits of the heavens. For example, when a planet is passing through a sign of the zodiac, particularly its ruling sign, the Banner of that sign and its sigils are powerful tools to command the spirits of that planet. They are effective when inscribed upon amulets made under their celestial influence, or when seeking results that fall into the domain of a particular sign, because each Banner is the God name of its sign of the zodiac.

The Banners are also used to rule the spirits that reside in the twelve directions of the Earth and the twenty-four hours of the day. They command the twenty-four Wings of the Winds (which are explained in Chapters VIII and XIV) and the Enochian angels that obey the twelve Enochian names of God and the twenty-four Enochian seniors. The Banners represent the enthroned authority of God acting through the houses of heaven and the hours of day and night. All the active agents of heaven—those beings called angels—who cause effects in the manifest universe are ruled and directed by the seated intelligences of the Banners. In this sense, they are no less powerful than the ten *sephiroth*.

VI

VVVVVVVVVVVVVVVVVVVVV

VIBRATING THE NAME

Because Tetragrammaton is before all else a word, its greatest force in magic is called forth only when it is shaped on the tongue and lips and animated by the living breath of the *Ba'al Shem,* or Master of the Name. In voicing the Name aloud, the magician imitates the initial creative act of God, who used the power of his own Name—his essential identity—to create both the universe (macrocosm) and man (microcosm).

The opening verses of Genesis reveal the way the macrocosm was made: "In the beginning God created the heaven and the earth. And the earth was without form, and void; and darkness was upon the face of the deep. And the Spirit of God moved upon the face of the waters" (Gen. 1:1–2). The word for "spirit" for the ancient Hebrews (and indeed, for the Greeks and Romans) was the same as for "breath." What is meant by the words "And the spirit of God moved upon the face of the waters" is that the breath of God caused visible ripples upon the dark mirror surface of the waters of chaos—form from formlessness. The breath of Spirit that shaped chaos into the archetypal pattern of the world was not exhaled silently, but was articulated by divine will.

That is why the next verse reads: "And God said, Let there be light: and there was light" (Gen. 1:3). First comes the verbal expression of the archetypal pattern through the mystical power of the Name; then follows the actual manifest structure. The apostle John understood this quite clearly when he wrote: "In the beginning was the Word, and the Word was with

God, and the Word was God" (John 1:1). This creative (and destructive) Word is Tetragrammaton.

When God created the microcosm, or Lesser Adam, he used the same method by which he had created the universe: "And the Lord God formed man of the dust of the ground, and breathed into his nostrils the breath of life; and man became a living soul" (Gen. 2:7). Human beings are made of dust only in the sense that our material bodies are formed from the elements of the earth. The shape of our souls was determined by the expressed Word in the vital breath of God when he inspired life into Adam.

The *Ba'al Shem* draws upon the divine life force that lies stored in the human blood, particularly the heart. This spiritual energy is the original gift of life from God that has been passed down generation after generation from Adam, the first man. It is carried out of the occult circle of the lesser self upon the vehicle of the breath, which is shaped for a specific magical act by the authority of the Name vibrated through the vocal cords and defined by the palate, lips, and tongue.

About the power of words, the great Renaissance magician Cornelius Agrippa wrote:

> Words therefore are the fittest medium betwixt the speaker and the hearer, carrying with them not only the conception of the mind, but also the virtue of the speaker with a certain efficacy unto the hearers, and this oftentimes with so great a power, that oftentimes they change not only the hearers, but also other bodies, and things that have no life. Now those words are of greater efficacy than others, which represent greater things, as intellectual, celestial, and supernatural, as more expressly, so more mysteriously. Also those that come from a more worthy tongue, or from any of a more holy order: for these, as it were certain signs, and representations, receive a power of celestial, and supercelestial things, as from the virtue of things explained, of which they are the *vehicula,* so from a power put into them by the virtue of the speaker. (Agrippa, *Three Books Of Occult Philosophy* 1.69)

Agrippa is saying that words have the power to affect, not only the mind of the hearer, but also inanimate things, particularly if they represent archetypal, astrological, or divine forces or beings. Their efficacy is greatly magnified when they are uttered by a person purified by prayer, ritual observances, austerities, and good works, because then the virtue inherent in the word is augmented by the virtue in the person voicing it. By "virtue," Agrippa means mana, or magical potency. Magical virtue has little to do with virtue in the conventional sense of propriety; it is rather a concentration and purification of the will.

The words that have the greatest power are names. In magic, names are not mere labels but embody the essence of the thing they represent. Agrippa writes: "Hence magicians say, that proper names of things are certain rays of things, everywhere present at all times, keeping the power of things, as the essence of the thing signified, rules, and is discerned in them, and know the things by them, as by proper, and living images" (*Occult Philosophy* 1.70). Among names, those are most potent that represent celestial or divine spirits and gods, and among these godly names the strongest are the names of Supreme Deity. But the greatest and most potent Name of all is Tetragrammaton, which is not merely a title, but the actual pattern and essence of God. It follows that in magic Tetragrammaton can be used to command all lesser names. This is why it was held in such esteem by kabbalists.

The legend of the Golem, an artificial man created out of clay by Rabbi Loew of Prague in the year 1580, gives useful insight as to how Tetragrammaton may have been used by the *Ba'alei Shem* of the Middle Ages.

Very troubled in his mind about how to protect the Jews of Prague against the malicious libels of a priest named Thaddeus, who preached their destruction, Rabbi Loew used his knowledge of kabbalah to obtain a dream oracle from God, who ordered him to create a Golem of clay to defend Israel. Loew called to him two disciples with the qualities he required. One had been born with the power of the fire element. The other had been born with the power of the water element. Loew himself had been gifted at birth with the power of air. It was necessary, he told the disciples, that all four elements be provided if such a creation was to succeed. He further informed them that he had been given ten words containing a combination of names by which a Golem might be formed.

The three prayed and meditated for seven days. Then, at "four after midnight," they went to the riverbank and used wet clay to fashion the figure of a man three cubits (about five feet) long lying on its back. The three stood at the feet of the Golem facing it. Loew ordered the disciple who had been gifted at birth with the power of the fire element to walk around the Golem seven times clockwise while reciting a "combination of letters" Loew had given him. Immediately, the clay figure began to glow like a bed of live coals. Then the second disciple gifted with the water element walked seven times around the Golem reciting a different combination of Hebrew letters. Steam issued from the body and cooled it. Hair grew from the head of the Golem, and upon the tips of its fingers appeared fingernails. Rabbi Loew himself circled the body seven times sunwise, reciting yet another combination of letters.

The three kabbalists stood together at the foot of the Golem and recited the words from Genesis 2:7—"And he breathed into his nostrils the breath of life, and the man became a living soul." The writer of the legend explains that, in the air of the breath, there must be found fire and water. The Golem opened his eyes and Rabbi Loew ordered him to stand up. It is significant that, although the Golem could see, hear, and understand, he "did not have the power of speech in his mouth."

Ten years following its creation, when the Golem had accomplished its task and the Jews of Prague were safe once again, Rabbi Loew decided it was time to dissolve the artificial man back into clay. He summoned the same two disciples, who met him in the attic room where the Golem lay sleeping on a cot. This time every action that had been done in the creation of the Golem was reversed. The three stood together at the head of the Golem rather than at his feet. They walked seven times around his cot in succession, this time beginning by walking down past the left side of the Golem, whereas in the creation ritual they had begun their circumambulations by walking up past the right side. Each recited the same "combinations of letters," but in reverse order. At the conclusion of this circling, the Golem lay inert upon his cot, "like a lump of hardened clay."

This legend is from the *Book of the Miracles of R. Loew,* published in Piotrkov in 1909 (see Raphael Patai, *Gates to the Old City* [Avon, 1980], pp. 636–42).

The numerology in the legend is highly instructive. Loew is given ten words of power by God that enable the creation of the artificial man. These were probably the divine names of the ten *sephiroth*. Although the *sephiroth* have their own descriptive titles such as Wisdom, Understanding, Beauty, and so on, fundamentally they consist of the "ten names of God that must not be erased." These are the ten essential names which collectively express Tetragrammaton. They are arranged upon the sephirothic tree in the following order:

Kether—Eheieh

Chokmah—Yah

Binah—IHVH (vocalized "Elohim")

Chesed—El

Geburah—Elohim Gibor

Tiphareth—IHVH (vocalized "Adonai")

Netzach—IHVH (vocalized "Adonai") Tzabaoth

Hod—Elohim Tzabaoth

Yesod—Shaddai, or El Chai

Malkuth—Adonai ha Aretz

It is important to understand that the true *sephiroth* are not the descriptive titles Kether, Chokmah, Binah, and so on; neither are they the spheres on the glyph of the tree of the kabbalah. The true *sephiroth* are nothing other than the ten names of God. All the rest is window dressing—an attempt to make the meanings and relationship of these ten names more comprehensible.

All four of the elements are said to be required in the creation of the Golem because four is the number of manifest being. The rabbis sought to create a physical man, not an ideal one. However, the "elements" of Loew and his disciples represent, not the four physical elements which are all present in the clay of the Golem's body, but the three active qualities or forces, represented in the kabbalah by the three Hebrew mother letters, *aleph* (א), *mem* (מ), and *shin* (ש). *Shin* stands for fire, but also for the cardinal quality of the zodiac. *Mem* stands for water, but also for the fixed quality. *Aleph* stands for air, but also for the mutable quality. The mutable lies between the cardinal and fixed (as is shown in the illustration on page 21). *Aleph* is said to be like the tongue of the balance.

The *Ba'alai Shem* meditated seven days because seven is a potent number in magic, the sum of three and four, the number of the wandering bodies of the heavens. For this same reason, they each circumambulated the clay figure seven times, moving sunwise to generate a creative vortex, as opposed to a counterclockwise, destructive vortex. They met at the riverbank at "four after midnight" (probably four hours after midnight) because four is the number of physical realization.

The "combinations of letters" each disciple was given by Rabbi Loew to recite were probably the four Banners of Tetragrammaton under each celestial quality. The first disciple, who possessed the gift of fire *(shin),* would have recited the letters of the cardinal IHVH, HVHI, VHIH, and HIHV. The second disciple, who had the gift of water *(mem),* would have recited the letters of the fixed IVHH, HHIV, VIHH, and HHVI. Finally, Rabbi Loew himself, who had the mediating gift of air *(aleph),* would have tied these extremes together by reciting the letters of the mutable IHHV, HVIH, VHHI, and HIVH.

It is possible that words of power other than the twelve Banners of Tetragrammaton were used in the creation of the Golem. However, the permutations of the Name would seem the most appropriate choice for this ritual, which imitates the creative act of Supreme Deity. It is worth noting that the Golem, although he could see, hear, and understand what was happening around him, did not possess the gift of speech. Since the Golem was created not by God, but by men who were themselves the creations of God, the spark of divinity that lies within each living human being was not passed on to him. Even though he looked like a man, he was a mere simulacrum. The

Golem could never have made another Golem by magic, because the Word which is in God and humans was not within him. This lack of a creative divine spark is symbolized by the muteness of the Golem.

It would seem that the author who recorded this legend of the Golem (Patai thinks it was Judah Rosenburg, who is listed on the title page of the *Miracles of R. Loew* as the editor) made an error in describing the dissolution of the Golem. Although it is said explicitly that "everything we did then was the reverse of what we had done at the creation of the Golem" (*Gates to the Old City*, p. 640), if the instructions are followed, they result in sunwise circumambulation (unless the Golem was lying on his face). Clearly the circumambulation should begin at the head and proceed counterclockwise seven times, against the course of the sun, in order to return the Golem to clay.

I have taken the trouble to discuss the Golem legend at such length because it illustrates the use of Tetragrammaton among the Jewish *Ba'alai Shem* of the Middle Ages. Although this ritual of the kabbalah would not actually cause a clay figure to become flesh and blood, it would induce a celestial intelligence to enter into that clay figure and reside within it, where it could be consulted as an oracle on important questions. This is likely the truth behind the Golem legend. Rabbi Loew probably created a manlike statue, then used the magic of the kabbalah to induce an angel of God to dwell within it and act as a protective and tutelary spirit for the Jews of Prague during their time of trial.

There are two aspects to any name, both of which must be considered in magic—the internal name and the uttered name. The internal name is what we understand the meaning of a name to be, and the inner silent expression of that name, as when we seem to speak names in our dreams, or voice them silently in our own thoughts. It is vital in magic that we understand completely the words of power, particularly the supreme Name, Tetragrammaton. The foregoing analysis of the structure of Tetragrammaton was intended to convey the inner understanding of the Name. The second aspect of any name is its correct vocalization. In the systems of modern magic that have descended from the Golden Dawn, this vocalization is called "vibrating" the name. Unless a name is correctly vibrated, it never becomes completely real in magic, and as a consequence its power is never fully realized.

The correct vibration of words of power, which in Eastern occultism go under the general title of "mantras," is the most jealously guarded secret of magic. Each magical system has its own hidden methods for vibrating words and names. Because these techniques are so closely protected, they are inevitably lost when a magical system becomes unable to sustain itself by the traditional transfer of secrets from master to disciple. The breaking of the chain of esoteric knowledge has many causes. Usually it results from the disruption of war, but political suppression, religious intolerance, lack of new initiates, and natural disasters all have caused the loss of magical knowledge at different times in human history.

We know that the Teutonic rune masters of ancient Europe used chants in conjunction with the rune symbols, but we no longer know what those chants were. More importantly, we do not know how they were vibrated, because they were never written down. The druids of the Celts conveyed their magical wisdom verbally. Because of the strong bardic tradition of the later druids, it very likely consisted of vocalizations of words of power, but again, the technique as well as the particular chants has been lost. The female worshippers of Dionysus among the ancient Greeks employed blood-curdling cries that were reported to freeze the blood of any man foolish enough to venture within hearing range. Some of these wild chants have been preserved, but the manner of their vocalization has been lost.

The universal features of language allow us to make some general observations on the magical vibration of names. Consonants for the most part cannot be extended or elongated on the voice without the support of vowels. For example, if we try to stretch the sound of the letter B with the breath, we must add an E sound after it, which gives us B-e-e-e-e. Even those consonants that are sustainable, such as F, L, M, N, R, S, V, and Z, all involve a tightness in the throat, compression of the lips, or pressure of the tongue against the palate or teeth. They are sounds held under constraint.

Only the vowels can be voiced with a fully opened throat. This allows them to be projected with considerable power, because the column of air within the open mouth and throat can be made to resonate like the hollow interior of a drum. When we loudly sustain a vowel on the voice, we can feel this vibration of air against our diaphragm and chest and feel it tickling inside our nose and at the back of our throat. The consequence of this inherent difference between vowels and consonants is that vowels have power and consonants, for the most part, do not. Both are necessary to form words, but the vowels are the vitality of the words, and the consonants merely act as a template to limit and shape that vital energy into a unique pattern. Magically, vowels are masculine and represent Shiva or Shakta, the creative god force that embodies everything but is itself without form; consonants are feminine and represent Shakti, the formative goddess force that has no inherent creativity but enables all creation.

The most famous of Eastern mantras, OM or AUM, involves the prolonged sustaining of the O sound, which causes a strong vibration in the diaphragm, chest cavity, and throat, followed by a gradual closing of the lips with the mouth cavity still held open, so that the M sound, which gradually emerges out of the O sound, transfers this vibration from the chest to the upper throat and nose. In this way the magical essence of the OM is drawn forth from deep in the abdomen and brought up into the head.

The awareness that the life force in a name lies in its vowels caused the ancient Hebrew priests to conceal the vowels of Tetragrammaton, initially from outsiders such as the Greeks and Romans, then ultimately from their fellow Hebrews, who were regarded by the priests as too worldly and corrupted to be entrusted with the true vibration of the Name. When the priesthood failed after the destruction of Herod's Temple, the correct vibration of the Name was lost.

It would perhaps be a hopeless task to attempt to restore the correct vibrations of all twelve Banners of the name when there is so much doubt over just the first Banner, IHVH. However, it is the custom in modern magic to vibrate names of power letter by individual letter. By this system, the first Banner of Tetragrammaton would not be sounded "Yahveh," but would be vocalized "Yod-Hay-Vav-Hay." This has the advantage of producing four distinct sounds for each Banner, echoing the fourfold nature of the Name.

Since it may sometimes be desirable to distinguish between the first and second H in vibrating the Banners, it is possible to vary their pronunciation slightly so that the first H is vibrated "He" and the second H is vibrated "Hay." Using this system, which I present here for the first time because of its practical utility in ritual magic, the overt Banner of Scorpio, **H**HIV, would be vibrated "He-Hay-Yod-Vav," whereas the occult Banner of Scorpio, **H**HIV, would be vibrated "Hay-He-Yod-Vav."

This vocalization of a name letter by letter is not as unusual as might first appear. The language called Enochian, which was received psychically from spirits by the Elizabethan philosopher John Dee and his seer, the alchemist Edward Kelley, is almost unpronounceable unless it is voiced letter by letter. When Enochian was adopted into the Golden Dawn as a magical alphabet and language suitable for vibrating words of power, this letter by letter method of speaking it was adopted and was carried on by the Great Beast, Aleister Crowley, in his own system of magic. The Golden Dawn also vibrated Tetragrammaton letter by letter.

The technique of Golden Dawn vibration of words and names is one of the most useful magical legacies of that Victorian occult order. It is set forth briefly, but quite clearly, in Israel Regardie's *Golden Dawn* (Llewellyn, 1989, p. 487). For those who do not own this book I will describe the method.

First, elevate your mind to the pure white radiance of Kether, the highest *sephirah* on the tree of the kabbalah. If this precaution is not taken, the vibration of a name will draw any astral forces that are in harmony with your inner emotions at the time of the vibration, and these spirits may hinder the desired effect of the vibration.

Second, take a deep breath and mentally fill your heart center with the white light of Kether, keeping your consciousness concentrated within your heart.

Third, while retaining the breath, formulate the letters of the name you intend to vibrate as though the name were written in your heart in brilliant white letters. Try to visualize the letters clearly as though they were formed out of scintillating white flame.

Fourth, emitting the breath, slowly pronounce the letters so that the sound vibrates strongly within you. At the same time, imagine that your body fills the entire universe and that the vibrations you feel within your own body are felt in every corner of creation. Imagine that your breath pervades the universe and that the sound of the letters in the name can be heard everywhere in time/space simultaneously.

The Golden Dawn method works well in vibrating the Banners of Tetragrammaton. Remember to keep your spine straight and your shoulders back to avoid pressure on your chest and diaphragm. Strive for openness in your throat and keep your mouth wide to produce the fullest sound. You should be able to feel the vibration strongly all through your chest. Notice how the vibration moves as you change from letter to letter.

While sounding the letters of an overt Banner in order, it is sometimes helpful to draw the invoking sigil of the Banner large upon the air with the right index finger, or the wand, and visualize the sigil floating at heart level in flaming white light. Vibrate the first letter as you point to the beginning of the sigil; then, as you move your finger from angle to angle, vibrate each letter in turn.

The Banners are highly effective when used as a mantra, either individually or collectively. When using a particular Banner for a specific purpose, vibrate the letters rhythmically one after the other, visualizing each Hebrew letter in turn shining with brilliant white light within your heart center. When you reach the end of the Banner, begin it again so that the letters are vibrated in a continuous spiral. This mantra technique is best practiced sitting comfortably in a dimly lit, quiet room. It is necessary that all the attention be focused inward upon the letters of the Name and upon the vibrations occurring in the body.

Another excellent mantra exercise is to vibrate each of the twelve overt Banners one after the other in their proper order, while visualizing within the heart center the invoking sigil of each Banner forming in white light as its letters are sounded. There is no better way to learn the technique of vibration and the correct ordering and shape of the Banners and their sigils.

Once you have mastered the way of vibrating words of power, you will be able to employ it in the "commanding voice." This can be very useful when it is necessary to cause others to react immediately below the level of conscious thought—for example, to make someone jump out of the way of a falling object. It can also be used to freeze an aggressor, such as a mugger, motionless for a second or two. Orders given in the commanding voice should be vibrated from the diaphragm in a deep forceful tone with an open throat.

The effect of an unexpected, forceful noise has long been known in the East. In karate, a loud cry is used to startle an opponent just prior to the delivery of a blow. We have all experienced the freezing of the heart that occurs when a large dog with a deep voice creeps up behind us and suddenly barks, or there is an unexpected clap of thunder. The commanding voice is an extension of this powerful effect, but instead of merely seeking to startle, we use the voice to implant simple commands in others below the level of their conscious judgement.

It is best to keep the instructions given by the commanding voice brief, if possible restricting them to a single word, or at most a few words. When the commanding voice is used for more complex commands, the mind of the person commanded must pause to analyze the instructions, and this allows time for judgement to come into play. If the command given consists only of such things as STOP or RUN or DROP IT the person receiving the command will react before he or she has a chance to analyze the action.

Never use the power of the commanding voice recklessly. It is capable of implanting commands directly into the subconscious and, if used with malicious intent, can impress permanent scars into the mind of an individual. The child whose father or mother continually cries "stupid!" in a deep, forceful voice has little chance of ever growing into a fully functional human being. When such hurtful commands are delivered with the commanding voice, their effect is multiplied tenfold.

VII

ʾ ʾ ʾ ʾ ʾ ʾ ʾ ʾ ʾ ʾ ʾ ʾ ʾ ʾ ʾ ʾ ʾ
PENTAGRAMMATON

The rebirth of ceremonial magic that occurred in Europe during the Renaissance was in no small measure driven by the amalgamation of the kabbalah of the Jews with the classical occultism of Greece and Rome. Central to this European hybrid was the tenet that a new name of power had been revealed by God that would supplant the ancient supremacy of Tetragrammaton. This new name expressed the essential being of God the Son, just as the old name expressed the nature of God the Father.

According to this theory, the magical name of Jesus was composed of the same four Hebrew letters as Tetragrammaton, but with one letter added in the middle, the Hebrew *shin* (ש), which stands for the element fire, or for the cardinal quality. The Fivefold Name, IHShVH (יהשוה), which can be rendered into English as "Yeheshuah," was held by the Christian kabbalists of the Renaissance to have deprived Tetragrammaton of all its power, even as Jesus Christ had supplanted the jealous God of the Hebrews and the Gospels had displaced the Old Testament.

This view was first explicitly set forth by Giovanni Pico della Mirandola (1463–94) in his seminal seventy-two *Conclusions* on the kabbalah, published in 1486. In the fourteenth conclusion, he argued that the insertion of the *shin* into Tetragrammaton represents the descent of the fiery holy Spirit into the fourfold realm of matter—the incarnation of God in human flesh.

Pico held that the addition of the Sh made the previously ineffable IHVH pronounceable.

This premise was defended by the first great non-Jewish kabbalist, Johannes Reuchlin (1455–1522) in his highly influential work *De verbo mirifico* (On the wonder-working word), published in Germany in 1494, and his later work *De arte cabalistica* (On the science of the kabbalah), published in 1517. Reuchlin quotes from Pico and argues that history can be divided into three periods: the first period, of Nature, in which God revealed himself to the patriarchs through the name of three letters, Shaddai (שׁדּי); the second period, of the Torah, in which God revealed himself to Moses through the name of four letters, Tetragrammaton; and the third period, of grace and redemption, in which God revealed himself to the apostles through the name of five letters, Yeheshuah.

Reuchlin held that with the birth of Jesus, the name of four letters had been rendered powerless, its ability to cause miracles having passed into the name of Jesus. This is why in the Gospels the name of Jesus has such force in casting out demons from the bodies of the possessed and in healing the sick. By using the holy tongue, Hebrew, and the numerical methods of the kabbalah, Reuchlin maintained that the truths of Christian doctrine could be proved and, more than this, that all occult secrets could be laid bare.

The importance of Pentagrammaton was further enhanced by the Venetian Francesco Giorgi (1456–1540), who, in his book *De harmonia mundi* (On the harmony of the world), published at Venice in 1525, demonstrated the ideas of Pico and Reuchlin through the use of kabbalistic numerology. These Christian kabbalists and others who followed in their footsteps were greatly aided by several Jewish scholars who converted to Christianity, such as Flavius Mithridates, who translated many kabbalistic texts for Pico, and Paulus Ricius, the private physician to the German Emperor Maximilian, who published Rabbi Joseph Gikatilla's influential *Portae lucis* (The gates of light) at Augsburg in 1516.

Concerning the power of the Fivefold Name of Jesus, Cornelius Agrippa quotes directly from the *Conclusions* of Pico della Mirandola when he writes:

> As John in the Revelations describeth that heavenly city, whose twelve gates are guarded with twelve angels, infusing on them what they receive from the divine name, twelve times revolved; and in the foundations of that city the names of the twelve apostles, and the Lamb; for as in the Law, in the stones of the ephod, and foundations of the holy city described by Ezekiel, were written the names of the tribes of Israel, and the name of four letters did predominate over them; so in the Gospel, the

names of the apostles are written in the stones of the
foundation of the heavenly city, which stones stand for
the tribes of Israel in the Church, over which the name of
the Lamb hath influence, that is, the name of Jesus, in
which is all the virtue of the four-lettered name; seeing
that Jehovah the Father hath given him all things.

Therefore the heavens receive from the angels, that
which they dart down; but the angels from the great
name of God and Jesu, the virtue whereof is first in God,
afterward diffused into these twelve and seven angels,
by whom it is extended into the twelve signs, and into
the seven planets, and consequently into all the other
ministers and instruments of God, penetrating even to
the very depths.

Hence Christ saith, whatsoever you shall ask the
Father in my name, he will give you; and after his resurrection saith, in my name they shall cast out devils, and
do as followeth; so that the name of four letters is no further necessary, the whole virtue thereof being translated
into the name Jesus, in which only miracles are done;
neither is there any other (as Peter saith) under heaven
given unto men, by which they can be saved, but that.

But let us not think, that by naming Jesus pro-
phanely, as the name of a certain man, we can do miracles by virtue of it: but we must invocate it in the holy
Spirit, with a pure mind and a fervent spirit, that we
may obtain those things which are promised us in him;
especially knowledge going before, without which there
is no hearing of us, according to that of the prophet, I will
hear him because he hath known my name.

Hence at this time no favour can be drawn from the
heavens, unless the authority, favour and consent of the
name Jesu intervene; hence the Hebrews and Cabalists
most skillful in the divine names, can work nothing after
Christ by those old names, as their fathers have done
long since; and now it is by experience confirmed, that no
devil nor power of hell, which vex and trouble men, can
resist this name, but will they, nill they, bow the knee
and obey, when the name Jesu by a due pronunciation is
proposed to them to be worshipped. (*Three Books Of
Occult Philosophy* 3.12)

When Agrippa writes of "knowledge going before," he is referring to the age-old belief, held by the ancient Egyptians and others, that knowledge of the true name of a spirit gives command over that spirit. When Agrippa writes of invoking the name of Jesus "in the holy Spirit," he means the elevation and focus of the mind that comes with magical purity of the will. When he writes of "a due pronunciation," he refers to the technique of vibrating the Fivefold Name.

Although the Christian Kabbalists of the Renaissance were quite sincere in their belief that the name IHShVH had displaced and rendered ineffective the name IHVH, we need not give their opinions too much credit. Tetragrammaton can never be displaced by another name, since it embodies in its very structure the order and plan of the universe. The Fivefold Name supplements Tetragrammaton, but it does not supplant it.

Reuchlin gives two ways of writing the esoteric name of Jesus. The first is with the added *shin* in the exact middle of Tetragrammaton—IHShVH (יהשוה), pronounced Yeheshuah. The second form uses the same five Hebrew letters, but places the *shin* after the *vau* of Tetragrammaton—IHVShH (יהושה), pronounced Yehovashah.

As I demonstrated in my book, *The New Magus** (pp. 110–1), both of these names can be extracted with supreme elegance from the occult figure of the pentagram, to the points of which the five letters of the name are attributed in modern magic, along with the five occult elements: spirit (Sh), fire (I), air (V), water (first H), and earth (second H):

If the continuous line of the pentagram is traced from point to point clockwise, beginning with the point of spirit, it reveals the natural order of these five elements, from the lightest and most active (spirit) to the heaviest and most inert (earth). If the Hebrew letters are read in a circle around the pentagram counterclockwise, beginning at the point of *yod,* the name IHShVH, Yeheshuah, results; but if the letters are read in a circle clockwise, the name IHVShH, Yehovashah, results.

This relationship is very similar to that which links the order of the seven days of the week with the astrological order of the seven planets on the heptagram (see illustration on page 53).

If the line of the seven-pointed star is traced clockwise from point to point, the order of the planets associated with the seven days of the week results. Beginning with Saturday, the Jewish Sabbath, this order is: Saturday (Saturn), Sunday (sun), Monday (moon), Tuesday (Tew—the Teutonic Mars), Wednesday (Woden—the Teutonic Mercury), Thursday (Thor—the Teutonic Jupiter), Friday (Frija—the Teutonic Venus). If a circle is traced clockwise around the heptagram from this same planet, Saturn, the order of the planets touched by the circle is their ancient astrological order based upon their apparent rate of progress across the heavens. From slowest

*New Millennium Magic, an updated and expanded version of The New Magus, will be available in May 1996 from Llewellyn Worldwide, Ltd.

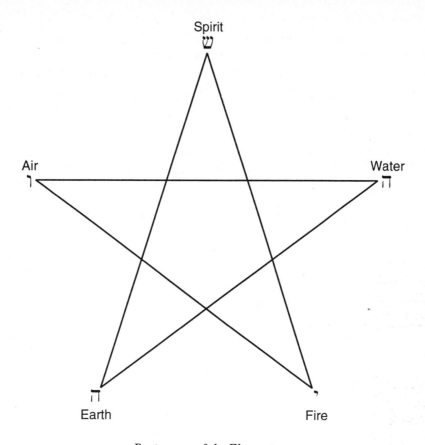

Pentagram of the Elements

heavens. From slowest planet to fastest, this order is: Saturn, Jupiter, Mars, sun, Venus, Mercury, moon.

The opposite directions of motion around the pentagram created by Yeheshuah and Yehovashah allow these two forms of Pentagrammaton to serve as words of power for banishing and invoking spirits, particularly those associated with the magical elements, the salamanders (fire), sylphs (air), undines (water), and gnomes (earth).

An effective technique is to hold the right arm extended straight out in front of the body at heart level with the fingers spread stiffly forward so that their tips define the points of an upright pentagram. This must be practiced a few times until the proper angle between the fingers is attained, so that as nearly as possible, a perfect pentagram is formed. The left palm should be pressed tightly over the heart center.

To create an invoking vortex, visualize the Hebrew letters of the invoking form of Pentagrammaton, Yehovashah (יהושה), flaming with white light in your heart center. Extend your right hand with the fingers stiffly forward to form an upright pentagram and vibrate the letters of the name one by one (pronounced "Yod-Hay-Vav-Shin-Hay"). As you vibrate each letter, visualize it flowing like liquid fire from your heart center into your left hand, up your left arm and across your body, and through your right arm to form itself upon the fingertip of your right hand associated with it on the pentagram— *yod* (little finger), *he* (thumb), *vau* (index finger), *shin* (middle finger), *he* (ring finger). Visualize a large vortex of white light begin to swirl clockwise upon the air in front of you, growing brighter as it gathers strength and spirals inward to a focus on the air in front of your extended hand. This blazing pinwheel of invocation may be contracted, expanded, or moved through the air by the force of your will.

To create a banishing vortex, stand as before and visualize the Hebrew letters of the banishing form of Pentagrammaton, Yeheshuah (יהשוה), flaming with white light in your heart center. Vibrate the letters of the name one by one (pronounced "Yod-Hay-Shin-Vav-Hay"). As you vibrate each letter, visualize it flowing out of your heart center into your left hand, up your left arm, across your body, and down your right arm to form itself on the fingertip of your right hand associated with it on the pentagram—*yod* (little finger), *he* (ring finger), *shin* (middle finger), *vau* (index finger), *he* (thumb). Visualize a vortex of white light begin to expand in a counterclockwise swirl from a point in front of your extended right hand. As it grows larger, it gradually loses energy and becomes less brilliant, until at last it dissipates into the distance like an ever-expanding swirl of smoke.

The invoking and banishing vortices of Pentagrammaton can be used in conjunction with the invoking and banishing pentagrams of the elements, to activate them more powerfully, or indeed in any magical operation where spirits or occult energies are to be concentrated or dissipated.

The invoking vortex of IHVShH is excellent for causing a spirit to indwell a talisman. For this purpose, it should be visualized surrounding the talisman with the right hand held a few inches over it as the name Yehovashah is vibrated. Once the invoking vortex has been established, the name of the spirit you wish to invoke into the magical object should be vibrated as you draw the sigil of that spirit in the air directly over the object with your right index finger. This process of creating the vortex and invoking the name of the spirit should be repeated several times in succession until you have an inner sense that the spirit had been successfully induced to dwell within the talisman.

Conversely, the banishing vortex created by the vibration of IHShVH can be used to purge or purify an object that retains strong astral associations. It is also useful in the exorcism of objects, places, or persons haunted or possessed by discarnate intelligences. Some doorways, because of evil spirits or humans that may have crossed their thresholds, are unlucky for

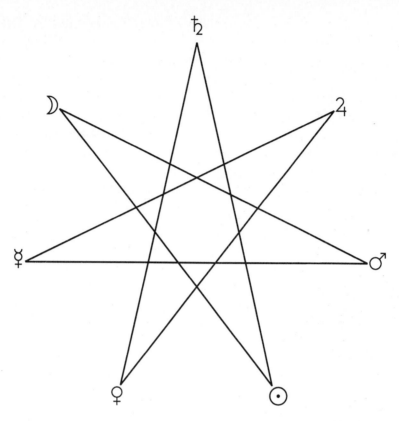

Heptagram of the Planets

those who must pass through them regularly. These can be successfully purged of their malevolent associations by the name Yeheshuah coupled with the banishing vortex. Even the name IHShVH alone, strongly vibrated upon the air without the visualization of the banishing vortex, is potent in cleansing spaces.

Of all names of power, the name of Yeheshuah is the most potent, when properly vibrated, for curing sickness or banishing malicious spirits. It is the esoteric name of the Messiah of the Jews and the Christ of the Christians. The magical power that has always been most closely associated with Jesus is the ability to drive out sickness from the mind and body. Thus the name IHShVH is not only a banishing formula, but a healing formula as well. To free a person from nightmares, possession, depression, or obsession (persistent destructive thoughts), place your right hand upon the forehead of the sufferer and your left hand over your heart center. Visualize the Hebrew letters IHShVH glowing in your heart and vibrate the letters so that your breath touches the face of the person. This should be done in a rhythmic chant, repeating the letters of Yeheshuah over and over. Time the rhythm of your vibrations of the name so that, as you sound the letters, the sufferer inhales. In this way your breath will be drawn directly into the body of that person through the lungs and spread to every point by the circulation of the blood. You should visualize the white light of the name flowing from your heart center, up your left arm, across your body, and out your right hand into the forehead of the sufferer. Visualize the body of the sufferer filling with white light, and dark shadows fleeing from this light through the top of the person's skull and out the soles of the feet.

To heal sickness, the right hand should be placed firmly over the site of the illness and the white light of IHShVH concentrated in this area. Vibrate the name with the lips close to the part of the body that is sick so that the breath touches the skin in this place. It sometimes helps for the ill person to also visualize the healing white light flow into the sick organ or other part of the body. For example, a person with bone cancer would visualize the white light filling the marrow and causing the entire skeleton to radiate with a cool and soothing energy. The name should be repeated over and over in time with the inhalations of the patient for a period of from fifteen minutes to half an hour, and this treatment repeated each day until there is a complete recovery.

Healing by means of Yeheshuah should only be attempted in conjunction with regular medical treatment. It is never wise to depend solely upon magical methods of healing. The body responds weakly to the commands of the spirit when the spirit is clouded by daily cares, emotions, desires, and thoughts. This is almost always the case, even with the most skillful and dedicated healers. Medical science may be limited, but within its limits it is effective and should be turned to first, not last, for the treatment of sickness. Only after you have consulted a doctor should you consult a magical healer or attempt to use magical healing techniques on yourself.

VIII

THE HIEROGLYPHIC MONAD

In 1564, the great English philosopher, astrologer, and magician John Dee wrote a short Latin tract in the form of twenty-four theorems titled the *Monas hieroglyphica* (The hieroglyphic monad). It was begun on January 13th and finished on the 25th of the same month while Dee was visiting the city of Antwerp. The work was printed at Antwerp by William Silvius in March of 1564.

In structure, it follows the pattern of classical texts on geometry—Dee was famed for his brilliant introduction to the *Elements* of Euclid, and he was a skilled mathematician and geometer. Each theorem of the *Monad* involves the examination of a different symbolic aspect of a single geometric figure, which Dee called the hieroglyphic monad, using its mathematical proportions as an aid to understanding. This curious symbol is similar to the planetary glyph of Mercury, except that a dot has been added to the middle of the circle and the sign of Aries attached to the bottom of the cross.

For Dee, the hieroglyphic monad represented in a graphic way the entire universe, which he believed might be understood by a close examination of the glyph's parts and proportions. He considered the work of supreme importance—it was dedicated to the German Emperor Maximilian II—and thought it had been divinely inspired. In Theorem XXIII, he declares: "In the name of Jesus Christ crucified upon the Cross, I say the Spirit writes these things rapidly through me; I hope, and I believe, I am merely the quill which traces these characters" (J. W. Hamilton-Jones translation [1947], *The Hieroglyphic Monad* [New York: Samuel Weiser, 1975], p. 41).

The work created a great sensation in its own time. A second edition was brought out by Dee at Frankfurt in 1591. Despite the interest it aroused, no one understood it. Dee deliberately concealed the plain meaning of the symbol under a cloak of alchemical and mathematical allusions. Diane di Prima, who provides a brief biographical note to the Weiser edition of the *Monad*, states: "We have the assurance of the several Dee scholars of the present day that the key to the interpretation of 'The Hieroglyphic Monad' is lost." She goes on to say that the understanding of the symbol of the monad seems to require the assistance of an "oral teaching" that has not come down to us, although Dee probably communicated it to others in his lifetime.

I believe I have the key, or one of the keys, to a true understanding of Dee's monad symbol. While I do not pretend to a complete gnosis of the glyph, it is necessary to examine it here because it bears directly on the structure and symbolism of Tetragrammaton, particularly as the Name relates to the symbolism of the planets.

There can be no doubt that Dee was a Christian kabbalist. He was familiar with all the major magical texts of the Renaissance, including the *Occult Philosophy* of Cornelius Agrippa. He was skilled in the art of ceremonial magic and knowledgeable in the numerical and positional manipulations of the kabbalah—indeed, in Theorem XXIII of the *Monad,* he specifically names a technique for substituting Hebrew letters based upon systems of permutation of the Hebrew alphabet: "Tziruph or Themura."

Since Dee was both a skilled kabbalist and a devoted Christian, it is virtually certain that he knew and embraced the doctrine, held by Pico della Mirandola, Johannes Reuchlin, Francesco Giorgi, and Cornelius Agrippa, that the Fivefold Name of Jesus had supplanted the place of Tetragrammaton as the supreme wonder-working name. It is this esoteric name of Jesus that is the lost key to understanding the hieroglyphic monad.

The glyph of the monad is drawn by Dee according to very exact proportions, which I have reproduced in the figure on the opposite page, although these proportions do not enter into the basic examination of the figure we will undertake here.

Dee begins the construction of the monad with a single point, the origin of all things. He extends from this point a line, and by revolving the line inscribes a circle. This circle with a point at its center finds its astrological correspondence in the sun. Above the circle of the sun but interlocked with it, Dee places the crescent of the moon, which he explicitly states to be semicircular. Below the circle of the sun he places a cross, which he later says corresponds with, among other things, the four elements. Below the cross he puts the symbol for the zodiac sign Aries.

These parts of the monad may be assigned to the letters of Pentagrammaton. The point in the center of the circle of the sun represents the invisible point at the upper tip of the Hebrew letter *yod* (ʾ), and the circle represents the entire *yod,* as well as the cardinal quality of astrology. The semicircle of the moon represents the first *he* (ה) and the mutable quality. The vertical bar of the cross of the elements represents the *vau* (ו) of the Name and the horizontal bar the second *He.* The entire cross stands for the earth and the fixed quality. The symbol of Aries, which is the first of the fire signs, and as Dee observes, "the origin of the fiery triplicity" (*Hieroglyphic Monad,* p. 13), stands for the *shin* (ש) of the esoteric name of Jesus. Notice that *shin,* which is the Hebrew letter associated with fire, has three points, even as the fiery symbol of Aries has three points. These may be taken to stand for the divine trinity.

Dee states that he has added the sign of Aries to the monad "to signify that in the practice of this Monad the use of fire is required" (Theorem X). Had Dee not added the sign of Aries, the symbol of the monad would accurately represent Tetragrammaton. He regarded the insertion of the fifth symbol, the Sh in IHShVH, as necessary to act as a channel through which the power of the ternary (sun, moon, earth, or cardinal, mutable, fixed) might pass into the septenary.

The Hieroglyphic Monad

The cross in the glyph of the monad exhibits these essential principles of trinity, quarternity, and septernity, as well as the role played by the fifth factor in joining and balancing these principles. It is a Christian cross, having a lower arm that is longer than the upper arm. In Theorem VI, Dee says that the cross may signify either the ternary or the quaternary. The ternary is expressed by the cross of two straight lines "having a copulative centre." The quaternary is expressed by the separation of the arms of the cross from this central point to form four lines at right angles to each other, as shown in the illustration on the following page.

Writing about the Roman numeral for the decad, X, Dee says somewhat obscurely that it defines the place "where the Ternary conducts its force into the Septenary" (Theorem VIII). His comments in Theorem XVI clarify what he means, where he observes that the Roman numeral X, which stands for the number ten, may be divided through the center to produce two Vs,

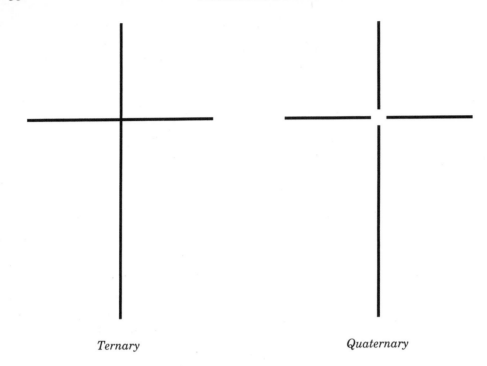

Ternary   *Quaternary*

equalling five and five. Each V points like an arrow to the intersection of the cross. It is this central point that conducts the force of the ternary into the septenary. He is in effect saying that the fifth letter inserted into Tetragrammaton, the fiery *shin,* is the conduit through which the power of the three qualities of cardinal, mutable, and fixed flow into the seven astrological planets.

It is not difficult to see how Dee gets divisions of three and seven from the cross. Without a definite point of intersection at the center of the cross, there are only three possible parts or divisions to this figure—the whole cross, the vertical axis, and the horizontal axis. However, if we add a central point that interrupts the two axes and breaks them in the middle, to these three parts we can add the four L-shaped quarters of the figure for a total of seven possible forms (see illustration on opposite page).

From the circle of the sun, the semicircle of the moon, the cross of the elements, and the sign of Aries, Dee forms all seven of the planetary glyphs, rightly observing that the glyphs of the planets are merely combinations of these basic symbols. For example, the sign of Jupiter (♃) is made up of the crescent of the moon over the cross of the earth. He makes the error, as it seems to me, of assuming that the sign of Aries is an essential component of the planetary glyphs. I believe that the arrow in the glyph of Mars is no more than a corrupted form of the cross.

The prominence of the number twenty-four in the *Hieroglyphic Monad* is conclusive proof that the work is indeed concerned with the esoteric name of

Divisions of the Cross

God. You will remember that there are actually twenty-four Banners of Tetragrammaton, but because the second and fourth letters of the Name are the same, only twelve distinct forms may be written, unless the first H is distinguished in some way from the second H.

Dee relates these twenty-four Banners to the twenty-four hours of the day, which he divides into two groups of twelve by the equinoctial sign Aries. The manifest set of Banners he intends should be associated with Aries and the sun. The occult set of Banners he associates with Taurus and the moon. These zodiac signs form the top and bottom parts of the Monad, connected by the cross of the elements.

Dee explains the glyph of Taurus as the thin crescent which the moon reveals in the sign of Taurus just after emerging from conjunction with the sun in the sign of Aries. He explains the sign of Aries as two semicircles representing the waxing and waning halves of the moon, which, when united, reveal the full circular glory of the reflected solar orb.

In Theorem XI, he writes concerning Aries that the period of twenty-four hours divided by the equinox "denotes most secret proportions." It is significant that the *Hieroglyphic Monad* is divided into twenty-four theorems. This was not an accident, as Dee states in the final theorem of his work, saying: "so now at last we consummate and terminate the metamorphosis and the metathesis of all possible contents of the Quaternary defined by the number 24 by our present twenty-fourth theorem" (Theorem XXIV).

Almost the last words of the work refer to the fourth part of the fourth chapter of Revelation, the chapter in which the heavenly throne of Christ is described. It is worth quoting a portion of this chapter, because it shows so clearly that Dee intended the permutations of Tetragrammaton:

> And immediately I was in the Spirit: and behold, a throne was set in heaven, and one sat on the throne.
>
> And he that sat was to look upon like a jasper and a sardine stone: and there was a rainbow round about the throne, in sight like unto an emerald.
>
> And round about the throne were four and twenty seats: and upon the seats I saw four and twenty elders sitting, clothed in white raiment; and they had on their heads crowns of gold.
>
> And out of the throne proceeded lightnings and thunderings and voices: and there were seven lamps of fire burning before the throne, which are the seven Spirits of God.
>
> And before the throne there was a sea of glass like unto a crystal: and in the midst of the throne, and round about the throne, were four beasts, full of eyes before and behind.
>
> And the first beast was like a lion, and the second beast like a calf, and the third beast had a face as a man, and the fourth beast was like a flying eagle.
>
> And the four beasts had each of them six wings about him; and they were full of eyes within: and they rest not day and night, saying, Holy, holy, holy, Lord God Almighty, which was, and is, and is to come. (Rev. 4:2–8)

In this text, the manifest and occult permutations of Tetragrammaton appear in the form of the twenty-four elders seated about the throne of Christ, but also as the twenty-four wings of the four beasts. The elders are the actual Banners of the Name. They must be seated in pairs, because every Banner has two forms that appear the same but are distinguished by the placement of the first H and second H. These two sets of Banners correspond to the twelve hours of the day and the twelve hours of the night. Each beast has three pairs of wings. Each pair represents the two angels associated with a particular Banner, an angel of mercy on the right who protects and rewards and an angel of severity on the left who administers judgments.

Since the four beasts stand for the elements fire, air, water, and earth, it is clear that six angels of Tetragrammaton administer to each element, three that are merciful and kind and three that are severe in judgment. They are in pairs ruled by the three Banners of the Name set over each element, the cardinal, mutable, and fixed. Each pair of angels is associated with one of the twelve signs of the zodiac, and by understanding the nature of the signs we can understand the nature of their angels and their allotted works.

The merciful and severe angels of each sign may be invoked and banished by means of the sigils of the Banners described in Chapter V. The invoking sigil of a Banner invokes the angel of mercy that labors under that Banner. This angel can then be banished by the banishing sigil. However, if the banishing sigil is used first, it acts to invoke the angel of severity set under that Banner. The angel of severity can then be banished by means of the invoking sigil. In fact, the "invoking" sigil of the merciful angel is the banishing sigil of the severe angel, and the "banishing" sigil of the merciful angel is the invoking sigil of the severe angel. Whether a sigil invokes or banishes depends upon whether it is used first or second. Either sigil invokes when used first—but they invoke different spirits, and opposite forces.

It would be useful in practical magic if we could find names for these twenty-four spirits under the Banners of Tetragrammaton. There is a kabbalistic rule for determining the names of angels from the Bible, which is given by Cornelius Agrippa:

> The general rule of these is, that wheresoever anything of divine essence is expressed in the Scripture, from that place the name of God may rightly be gathered; but in what place soever in the Scripture the name of God is found expressed, there mark what office lies under that name. Wheresoever therefore the Scripture speaks of the office or work of any spirit, good, or bad, from thence the name of that spirit, whether good, or bad, may be gathered... *(Three Books Of Occult Philosophy* 3.25)

If we examine the fourth chapter of Revelation referred to by Dee, we find the office of the four beasts with the twenty-four wings, representing the angels of the Banners, stated in the eighth verse: "and they rest not day and night, saying, Holy, holy, holy, Lord God Almighty, which was, and is, and is to come." Notice the reference to day and night, which comprehends both the manifest and occult sets of the Banners. It is interesting that this is in the eighth verse, since Dee refers to the "fourth and last part of the fourth chapter of the Apocalypse, who is seated on His Throne, around and in front of which the four animals, each with six wings, chant night and day without repose: 'Holy, Holy, Holy is the Lord God Omnipotent, who was, is and is to come'" *(Hieroglyphic Monad,* p. 53).

The actual office of these wings, or angels, is given in the chant they proclaim before the throne of Christ, which Dee took the trouble to write out. It is from this that their names may be kabbalistically extracted. If we refer to a Hebrew Bible, we find that this chant consists of exactly thirty-six letters. Following established methods of the kabbalah, we can write these Hebrew letters out in three rows of twelve, the first row from right to left, the second row from left to right beneath the first row, and the third row from right to left beneath the second row.

These three rows of twelve letters naturally divide themselves into three groups because of the triple repetition of the word "holy" (QDVSh) in the top row. It is reasonable to assign these three groups to the cardinal, mutable, and fixed qualities. Note that the order of the letters in the table below is reversed because the Hebrew letters have been transliterated into English letters, which are written from left to right. Thus, the first row of the transliterated letters runs from left to right, the second row from right to left, and the third row from left to right:

	Cardinal				Mutable				Fixed		
Q	D	V	Sh	Q	D	V	Sh	Q	D	V	Sh
Th	V	A	B	Tz	M	I	H	L	A	I	I
H	I	H	V	H	V	H	V	I	B	V	A

The twelve names of the benevolent and merciful angels are extracted by reading down the columns. Each name has three Hebrew letters. To empower these names, the divine suffixes AL or IH must be added to each and vowels inserted to render them pronounceable. The related twelve names of the severe angels of judgment are extracted by reading *up* the columns, adding the divine suffixes, and inserting vowels as before.

It might be objected that Revelation is a book of the New Testament, was not originally written in Hebrew, and has little connection with the kabbalah of the Jews, which relies on verses extracted from the books of the Old Testament. This overlooks the strong reliance placed on the metaphors of the ancient Hebrew prophets by the New Testament writers. There is a direct link between Revelation 4:8 and Isaiah 6:3. In both places the word "holy" (QDVSh) is repeated three times in succession. This repetition was regarded by kabbalists as of supreme significance. They called the verse in which it appears in Isaiah the "Kedushah."

The sixth chapter of Isaiah begins with a description of the heavenly throne of God, just like the fourth chapter of Revelation. In Isaiah, instead of four beasts with six wings each, the two seraphim, each with six wings, are described. It is the seraphim who cry "holy, holy, holy" here rather than the beasts. However, there can be little doubt that the author of Revelation drew upon the imagery of this chapter of Isaiah.

In the *Bahir,* the Kedushah is discussed at length (see *Bahir,* secs. 126–31). It is said that in the mystery of the arrangement of the great Kedushah is the "fearsome and terrible King" crowned with three holies. Although the wording of the Kedushah of Revelation does not agree with that in Isaiah, there is a fascinating bridge between the two verses that occurs in the *Bahir* (sec. 111). This reads in translation: "IHVH is King, IHVH was King, IHVH will be King forever and ever." Notice that the name of God is repeated three times, and that the meaning expressed by the verse is the same as that expressed in Revelation 4:8. Aryeh Kaplan notes that this is not a biblical verse but occurs in the prayer book of *Yehi Kavod* (*Bahir,* p. 197). In the text of the *Bahir,* this mystical verse is called the Explicit Name (Shem ha-Mephoresh) "for which permission was given that it be permuted and spoken." Clearly there is more than a passing connection between Revelation 4:8 and the kabbalah.

The method for extracting the names of the angels described here would have been completely familiar to John Dee, who had read Agrippa and Reuchlin. It is the same technique that is used to extract the seventy-two names of the Shem ha-Mephoresh from Exodus 14:19–21 (see Christian Ginsburg, *The Kabbalah* [London: Routledge and Kegan Paul, 1955], pp. 132–6).

In order to distinguish these two sets of angelic names, I have added the divine suffix AL to the merciful angels and the suffix IH to the angels of judgment. The results are tabulated below. The position of the second H in each of the twenty-four permutations of Tetragrammaton is indicated by boldface type:

IHVH: Aries (Fire—Cardinal)
  1. Angel of Mercy: QThH + AL (Kethahel)—IHV**H**
  2. Angel of Severity: HThQ + IH (Hatakiah)—IH**V**H

IHHV: Sagittarius (Fire—Mutable)
  3. Angel of Mercy: QTzH + AL (Kazahel)—IH**H**V
  4. Angel of Severity: HTzQ + IH (Hazekiah)—IHH**V**

IVHH: Leo (Fire—Fixed)
  5. Angel of Mercy: QLI + AL (Keliel)—IV**H**H
  6. Angel of Severity: ILQ + IH (Yelekiah)—IVH**H**

HVHI: Cancer (Water—Cardinal)
  7. Angel of Mercy: DVI + AL (Daviel)—HV**H**I
  8. Angel of Severity: IVD + IH (Yodiah)—**H**VHI

HVIH: Pisces (Water—Mutable)
    9. Angel of Mercy: DMV + AL (Demuel)—HVI**H**
   10. Angel of Severity: VMD + IH (Vamediah)—**H**VIH

HHIV: Scorpio (Water—Fixed)
   11. Angel of Mercy: DAB + AL (Dabael)—HH**I**V
   12. Angel of Severity: BAD + IH (Badiah)—**H**HIV

VHIH: Libra (Air—Cardinal)
   13. Angel of Mercy: VAH + AL (Vahael)—**V**HIH
   14. Angel of Severity: HAV + IH (Haviah)—VHI**H**

VHHI: Gemini (Air—Mutable)
   15. Angel of Mercy: VIH + AL (Vihael)—**V**HHI
   16. Angel of Severity: HIV + IH (Hiviah)—V**H**HI

VIHH: Aquarius (Air—Fixed)
   17. Angel of Mercy: VIV + AL (Vivael)—VIH**H**
   18. Angel of Severity: VIV + IH (Viviah)—VI**H**H

HIHV: Capricorn (Earth—Cardinal)
   19. Angel of Mercy: ShBV + AL (Shabuel)—**H**IHV
   20. Angel of Severity: VBSh + IH (Vabashiah)—HI**H**V

HIVH: Virgo (Earth—Mutable)
   21. Angel of Mercy: ShHV + AL (Shahavel)—**H**IVH
   22. Angel of Severity: VHSh + IH (Vaheshiah)—HIV**H**

HHVI: Taurus (Earth—Fixed)
   23. Angel of Mercy: ShIA + AL (Shiael)—**H**HVI
   24. Angel of Severity: AISh + IH (Aishiah)—**H**HVI

These twenty-four wings of the four beasts, who are the angels of the elements, would seem to be the same as the "Wings of the Winds," an order of angels that is mentioned in the second of a series of forty-eight invocations called the Enochian Keys, or Calls, received by John Dee through the mediumship of Edward Kelley in the form of complex ciphers.

The second Key was translated by Dee into English in his personal record of his communications with the Enochian spirits. It is relevant to our inquiry because it shows that the order of angels known as the Wings of the Winds are elemental angels of the earth:

Can the Wings of the Winds understand your voices of wonder, O you, the Second of the First? Whom the Burning Flames have framed within the depths of my jaws; whom I have prepared as cups for a wedding, or as the

flowers in their beauty for the chamber of righteousness.
Stronger are your feet than the barren stone, and mightier are your voices than the manifold winds: for you are
become a building such as is not, but in the mind of the
All-powerful. Arise, saith the First! Move, therefore, unto
his servants! Show yourselves in power, and make me a
strong see-thing; for I am of Him that liveth forever.

The "Wings of the Winds" signify the angels of the four elements of the
world. The "Second of the First" may mean Christ as the articulated Word of
God. There are four elemental associations for the four beasts. The "Burning Flames," an order of angels about which more will be said in Appendix
A, signify elemental fire. The "cups for a wedding" stand for water. The
"flowers" are a common magical symbol for air. The "barren stone" (which
perhaps should be "stones") is evocative of the element earth. The "manifold
winds" are all the twenty-four angels considered together.

It is stated that the "voices of wonder" of the "Second of the First"
(IHShVH) are "mightier" than the "manifold winds." This signifies that
Christ rules the angels of the elements by means of the vocalization of the
twenty-four permutations of Tetragrammaton (twelve overt and twelve
occult). The "voices of wonder" are these Banners of IHVH, which the magician vibrates after first assuming the authority of IHShVH by invoking the
god-form of heavenly Christ, as this deity is described in Revelation 1:13–16.

Only by taking on the persona of Christ can the magus use the Pentagrammaton with maximum effect in commanding the Wings of the Winds.
This is a poorly understood secret of magic, but absolutely vital: the magician in him or herself is a fallible human being, and can perform no more
than the works of a human, but when he or she takes on the identity of a
god, the magician is rendered able to perform the works of a god.

The winds are usually considered to be four in number, blowing from the
four corners of the earth, and for this reason have a close association with
the four elements. In fact, the Wings of the Winds are a legitimate class of
angels—the term occurs in the Bible in connection with descriptions of God's
wrathful descent from heaven to the earth to punish the wicked in response
to prayers: "And he rode upon a cherub, and did fly; yea, he did fly upon the
wings of the wind" (Ps. 18:10); "Who layeth the beams of his chambers in the
waters; who maketh the clouds his chariot; who walketh upon the wings of
the wind" (Ps. 104:3).

We have been following a single golden thread of discovery. From the
symbolic interrelationship of Dee's hieroglyphic monad, we gained insight

into the Fivefold Name of Jesus of the Christian kabbalists and the twenty-four permutations of Tetragrammaton, twelve under the sun and twelve under the moon. The final theorem of Dee's book pointed the way to the extraction of the names of the twenty-four Wings of the Winds, three pairs for each element, each pair made up of a left-hand spirit of judgment and a right-hand spirit of compassion. Dee's Second Enochian Key, where the Wings of the Winds are mentioned, demonstrated that it is necessary to assume the god-form of Yehovashah (IHVShH), the creative and compassionate aspect of the heavenly Christ, when we seek to command and direct the twelve Wings of mercy on the right side through the "invoking" sigils of the Banners; and to assume the god-form of Yeheshuah (IHShVH), the judicative and vengeful aspect of heavenly Christ, when we seek to command and direct the twelve Wings of severity on the left side through the "banishing" sigils of the Banners.

The symbolism in the fourth chapter of the Revelation of St. John the Divine is not only the key to understanding Dee's hieroglyphic monad, but also to a true comprehension of his four Enochian Watchtowers and forty-eight Enochian Keys. This is a very bold statement, I know, but I believe I have completely justified it in Chapter XVI and in Appendix A.

It may be argued that when Dee wrote his *Hieroglyphic Monad* he had not yet established communication with the Enochian angels. This overlooks the magical phenomenon of synchronicity, the fact that magic is not dependent upon causal or temporal relationships. Besides, whatever their source of inspiration, both the monad and the system of Enochian magic were refined and expressed by a single human brain—that of John Dee.

IX

ʼ ʼ

THE TWELVE STONES

When the Israelites crossed over the River Jordan, their leader Joshua ordered a man from each of the twelve tribes to take up a large stone from the riverbed and carry it with him on his shoulder onto the opposite bank. He then had twelve other stones mortared together to form an altar in the middle of the riverbed at the fording place opposite Jericho.

These things were done at the command of Moses, for the purpose of magically establishing the presence of the Israelites in the land across Jordan. Although it is not expressly stated, there is good reason to speculate that the twelve stones were sacrificial, and that each stone was inscribed, or at least associated, with one of the Banners of Tetragrammaton. Moses says to the Israelites:

> And it shall be on the day when ye shall pass over Jordan unto the land which the Lord thy God giveth thee, that thou shalt set thee up great stones, and plaster them with plaster:
> And thou shalt write upon them all the words of this law, when thou art passed over, that thou mayest go in unto the land which the Lord thy God giveth thee, a land that floweth with milk and honey; as the Lord God of thy fathers hath promised thee.

> Therefore it shall be when ye be gone over Jordan, that ye shall set up these stones, which I command you this day, in mount Ebal, and thou shalt plaster them with plaster.
>
> And there shalt thou build an altar unto the Lord thy God, an altar of stones: thou shalt not lift up any iron tool upon them.
>
> Thou shalt build the altar of the Lord thy God of whole stones; and thou shalt offer burnt offerings thereon unto the Lord thy God:
>
> And thou shalt offer peace offerings, and shalt eat there, and rejoice before the Lord thy God.
>
> And thou shalt write upon the stones all the words of this law very plainly. (Deut. 27:2–8)

It is not perfectly clear in the words of Moses, but there seem to be two piles of stones intended, one of "great stones" that are plastered (mortared) together, and another of "whole stones" that serve as an altar. Both (if indeed they are two piles) are to be inscribed with the law of God.

In following out the command of Moses, Joshua first has the representatives of the tribes carry the stones across the river before allowing the ark of the covenant to pass: "And Joshua said unto them, Pass over before the ark of the Lord your God into the midst of Jordan, and take you up every man of you a stone upon his shoulder, according to the number of the tribes of the children of Israel" (Josh. 4:5). The twelve representatives of the tribes took up a stone each "and carried them over with them unto the place where they lodged, and laid them down there" (Josh. 4:8). But it is also said "And Joshua set up twelve stones in the midst of Jordan, in the place where the feet of the priests which bare the ark of the covenant stood" (Josh. 4:9). This seems to indicate that there were two sets of twelve stones, one a monument of the crossing, and the other a sacrificial altar.

It is absurd to think that all the words of the law delivered by God to Moses could be written upon the mortared stones of the monument—there would not be enough space, or time, to write them. What is probably intended is the list of twelve commandments spoken by Moses in the form of twelve curses (Deut. 27:15–26), one for each stone.

The purpose behind all this carrying and setting up of stones was to sanctify the ground on the far bank of the Jordan River, which was until the day of the crossing the land of foreign gods. This was done with the Banners of IHVH, symbolized by the twelve stones taken out of the riverbed and assembled on the far bank in the form of an altar, or pair of altars. Sacrifice was essential to attract the God of the Israelites through its blood offering and entice this God across the river.

The twelve commandments in the form of curses are part of a magic ritual conducted by Joshua on the far bank of the Jordan to exorcise the foreign soil and prepare it to receive the spirit of God that is resident within the ark. This is the reason the priests carrying the ark remain standing in the middle of the river, which the ark has miraculously caused to dry up, "until everything was finished that the Lord commanded Joshua to speak unto the people, according to all that Moses commanded Joshua: and the people hasted and passed over" (Josh. 4:10).

The rite of passage is partially described by Moses. After the twelve stones are carried across the riverbed, six of the stones that represent the six tribes of Simeon, Levi, Judah, Issachar, Joseph, and Benjamin are piled up in a symbolic representation of Mount Gerizim, probably on the right side of the path to be followed by the Israelites. The other six stones that represent the tribes of Reuben, Gad, Asher, Zebulun, Dan, and Naphtali are piled up in a representation of Mount Ebal, probably on the left side of the path (Deut. 27:12–3). It is also possible that the stones form the right and left sides of a single altar,or even a stone circle—Gilgal, the place where the stones are said to be piled, is Hebrew meaning "circle."

It is clear that the real Mount Gerizim and Mount Ebal play no part in this passage ritual, since these hills are nowhere near Jericho, and in fact stand some forty miles north of Jerusalem on opposite sides of a pass through which runs a road. It may be that the stones from Jordan were eventually transported to these twin peaks and erected there as a permanent embodiment of the cursing, and blessing, of God. There is some suggestion that they may have been erected as a single altar on Mount Ebal that represented both hills (Deut. 27:4).

These piles of unhewn stones act as symbolic pillars and form a gateway into the promised land. The six stones of Mount Gerizim bless the people who come over the Jordan and uphold the covenant, and the six stones of Mount Ebal curse those that pass the river and break the covenant. They are the carrot and the stick offered to the Israelites as they enter through the gate to the land of milk and honey, designed to keep them obedient to the laws of Moses.

Although it is not explicitly stated in the Bible, it would be reasonable to assume that the twelve representatives who carried these stones on their backs across the Jordan were sacrificed to insure a safe entry into the new land for the rest of the tribes. They may have been slain with the very stones they carried. Their blood would form the offering to God that would attract Him across the river. As a part of this sacrificial ritual, the Levites recite the twelve curses before the assembled people of Israel, who respond to each with an

"Amen," thereby confirming their obedience. During this ritual, the Israelites were probably required by Joshua to stand in the ford of the Jordan River, half the tribes on one side of the ark and the other half on the opposite side.

Those who remain obedient are promised six blessings from the stones on Gerizim, washed with the blood of the tribes of Simeon, Levi, Judah, Issachar, Joseph, and Benjamin:

> Blessed shalt thou be in the city, and blessed shalt thou be in the field.
> Blessed shall be the fruit of thy body, and the fruit of thy ground, and the fruit of thy cattle, the increase of thy kine, and the flocks of thy sheep.
> Blessed shall be thy basket and thy store.
> Blessed shalt thou be when thou comest in, and blessed shalt thou be when thou goest out. (Deut. 28:3–6)

Those who lapse into disobedience are threatened with six curses from the stones on Ebal, washed with the blood of the tribes of Reuben, Gad, Asher, Zebulun, Dan, and Naphtali:

> Cursed shalt thou be in the city, and cursed shalt thou be in the field.
> Cursed shall be thy basket and thy store.
> Cursed shall be the fruit of thy body, and the fruit of thy land, the increase of thy kine, and the flocks of thy sheep.
> Cursed shalt thou be when thou comest in, and cursed shalt thou be when thou goest out. (Deut. 28:16–9)

It is no accident that the two passages quoted above are parallel. These are the specific curses and blessings attached to the twelve stones set up on the left and right side of the pathway into the new land of the Israelites (or on the left and right sides of a single altar) empowered by the blood of the human sacrifices and rendered binding by the presence of the living spirit of God. The spirits of the sacrificed representatives of the tribes were magically infused into the stones, which each had personally selected as his instrument (quite possibly the instrument of his death), by the application of the blood of the sacrifices. This blood served as a kind of baptism of the stones, necessary if the spirits of the tribes, acting as the angels of blessing or wrath, were to be induced to dwell within them.

It seems that this initial ritual of passage confirming the obedience of the children of Israel to the laws of the covenant of God the Father was reenacted in later times on a regular basis, probably in the pass between mounts Gerizim and Ebal, where the stones eventually resided. This may have occurred annually (see John L. McKenzie, *Dictionary of the Bible,* Macmillan, New York, 1965, page 209). It would not have involved sacrifice, but a shared feast.

Only after this complex rite of passage has been accomplished and all the peoples of the twelve tribes are permitted to cross the river does Joshua allow the priests who carry the ark of the covenant to step up onto the far bank of the Jordan. The ground on the west has been prepared for the reception of the ark, where God dwells, by the sacrifice of the twelve and the faith of all the people.

How do we know that the spirits of the twelve unfortunate men "prepared of the children of Israel" by Joshua really entered into the twelve stones? It is suggested by another act of Joshua, where he erects a stone in Shechem as a "witness" of the renewed covenant: "And Joshua said unto all the people, Behold, this stone shall be a witness unto us; for it hath heard all the words of the Lord which he spake unto us: it shall be therefore a witness unto you, lest ye deny your God" (Josh. 24:27). To bring the twelve stones alive, so that they could "hear" the affairs of the Israelites and dispense the curse or blessing appointed to each stone, it was necessary to make each stone a member of its particular tribe by a tie of blood.

The most primitive form of altar in the Old Testament is that erected by piling unshaped stones together: "And Jacob said unto his brethren, Gather stones; and they took stones, and made an heap: and they did eat there upon the heap"(Gen. 31:46). It is worth noting that Laban calls upon the heap of stones to "be witness" to his personal covenant with Jacob. We are not told how many stones were in the heap, but when the prophet Elijah erects a similar altar for magical purposes, it is said: "he took twelve stones, according to the number of the tribes of the sons of Jacob, unto whom the word of the Lord came, saying, Israel shall be thy name; And with the stones he built an altar in the name of the Lord" (1 Kings 18:31–2).

The words "in the name of the Lord" may be an intentional pun, since an altar erected of twelve stones, each of which symbolically represents one of the twelve Banners of Tetragrammaton, would truly be built in, or more properly of, the Name of IHVH.

In later times the altars of sacrifice became square to reflect the fourfold nature of Tetragrammaton. The altar of Solomon was twenty cubits in length and twenty cubits in breadth (2 Chron. 4:1). They also developed horns at the corners (Exod. 27:2), which seem to have symbolized the power of God. In sacrifices, blood was smeared over these horns. Altars in those degenerate times began to be made of cut stones, or a single cut stone, wood, and even brass. The rationale for the use of natural stone is that it is a product of God, who is perfect, and not the result of the craft of imperfect men. Probably the same reasoning was used in the construction of the pagan stone circles of Europe.

Human sacrifice was extremely uncommon, even in earliest times, among the ancient Hebrews. However, there is evidence that it did take place, and it may have been deleted from the religious records at a later date by revisionists to bring the Scriptures more in line with the religious practices contemporary with the editors of the Old Testament books. In the most famous incident, where Abraham is tempted by God to sacrifice his first-born son, Isaac, as a test of faith, it is said: "and Abraham built an altar there" (Gen. 22:9), presumably of unhewn stones in the prescribed manner.

In demanding the sacrifice of Isaac, God was only asking for what was rightfully his. By law, the first-born male of every mother, human or animal, belonged to God (Exod. 34:19–20). The first-born males of sacrificial animals were sacrificed before the altar. The first-born males of non-sacrificial animals were simply destroyed, or redeemed by substituting a sacrificial animal. First-born sons were redeemed by the offering to the priests of five shekels of silver (Num. 18:15–7), but strictly speaking they belonged to God in return for sparing the first-born of the Hebrews during the last plague of Egypt, when the first-born of the Egyptians, including the son of the Pharaoh, were taken (Exod. 13:15). It is very possible that the twelve selected by Joshua to carry the stones across the Jordan were first-born sons.

Again, there is no mention of the number of the stones erected by Abraham, but it would be reasonable to suspect that it was a set number and that the stones were erected in an established pattern. We can make some general observations about the stones used in altars. They were small enough to be carried on the back of a single man, probably about the size of the human head or smaller. They may have been rounded—at least, the stones taken from the bed of the Jordan River were likely to have been rounded by the action of the water. It is reasonable to suspect that they were chosen for their regular size and shape.

If the twelve stones of the altar were erected in two parallel rows, the bottom rows would consist of three stones, the middle rows of two stones, and the top rows of one stone, so that each side of the altar would form a pyramid of six stones piled on top of each other. In this way, the structure of the altar would reflect the division of the tribes into groups of six and six, one group on the left and the other on the right, which occurs a number of times in the Old Testament, most notably in the onyx stones on the shoulders of the high priest, which are each inscribed with the names of six of the tribes.

Sacrifice involved the sprinkling of the blood of the sacrificed animal, or human, upon the stones of the altar; alternately, the blood was dashed down at the base of the altar, but this was probably a later practice. It was magically important that the blood baptize the altar stones if the spirit of God was to be made to reside within the stones. Blood was believed to be the vehicle of the life force. Blood splashed upon the stones conveyed the life force of the sacrifice, which rested in the blood, to God, who resided in the stones. The act of killing itself was not nearly so significant, magically, as the sprinkling of blood.

Stones had other uses besides the building of altars. When the prophet Jeremiah wished to punish the men and women of Judah who had gone to live in Egypt, he took "great stones" and buried them in the soft clay in the brickkiln in front of one of the Pharaoh's houses, speaking to the men of Judah in the voice of God: "Behold, I will send and take Nebuchadrezzar the king of Babylon, my servant, and will set his throne upon these stones that I have hid; and he shall spread his royal pavilion over them" (Jer. 43:10). The stones in this way accomplished the destruction of Egypt. We are not told how many stones Jeremiah used for this magic, only that there were more than one, but four would seem the most appropriate number—one for each letter of Tetragrammaton, and for each leg of Nebuchadrezzar's throne. Alternately, it is possible that twelve stones, one for each tribe and each overt Banner of IHVH, were buried in a circle to surround the place where the throne would eventually reside.

The twelve stones of the altar surface in various places later in both Old and New Testament writings. They are, of course, the twelve jewels in the breastplate of Aaron, about which much more will be said in the next chapter. They are the twelve pillars placed by Moses on either side of the altar of sacrifice (Exod. 24:4). They are the twelve cakes of the sabbath eaten by the priests: "Thou shalt take fine flour, and bake twelve cakes thereof: two tenth deals shall be in one cake. And thou shalt set them in two rows, six on a row, upon the pure table before the Lord" (Lev. 24:5–6). They are the twelve oxen that support the great molten sea (a large basin cast from molten brass) upon their backs in the temple of Solomon (2 Chron. 4:4).

By far the most elaborate appearance of the stones is as the twelve foundations of the heavenly city of New Jerusalem. The entire plan of this city is based upon the twelve Banners of the Name. It is in the shape of a cube twelve thousand furlongs on each side, corresponding with the number from each tribe who will be sealed with the mark of God in their foreheads (Rev. 7:4–8). Its area is 144,000 square furlongs, the number of all the servants of God from all the tribes. Each wall has three gates, for the three Banners of each element. Each gate is made of pearl. At the twelve gates, twelve angels stand guard. Upon each gate is written one of the names of the twelve tribes. The walls of New Jerusalem are founded upon twelve foundations— that is, twelve foundation stones, every stone inscribed with one of the names of the twelve apostles of Christ and garnished with a different variety of precious jewel:

> And the foundations of the wall of the city were garnished with all manner of precious stones. The first foundation was jasper; the second, sapphire; the third, a chalcedony; the fourth, an emerald;
>
> The fifth, sardonyx; the sixth, sardius; the seventh, chrysolite; the eighth, beryl; the ninth, a topaz; the tenth, a chrysoprasus; the eleventh, a jacinth; the twelfth, an amethyst. (Rev. 21:19–20)

In the exact center of the city sits the throne of God, from which flows a river of the "water of life," which refreshes the tree of life. This tree has twelve manner of fruits and bears twelve times a year. It is described in a rather puzzling manner as growing in the midst of the street and at the same time on either side of the river, which suggests that there is more than one tree, or that the tree has three trunks. This calls to mind the tree of the *sephiroth* in the kabbalah, which indeed has three pillars, but I am inclined to accept the former explanation, that the tree referred to is a species, not an individual specimen.

We encounter the numerical pattern of the Name again and again in the symbolism of those things that represent God in the Bible. At its most fundamental, the name is square. This is the shape of the later altars, which have a square top and which approach a cubic shape: "So the altar shall be four cubits; and from the altar and upward shall be four horns. And the altar shall be twelve cubits long, twelve broad, square in the four squares thereof" (Ezek. 43:15–6).

A square is presumably also the shape of the great white throne of God, which seems to be supported upon, or composed of, the four beasts (Rev. 4:6). Around the heavenly throne are the twenty-four lesser thrones of the elders, who represent karma, or cause and effect in time, at the most fundamental level. These seats are probably arranged in opposite crescents of six, one circle of twelve above a second circle of twelve, with the upper and lower elders forming pairs that represent the hours of the day and the equivalent hours of the night. For a justification of this division of the seats of the elders, see Appendix A, the Third and the Fourteenth keys.

The divisions of the heavenly throne are reflected in the throne of Solomon, God's representative upon the Earth. Solomon's throne had six steps leading up to it, and upon these steps were twelve lions, representing the twelve tribes (1 Kings 10:18–20). The symbolism of Solomon's throne gained considerable importance in Islamic folklore, where it was merged with the throne of God (see the description in Chapter XI). On the symbolic level, the throne and the altar are the same. Both are, at root, cubic stones that contain the awareness and power of God. Both express Tetragrammaton in a concrete manner, numerically in divisions of four, six, twelve, and twenty-four.

X

ʾ ʾ

THE BREASTPLATE OF AARON

In the Bible, there are a number of magical objects associated with Tetragrammaton and its permutations. The most important of these is the breastplate of Aaron, who was the brother of Moses and the first high priest of Israel. This breastplate is described in considerable detail in Exodus 28:15–30, where it is called the "breastplate of judgment," and also in the *Antiquities* of Josephus (3.7.5).

The name "breastplate" is misleading. The Hebrew word used to describe this object is *chosen* (ChShN). Its meaning is unknown, but it has been translated as "ornament" or "breast-piece." It consisted of a linen pouch used in divination that was worn against the breast of the high priest. To allow the *chosen* to be worn in this manner, a hole was cut in the front of the ephod, or upper garment, of the priest.

The ephod, which was always intimately joined with the breastplate, is another mysterious instrument. It seems in earliest times to have been an oracular idol or image (see Judg. 8:27). However, the word may simply have been used as a synonym for "oracle;" or it is possible that an oracular idol was arrayed in a special garment that was later adopted by the high priest for divination purposes. Whatever its origin, the ephod was an integral part of the breastplate and its contents.

On its front, the breastplate held twelve large precious and semiprecious stones arranged in four rows and three columns. The deep golden settings of the stones were joined together by a woven linen frame one span (about eight inches) wide and two spans long, which was folded over once like a towel and hung from the ephod by two gold loops so that the back panel lay against the undergarment of the priest over his heart. Two more gold loops secured the bottom corners of this linen frame to the ephod by blue thread. The threads of the breastplate itself were of four colors: gold, blue, purple, and scarlet.

Josephus assigns these threads to the four elements, but not in the way we might expect. Blue, he says, signifies the sky and the air; purple signifies the sea and water, because it is the color of the dye extracted from shellfish; the scarlet threads "will naturally be an indication of fire" (*Antiquities,* 3.7.7). However, he does not assign the remaining color, gold, to earth, but says that the linen threads that make up the body of the breastplate itself accord with the earth "because the flax grows out of the earth." About the golden threads, which he understood to be of pure metallic gold, he says: "I suppose it related to the splendour by which all things are enlightened." I would be more inclined to assign the colors scarlet-fire, gold-air, blue-water, purple-earth.

Each stone was probably rectangular, wider than it was high, and rounded in front like a half a cylinder cut through the length of its axis. Josephus says these stones were "extraordinary in largeness and beauty; and they were an ornament not to be purchased by men, because of their immense value." Each stone was said to be engraved with the name of one of the twelve tribes of Israel "like the engravings of a signet" (Exod. 28:21). However, since the names of the tribes are also said to be engraved upon the onyx stones on the shoulders of the high priest (Exod. 28:9), it has been speculated that the breastplate stones were engraved with standards of the tribes rather than with their names. It is very possible that the stones bore the twelve Banners of the Ineffable Name set over the twelve tribes. It is also possible, though less likely, that the Banners were engraved backward in mirror inversion "like the engravings of a signet."

There is considerable disagreement among authorities as to the correct ordering of the stones, partly arising from the fact that the names of some stones have changed since biblical times, making it difficult to know exactly which stones were intended. Of the seven authorities I have studied who are bold enough to name the stones, no two agree in every particular. Many biblical scholars will not even hazard a guess about the exact type and placement of the stones. The order given here is based upon my own study and best judgement.

Row One:
Stone One: Sard, or carnelian, both of which are orange-red types of chalcedony, a kind of milky quartz said to have the luster of wax.

Stone Two: Topaz, a transparent yellow stone; or perhaps peridot, a transparent yellow-green stone.

Stone Three: Emerald, a transparent green stone.

Row Two:

Stone Four: Carbuncle, specifically garnet, a deep red transparent stone. Probably not ruby.

Stone Five: Sapphire, a transparent blue stone; or perhaps lapis lazuli, an opaque deep-blue stone.

Stone Six: Jasper, which was a green gemstone for the Greeks who translated the Bible, but which today is a reddish, yellowish, or brown variety of opaque quartz.

Row Three:

Stone Seven: Jacinth, specifically ligure, which is a yellow form of jacinth.

Stone Eight: Agate, a clouded or striped stone, another variety of chalcedony.

Stone Nine: Amethyst, a transparent purple or violet stone.

Row Four:

Stone Ten: Chrysolite, a yellow-green stone, which is called peridot when it is of gem quality.

Stone Eleven: Onyx, a whitish-pink variety of agate.

Stone Twelve: Beryl, a sea-green gem stone; possibly aquamarine is intended.

Clearly a magical relationship exists between the choice of stones, the tribes associated with them, the signs of the zodiac and their related months of the year, and the permutations of Tetragrammaton. Each tribe probably had its own complex occult associations, which were reinforced by the ancient accepted meanings of the zodiac signs, and these associations were linked with the twelve overt Banners of the name and their shadow twins, the twelve secret Banners.

For some reason biblical scholars have nothing to say about the connection between the Banners of Tetragrammaton and the breastplate of Aaron—probably because the Banners are not explicitly named in Exodus. Nonetheless, if we accept that the arrangement of the stones on the breastplate is not an accident, we can speculate that the three columns are intended to signify the cardinal, mutable, and fixed qualities and that the four rows are meant to stand for the elements fire, water, air, and earth.

Using this grid of qualities and elements, it is a simple matter to assign the twelve Banners to the stones of the breastplate and to the corresponding tribes of Israel. An occult correspondence between the tribes and the zodiac signs is forged that hinges on the double link between the signs and the Banners, and between the Banners and the tribes. These connections are not arbitrary but are clearly indicated by the numerical structure of the permutations of IHVH. The illustration of the breastplate on the opposite page sets forth the occult correspondences between the Banners and the stones, the sons of Jacob who stand for the tribes of Israel, and the zodiac signs, as this relationship is revealed by the key of Tetragrammaton.

This set of occult relationships will not be found in books on the kabbalah, which give conflicting assignments of the tribes to the signs of the zodiac, the stones of the breastplate, and the months of the year (see Appendix F for the occult correspondences of the Banners given by the great Renaissance magician, Henry Cornelius Agrippa, in his *Three Books Of Occult Philosophy,* to the the tribes, the zodiac signs, the apostles, the months, and the stones). However, it seems reasonable to assign the sons of Jacob to the stones of the breastplate in order of their birth. This assignment is provided in the notes to the King James Bible for Exodus 39:10–3, and also appears in Aryeh Kaplan's *Meditation and the Bible* (Weiser, 1978, p. 143).

Because of the explicit correspondence presented in the notes of the King James Bible between the stones on the breastplate and the twelve tribes, I have not felt bold enough to depart from this placement of the tribes on the stones. However, were this correspondence not present in the Bible notes, I would be strongly inclined to assign the names of the six tribes who dispense blessings on the children of Israel (Simeon, Levi, Judah, Issachar, Joseph, and Benjamin; Deut. 27:12) to the two upper rows of the stones, which relate to the Urim, and the six tribes who dispense curses (Reuben, Gad, Asher, Zebulun, Dan, and Naphtali; Deut. 27:13) to the two lower rows of stones, which relate to the Thummim. There is also reason to suspect that these sets of tribes correspond with the names on the onyx stones on the shoulders of the high priest, in spite of Exodus 28:10.

It is curious that the names of Jacob's sons are assigned to the breastplate in a slightly different order than they appear in Genesis 49:3–27, where their father blesses them on his deathbed. This blessing has great occult significance, because it provides a key to the nature of each son and therefore to the tribe he represents. There seems to be a veiled reference in this blessing to the twelve signs of the zodiac. For example, Judah is said to be a lion, perhaps a reference to Leo; Simeon and Levi are said to be

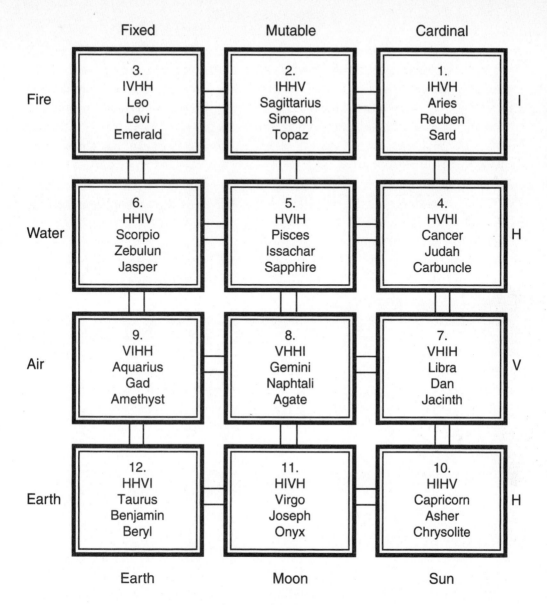

	Fixed	Mutable	Cardinal	
Fire	3. IVHH Leo Levi Emerald	2. IHHV Sagittarius Simeon Topaz	1. IHVH Aries Reuben Sard	I
Water	6. HHIV Scorpio Zebulun Jasper	5. HVIH Pisces Issachar Sapphire	4. HVHI Cancer Judah Carbuncle	H
Air	9. VIHH Aquarius Gad Amethyst	8. VHHI Gemini Naphtali Agate	7. VHIH Libra Dan Jacinth	V
Earth	12. HHVI Taurus Benjamin Beryl	11. HIVH Virgo Joseph Onyx	10. HIHV Capricorn Asher Chrysolite	H
	Earth	Moon	Sun	

The Breastplate of Aaron

brethren, which may refer to Gemini, the sign of the twins; Dan is said to be a judge (Libra); Joseph is linked to the bow (Sagittarius); and two of the brothers, Reuben and Zebulun, are linked with water.

I am not the only person to notice the allusions to the zodiac in the blessing of Jacob. Alfred J. Pearce in his classic work *The Text-Book of Astrology* gives the assignment of the blessings to the signs arrived at by one Dr. Hales, based upon the researches of a General Vallancey (see *Text-Book of Astrology,* reprinted by the American Federation of Astrologers, Washington, DC, 1970, p. 6).

It is obvious from references in scripture that the breastplate was a divinatory device used by the high priest or king of Israel in times of great trial. Within a pouch hidden inside the fold of the breastplate behind the twelve stones resided the two mysterious and sacred objects, Urim and Thummim. When Moses robes Aaron in the vestments of a priest, it is written: "And he put the breastplate upon him: also he put in the breastplate Urim and Thummim" (Lev. 8:8). When God instructs Moses about the making of the priest's apparel, he says: "And thou shalt put in the breastplate the Urim and the Thummim; and they shall be upon Aaron's heart when he goeth in before the Lord: and Aaron shall bear the judgment of the children of Israel upon his heart before the Lord continually."

Precisely what these objects were is never described clearly, but they were used as an oracle. When Saul sought guidance from God, "the Lord answered him not, neither by dreams, nor by Urim, nor by prophets" (1 Sam. 28:6). Joshua was publicly chosen to succeed Moses as the leader of Israel by the divination of the breastplate: "And he shall stand before Eleazar the priest, who shall ask counsel for him after the judgment of Urim before the Lord" (Num. 27:21).

It is generally believed that this oracle consisted of a simple yes-no. Brewer in his *Dictionary of Phrase and Fable* says that it was composed of three pebbles, one signifying yes, one signifying no, and a third signifying uncertainty. However, this seems highly unlikely, because two, not three, objects are named. The notion that the oracle gave a simple yes-no response stems from its description in the Bible, where in several places a yes or no seems to answer the question (see for example 1 Sam. 23:9–12). However, merely because a yes or a no will suffice for some questions does not mean that all questions posed to the oracle of Urim and Thummim were satisfied by a simple yes or no. If only a yes-no response were needed, the oracle might easily have consisted of a single disk or tablet, one side of which indicated yes and the other no. But it was two objects.

The great Jewish commentator on the Bible, Rashi, states unequivocally in his commentary on Leviticus 8:8 that Urim and Thummim are "the letters of the Ineffable Name" (*The Pentateuch and Rashi's Commentary* [Brooklyn: S. S. & R. Publishing, 1949]). Regarding Exodus 28:30, where Urim and Thummim are first described, he says explicitly: "This was the writing of the Divine Name." Surely nothing could be more clear. Yet biblical scholars persist in regarding Urim and Thummim as colored pebbles.

I believe the entire breastplate was a magical device structured around the permutations of Tetragrammaton. Upon the stones were written the Banners that related to the tribes, each tribe having its own color of stone with an occult significance. Within the pocket of the breastplate was a divinatory device for generating the twelve Banners. Each Banner, along with its set of associations, gave a specific divination.

It is impossible to be certain what form this double oracle took. We can be confident that it was in two parts, because of the two names Urim and Thummim and because, on the onyx stones on the shoulders of the priest, the twelve tribes are divided into two sets of six names: "And thou shalt take two onyx stones, and grave on them the names of the children of Israel: six of their names on one stone, and the other six names of the rest on the other stone, according to their birth" (Exod. 28:9–10).

The name Urim, AVRIM, literally translates as "lights." This name was often used alone to stand for both parts of the oracle. The name Thummim (ThMIM) is literally translated as "truth." Both of these are plural forms in Hebrew. The names are translated in the Septuagint as "Revelation" and "Truth." Philo Judaeus believed that Urim and Thummim were two little images, the first symbolically representing revelation and the second representing truth. Since revelation is truth of a kind, apparently two types of truth are intended. The name Urim (Lights) calls to mind the *sephiroth* of the kabbalistic tree, specifically the second and third *sephiroth, Chokmah* (Wisdom) and *Binah* (Understanding). These may be understood as inspired truth and reasoned truth, or truth that is above words, and truth that may be expressed in the form of words. The names Urim and Thummim probably conveyed a very similar meaning. Thus, Urim would mean inspiration and Thummim ratiocination.

Once we accept the idea that Urim and Thummim were designed to generate the twelve Banners of Tetragrammaton, we might naturally speculate that they were two cubes, each facet of which was engraved with one of the Banners. By reaching into the pouch in the fold of the breastplate, the priest could draw out a cube, standing either for the set of names on his right shoulder or the set on his left shoulder, and by casting the cube could select one of these six names. However, Rashi says that Urim and Thummim were the letters of the Name, not the Banners of the Name.

I believe that Urim and Thummim consisted of two round disks, like coins. The disk of Urim was probably of gold, and that of Thummim was likely of silver. Upon the face of Urim was engraved the Hebrew letter *yod*. On the back was engraved the letter *he*. Upon the face of Thummim was engraved the letter *vau;* on the back was engraved the second letter *he* in the Ineffable Name.

The oracle may have been obtained in the following manner. Seeking a response to a question by one of the twelve Banners of the tribes, the priest reached into the pocket of the breastplate with his right hand and took out a disk. He reached into the pocket with his left hand and took out the remaining disk. Holding his hands before him and turning them so that the nails were uppermost, he slowly opened his right hand. The letter of the Name upon the disk represented the first letter in the oracular Banner. Opening his left hand, he obtained the second letter of the Name.

Returning the disks to their pouch in the breastplate, he mixed them and drew them forth again in the same manner. Opening his right hand, he obtained the third letter of the Name. If the disk in his right hand showed either an I or a V which he had previously drawn, he turned it over and got H as the third letter of the Name. If he had drawn two Hs the first time, and the disk showed an H on the second drawing, he turned it over and got either an I or a V for the third letter. Opening his left hand, he obtained the fourth letter in the Name in exactly the same way that he obtained the third letter.

If only a simple yes-no response were required, this might be obtained by drawing only one of the disks. Gold may have signified yes and silver no. Or perhaps *yod* meant yes, *vau* meant no, and *he* indicated uncertainty. In this way the oracle can be both twofold, as suggested by the two names Urim and Thummim, yet at the same time threefold as indicated by Brewer. If this was the technique employed with these disks, there was one chance in two of gaining an uncertain response but only one chance in four of either a yes or a no. Thus, a yes or no answer would have been taken to be emphatic if obtained on the first drawing.

Of course, the elemental associations of the letters in the name allow the oracle of Urim and Thummim to give four different responses from a single drawing of a disk—fire, water, air, or earth. Josephus placed great importance on the elemental significance of the apparel of the high priest.

Another occult association that may have played a part in the divination is the polarity of the human body. The right side is masculine, the left side feminine. If the gold disk is drawn in the right hand and the silver disk in the left, this is in harmony with the polarity of the body. However, if the gold disk is drawn in the left hand and the silver disk in the right, this is in discord with the natural balance of the body.

Another polarity is with the sets of six names signifying the tribes of Israel worn by the high priest on his shoulders. According to Josephus, the names of the six elder sons of Jacob were engraved into the onyx stone on the priest's right shoulder, and the names of the six younger sons were engraved into the onyx stone on his left shoulder. He further states: "Each of the sardonyxes declares to us the sun and the moon; those, I mean, that were in the nature of buttons on the high priest's shoulders." Clearly there is a direct correspondence between these shoulder stones, which were flat and round in the form of disks, and the two disks of Urim and Thummim.

The six elder names of the disk on the right shoulder were the overt expression of the occult disk of Urim, made of gold to signify the masculine right side. The six younger names of the disk on the left shoulder were the overt expression of the occult disk of Thummim, made of silver to signify the feminine left side. What the IH of the Ineffable Name embodies in the macrocosm, the six elder sons of Jacob embody in the microcosm; similarly, the VH of the Name embodies the same meaning in the macrocosm that is signified by the six younger sons in the microcosm. This division of the Name occurs in kabbalistic illustrations of the human hands raised in blessing, where the letters IH are inscribed on the back of the right wrist and VH on the back of the left wrist.

By studying the prophecies pronounced by Jacob on his deathbed to his twelve sons (Gen. 49), it is possible to gain some notion of the divinatory significance of those names, and of the tribes to which they are linked. The meanings are listed below:

Reuben: beginning of strength, the excellence of dignity, the excellence of power.

Simeon: anger as an instrument of cruelty.

Levi: wrath as an instrument of cruelty.

Judah: glory, praise, triumph, dominion.

Issachar: labor, service, debt.

Zebulun: a safe haven, place of peace, tranquility.

Dan: stern judgement, retribution.

Naphtali: eloquence, free speech, true testimony.

Gad: triumph after adversity.

Asher: abundance, wealth, luxury.

Joseph: fruitfulness, blessings.

Benjamin: lawlessness, violence.

To employ Urim and Thummim as an oracle, it would be necessary to consider the meaning of the tribes in concert with the astrological meaning of their related signs of the zodiac. The particular Banner of the Name selected shows which tribe and related sign should be applied to the question. For example, if the question were put to the oracle, "What is the likely outcome of my forthcoming visit to relatives?" and the Banner drawn was VHHI, pointing to Naphtali and the sign Gemini, the response would be free speech and true testimony, indicating the revelation of some family secret.

It is possible that Urim and Thummim were used for more than just divination by lot. According to the Torah, the high priest employed them as a focus during deep meditation until he attained the exalted state of *Ruach ha-Qadesh,* the holy Ruach, during which the enlightenment of God enters into a human. At this point the letters on Urim and Thummim lit up and spelled out the answer sought by the priest (see Kaplan, *Meditation and the Bible* [Weiser, 1978], p. 142).

This notion that the stones worn by the high priest emitted holy light was pervasive. Josephus declares that the onyx stone on the priest's right shoulder shone when God was present at the sacrifice, "bright rays darting out thence, and being seen even by those that were most remote" (*Antiquities,* 3.8.9). He goes on to say that the twelve stones on the breastplate shone with light just before a battle to indicate that the Jews would be victorious, but adds: "Now this breastplate, and this sardonyx, left off shining two hundred years before I composed this book [published A.D. 93], God having been displeased at the transgressions of his laws."

To construct the oracle of Urim and Thummim, cut two identical disks of metal, wood, or cardboard. They should be of a size easily held in the hand—about two inches in diameter. Paint one disk gold and the other silver. Paint in black on the face of the gold disk a large Hebrew letter *yod* (') and on the back a large Hebrew letter *he* (ה). On the face of the silver disk, paint in black a large Hebrew letter *vau* (ו) and on the back paint a second *he* identical to the first.

Construct a pouch about eight inches wide and eight inches deep out of linen that is a natural color; or, if you cannot obtain undyed linen, use white linen. Sew a drawstring into the mouth of the pouch that can be used to close it while the disks are being mixed prior to drawing them forth. This drawstring can be made in such a way that the pouch may, if desired, be hung from a belt for easy carrying.

This oracle will give the same response delivered by Urim and Thummim to the high priest or king of Israel, but is much easier and cheaper to make than the full sacred regalia. The pouch should be ornamented with scarlet, gold, blue, and purple thread—embroidery thread, which comes in many bright colors, is ideal. The threads should be sewn into an appropriate symbolic design. One possible pattern is the single eye of God set within the hexagram of two interlocking triangles.

XI

THE RING OF SOLOMON

T he greatest magician after Moses was Solomon, yet none of his magic actually appears in the Bible. It has come down to us through such diverse sources as the Talmud and Jewish folk tales, the Koran and *The Book of a Thousand Nights and a Night* of the Arabs, and the magical manuscripts of the Ethiopians.

This widespread fame of Solomon as a magician may result from a confusion of names. Arabian and Persian legends speak of a prehistoric race ruled by seventy-two kings named Suleiman. These kings were great masters of magic and commanded all the spirits and demons of the world. The last monarch ruled for a thousand years. Some scholars believe that these mythical Persian kings are unconnected with the biblical Solomon but became merged with him due to the similarity of names. However it may have happened, the fables of Solomon as a wonderworker have always been much more popular in Islam than in Judaism or Christianity.

According to Arab and Jewish legends, Solomon had the power to control the four winds of the world. Borne upon the wind, he flew sitting upon his throne across the face of the whole earth each day, then returned each night to Jerusalem. The wind was able to accomplish this amazing feat because the throne rested upon an enormous green carpet, which the wind blew under and lifted.

So large was this carpet that all of Solomon's army of men could stand upon it at the right side of the throne, and all of his equally numerous army of spirits could stand on the left side. Above his head flew a third army of birds whose innumerable wings formed a canopy over this carpet and shielded it from the hot rays of the sun. Solomon was able to communicate with the birds, as well as with all the beasts of the field, because he understood their languages.

From the legends of the Jewish Midrash, we learn something about the throne itself, which Solomon is said to have fashioned in the shape of the "Throne of Glory which is above" with the help of the Holy Spirit. In the throne were the shapes of the four living creatures—the man, the lion, the ox, and the eagle. The lion was placed opposite the ox, probably on the arms of the throne, and presumably the man was opposite the eagle on the two sides of the back. Behind the throne was the likeness of a wheel and cherubim. The throne was made of pure gold studded with pearls and precious stones. Inside its seat was hidden "a tablet engraved with a serpent on a pole." A great sapphire stone served Solomon for a footstool.

In the mouths of the animals that composed the throne were golden bells that rang when the wind blew, and above the throne hung a canopy of colored cloths that fluttered with the appearance of lightning and flaming torches and a shimmering rainbow. Around the throne were seventy chairs for seventy elders, and two more chairs opposite the throne for the seer Gad and the prophet Nathan, making a total of seventy-two, the same as the "divine name of seventy-two words" extracted kabbalistically from Exodus 14:19–21 (see Ginsburg, *The Kabbalah,* pp. 132–6). The mother of Solomon, Bathsheba, sat in a chair on his right side.

From another Midrash legend we learn that the throne had six steps leading up to it and was made in the shape of the four-horse war chariot of God. It may be conjectured by combining the descriptions of the throne in the two legends that each step had the carved figures of beasts on the left and right side. It may be further speculated that these animals were, right to left and bottom to top: (1) a ram and a panther; (2) a lamb and a wolf; (3) a gazelle and a bear; (4) a deer and an elephant; (5) a unicorn and a griffin; (6) a man and a demon (see Raphael Patai, *Gates to the Old City* [New York: Avon, 1980], pp. 335–8). It should scarcely be necessary to point out the magical significance of these twelve beasts, six benevolent to bless on the right side and six malevolent to curse on the left side.

Besides the four winds, the birds, and the beasts, Solomon also commanded the spirits called jinn by the Arabs (the singular form is jinni). These spirits he captured when needed in a magical fishing net. He caused them to dive deep into the sea and harvest pearls, to build the Temple and other architectural marvels, and to perform many services for him at his bidding.

To punish the jinn and to keep them under restraint, the great king sealed them into brass vessels (Richard F. Burton's translation of *The Book of a Thousand Nights and a Night* says the vessels were of copper). These sealed vessels were cast into the sea, and from time to time they wash up on shore, giving rise to all the tales of jinn freed from lamps by fools. In modern popular stories, these "genies" are often good spirits, but in older tales they are evil demons—why else would Solomon have imprisoned them?

The instrument of Solomon's power was his magic ring. There are various descriptions of this object. We know it was a seal ring because the king used it to seal the jinn into their prisons. The brass (or copper) vessels were stopped with lead caps into which was pressed the symbol of Solomon's ring. Some early accounts say that the pentagram was engraved upon its bezel (the enlarged, flat part of a ring). In later accounts, this is changed into the hexagram, but the pentagram is the earlier and more authentic symbol. By other accounts *(Zohar* 3:233a-b), the ring is inscribed with the four letters of Tetragrammaton.

The seal of Solomon—the symbol inscribed upon his seal ring—figures prominently in the many magical books attributed to him. Among the many versions of the seal, the most common is that appearing in the accompanying illustration (see page 91), which occurs in manuscripts of the *Lesser Key of Solomon.* It is said that Solomon used it to bind and seal seventy-two wicked spirits within a large brazen vessel, then cast the vessel of brass into a deep lake.

There seems to be no magical link between the seal upon Solomon's ring, and the herb known as Solomon's seal *(Polygonatum multiflorum),* which was employed to heal green (fresh) wounds or stop menstrual blood, but it is interesting that, whereas the stone in Solomon's ring was credited with the power to cut open anything, this herb was used to close gaping wounds. No one knows for certain how this herb got its name, but Culpeper thought it came from "a flat round circle representing a seal [around the root] lying all along under the upper crust of the earth" (*Culpeper's Complete Herbal* [Manchester, 1826], p. 166).

Solomon's ring occurs in connection with a magical herb in an anecdotal account of an exorcism witnessed by Josephus, which took place in the presence of the Roman emperor Vespasian (first century A.D.). Josephus reports than a Jewish exorcist named Eleazar used "a ring that had a root [in it] of one of those sorts mentioned by Solomon" *(Antiquities* 8.2.5) to draw demons out through the nose of those that were possessed. He did this by placing the ring close to the nostrils of the possessed person. The evil spirit (*spiritus* means breath) was forced out upon the exhalation of the sick individual by the power of the ring, or the root contained in it, or both (this is not made clear). It is a common practice in magic for occult herbs to be placed under the stones of rings, so that the rings take on the virtues of the herbs.

As is true of the breastplate of Aaron, the power of Solomon's ring arose both from the magic symbol, or symbols, cut into its bezel and from the jewel, or jewels, with which it was set.

E. A. Wallis Budge says the ring was made of pure gold and bore a single, large *shamir* (diamond), upon which were engraved the four letters of the Ineffable Name or perhaps the symbol known as the "shield of Solomon," which was probably the pentagram (*Amulets and Talismans,* p. 281). Elsewhere (p. 424) Budge says that the *shamir* was regarded as a "living power" that preserved Solomon from harm and kept him upon his throne. The *shamir,* which seems to have entered the legend of Solomon through Jewish folk tales, served as a magic mirror wherein the king was able to see the reflected image of any distant place or person he wished (George F. Kuntz, *Rings for the Finger* (New York: Dover, 1973], pp. 288–9).

There is some doubt over exactly what the fabulous *shamir* may have been. In Talmudic legend, it seems to be described as a small worm that could eat through any stone, but this is far from clear. Rashi called it "A creature from the six days of creation that no hard object can resist." According to the Talmud, Solomon asked the rabbis how he could build the Temple without iron tools (see 1 Kings 6:7). They told him there was a thing called a *shamir,* which Moses had used to cut the stones on the breastplate of Aaron. To discover where this magical object lay hidden, Solomon caused the king of all the demons, Ashmodai, to be bound with a ring and a chain inscribed with Tetragrammaton. After learning from Ashmodai how to get the *shamir,* Solomon kept the demon prisoner to build the Temple (see Patai, *Gates to the Old City,* pp. 185–7).

It is easy to see how the diamond might be confused with a creature who can melt through stone, since the diamond is the hardest substance known and was used in ancient times to inscribe and carve other gemstones. Couple this with the fable that the Temple was built without iron tools (in fact, the stones were probably cut elsewhere and carried to the site of the Temple) and the fable that the *shamir* in Solomon's ring was indirectly responsible for the building of the Temple, in that it commanded the demons who built it, and we can see how the divine Name, the magical stone in the ring, and the demons commanded by Solomon were combined to create a fabulous stone-cutting creature, the *shamir.*

In a Sephardi folk tale, the date of which is unknown, the single stone in Solomon's ring is said to be blue in color, suggesting the sapphire. This is interesting, since the word *sephiroth* comes from the Hebrew word for sapphire. The brilliant, sparkling light of the sapphire was considered purer

The Seal of Solomon

than all other colors. In this folktale, Solomon uses his ring to command the four winds and activates the ring's power by kissing the blue stone.

Richard F. Burton presents a somewhat different picture of the ring. He says that it was composed of stamped stone, iron, copper, and lead (*The Book of the Thousand Nights and a Night*, 6.84), and elsewhere (7.317) says that it was set with four jewels presented to Solomon by four angels to rule the winds, the birds, the land and sea, and the spirits. Each of these jewels was inscribed with a holy verse. On the jewel that ruled the winds was written: "To Allah belong Majesty and Might." On the jewel that ruled the birds was written: "All created things praise the Lord." On the jewel that ruled the land and sea was written: "Heaven and Earth are Allah's slaves." On the jewel that ruled the spirits was written: "There is no god but the God, and Mohammed is His messenger."

An illustration in a Syriac magical text called *The Little Book of Protection* depicts the shield of Solomon as an eight-rayed star with a smaller four-rayed star cut into the middle of it. Seven names or words of power were engraved between two concentric circles on the ring, probably around its bezel, and on the hoop of the ring were cut twenty-nine more barbaric words in Syriac characters. It is likely that the seven around the bezel represented the seven planets and seven days of the week, while these coupled with the other twenty-nine, forming a total of thirty-six, stood for the thirty-six decans (divisions of ten degrees) of the zodiac.

It is impossible to arrive at any firm conclusion about the true form of the ring of Solomon, which has received so many different shapes throughout its long history. Perhaps the purest form, from a magical standpoint, is that of a pentagram inscribed within its center with the IHVH. There can be little doubt that the fourfold power of the ring, symbolized by the four jewels, originated with the fourfold Name of God.

The letters IHVH, cut deeply into the ring in the form of a seal in mirror inversion, when pressed into the hot lead that stopped the vessels holding the jinn, would appear written in the lead in its natural order, right to left. This lends some credence to the notion that the Banners of IHVH on the breastplate of Aaron were also cut into the stones in mirror inversion, allowing these twelve stones to act as seals for the twelve tribes of Israel. It seems significant that the fable of the *shamir* directly connects Solomon with the breastplate.

The most famous tale about the ring of Solomon involves the time it was stolen. There are several versions of this tale. In the Talmud, after Ashmodai completed the Temple for Solomon, he tricked the king into handing over his magic ring. At once Ashmodai swallowed the ring and hurled Solomon a vast distance away from Jerusalem, then took up the throne in his place under a false appearance. No one recognized Solomon because the demon had changed his features; moreover, the king was prevented by the magic of Ashmodai from telling anyone his identity. He wandered a long time as a beggar (some say for forty years) and eventually made his way back to Jerusalem. The rabbis became suspicious of him because he ceaselessly repeated a verse from the Torah: "I, Koheleth, was king over Israel in Jerusalem" (Eccles. 1:12). They did some checking and discovered from Solomon's wives that Ashmodai, in the guise of the king, was demanding sex from them during their menstrual periods, and also from Solomon's mother, Bathsheba, in violation of Jewish law. The rabbis gave the beggar a ring and a chain engraved with IHVH, and as soon as Ashmodai saw Solomon enter the palace, he flew away, releasing Solomon from his enchantment.

In a slightly different Arab version of the theft of the ring, Solomon took it off while bathing and entrusted it to a favorite concubine named Amina. A demon named Sakhar approached her cloaked in the appearance of the king and tricked her into giving him the ring. At once he assumed the throne, and Solomon, his features changed by magic, was forced to beg for forty days while the demon did anything he desired. At the end of this time, the demon threw the ring into the sea. It was swallowed by a fish, where Solomon found it when he cut the fish open. By means of the power of the ring he regained his kingdom. He captured Sakhar, tied a great stone around his neck, and threw the demon into a deep lake.

Throughout the stories about the ring runs a swallowing motif. Ashmodai swallows the ring to keep it from Solomon. In the Arab version, it is the fish who swallows the ring. According to a story in the *Zohar,* Solomon would ride on the back of an eagle to the dark gathering place of evil spirits, where the fallen angels Uzza and Azael lay bound in vast iron chains that were fastened to the roots of the abyss. Solomon would put his seal ring into the mouth of the eagle and hide under its left wing, and the power of the Name upon the ring would force the dark angels to tell him all the secrets of supernal wisdom.

In alchemy, a common image is the swallowing or devouring of the king (dominant conscious mind) by a dragon or other beast, representing the *prima materia* (unconscious mind). This brings about a state of *nigredo* (darkness) that eventually leads to the renewal and rebirth of the king (see Carl Jung, *Psychology and Alchemy* [Princeton, 1980], p. 417).

A distinction should probably be made between swallowing the ring and placing the ring in the mouth. In the first case, the occult virtues of the ring are taken hostage; in the second case, the ring confers the power of verbal command, which is expressed through the organ of the mouth.

The ring of Solomon represents not only his authority, but his wholeness as a person. When it is swallowed by the beast, he wanders lost, unrecognized, unable even to speak his own name. Only after he regains the ring does he become complete once again. The open hoop of a magic ring represents a portal to a higher dimension of reality. By passing through the ring, symbolically expressed by inserting the finger, we enter this higher dimension and partake of its power. The physical body represents another kind of magic circle that can be entered through the mouth, nose, ears, or in women the vagina, and exited either by the mouth (in vomiting) or the anus (in excretion) or the vagina (in birth) or through a cut in the skin. When Ashmodai swallows the ring, he takes its higher dimension of reality and submerges it within the shadows of the magic circle of his body, thereby isolating it, and to the extent it is possible for a creature of darkness to control an instrument of light, commanding it.

In magic, rings can be empowered in four ways. Either a spirit is caused through ritual procedures to enter into the ring and dwell within it, lending it the power of the spirit, which the possessor of the ring commands; or the ring derives its efficacy from its occult correspondences with the heavens; or the ring gets its power from natural objects possessing occult virtues such as stones, herbs, or parts of beasts; or it derives power from a symbolic shape or pattern or image that embodies the authority of a potent supernatural being. Usually this symbol is the name of that being, or an image representing its name.

The first great river of power that flowed through Solomon's ring issued from the Ineffable Name of God inscribed into it, which Solomon was able to employ during his early years for holy works because he lived according to the law of the Torah. In the folktales and legends of Solomon, he loses the ring after he has violated this law in some particular way. In one version, he loses the ring when he lusts after the daughter of a gentile king. In another, it is lost after he allows an idol to be erected within his palace to please his wife Jerada. In another version, he loses it when his pride is tempted by Ashmodai. Solomon can only wield the authority of the Name when he is in perfect harmony with it. At such a time, he becomes an expression of God's will upon the earth, fulfilling the purposes of God—in effect, an angel incarnate.

The second river of power flowing through the ring of Solomon issued from the *shamir* stone. The "living power" of the *shamir* indicates that it contained an angel of God, probably a very powerful and exalted angel, because the ring was used for the holiest works, such as erecting the Temple and binding evil spirits. It would be idle to speculate which angel resided within the brilliant radiance of the *shamir.* Perhaps it was Michael, who is the great warrior angel. I am more inclined to think that the light of Metatron, the highest of all angels, shone from the depths of the stone.

The third river of power flowed from any occult symbols that may have been inscribed upon the ring at the time of its making. These drew down the rays of the planets and the fixed stars or signs, or attracted the energies of the four earthly elements. Among these symbols is the pentagram and the hexagram, either of which may have been on Solomon's ring.

A fourth river of power flowed forth from the material substance, or substances, that formed the ring, or were enclosed within the ring. These were such things as the metal gold, of which the ring was made; the particular nature of the ring's stone (diamond or sapphire are most likely; or there may have been four different jewels, one for each of the letters of the Name); and any occult material that may have been set beneath the stone, such as a magic herb. These natural substances derive their power from the heavens also, through occult correspondences that connect them to the planets and

stars. For example, gold
draws down the solar virtue
of the sun; diamond is the
stone of Aries and Mars. The
sun represents Solomon as
an enlightened and benevolent ruler; Aries and Mars
reinforce his aspect as a powerful warrior king.

Many occult texts claim
to possess the true description of the ring, but since
each differs from all the others, it is difficult to know how
much faith to place in their
assertions. For example, the
Enochian angels conveyed
the supposed true image of
the ring to John Dee through
the seer Edward Kelley, who
observed the ring issue from
a flame that sprang out of

Enochian Ring of Solomon

the sword of the angel
Michael (see Geoffrey James,
The Enochian Magick of Dr. John Dee, pp. 26–7). Dee drew the ring accord-
ing to Kelley's direction, and the result is pictured above.

It is highly significant that the bezel of Dee's ring is square, since any
true ring of Solomon must have some close connection with the fourfold
Name of God. The letters on the face of the bezel may be an anagram for
some word, or words, of power. There are eight of them, counting the
enlarged letters superimposed one on top of the other in the center of the
ring: P, V, E, O, I, E, L, L. It may be that the four letters in the corners of the
ring, PELE, are substitutions for the letters of Tetragrammaton, IHVH. It
seems more than coincidence that the E repeats itself. The three-letter
Hebrew word *Pele* (PLA) occurs in Judges 13:18, and signifies a worker of
miracles (see Agrippa, *Occult Philosophy*, 3.11).

We cannot begin to reconstruct the true ring of Solomon. There are too
many conflicting descriptions. However, we can devise modern rings of
power based upon the same magical principles that went into the design of
Solomon's ring and which also rely upon the authority of Tetragrammaton
for their effectiveness. The method of making and empowering a set of
twenty-four magic rings is described in the following chapter.

XII

׳׳׳׳׳׳׳׳׳׳׳׳

BANNER RINGS

The following set of magic rings is intended to appeal to serious ritualists interested in working with the Banners of Tetragrammaton and their associated angels, the Wings of the Winds. Because the construction of the rings entails considerable work and expense, it should be undertaken only by occultists who are certain they know what they want and what they are doing. Kabbalists will be especially interested in this unique magical machine.

Obtain twenty-four identical blank signet rings, twelve made of silver and twelve of gold. A cheaper substitute for silver is pewter. A cheaper substitute for gold is brass. Gold-plated and silver-plated rings may be used if these can be found. In the latter case, the base metal under the plating should be the same material. Do not mix solid silver rings with gold-plated rings.

If you are skilled in jewelry making, you can manufacture your own set of rings. Or you may wish to have a jeweler friend make them for you. They should have a square or rectangular plain bezel suitable for engraving. A small, blank signet ring is very close to the ideal pattern. If necessary, the shape of the gold rings can differ slightly from the shape of the silver rings, but all twelve rings of gold should be the same and all twelve silver rings the same.

Upon the bezels of the gold rings, engrave, or have engraved, the twelve *overt* Banners of Tetragrammaton, each in Hebrew letters, right to left, so that the four letters of the Name fill the bezel. On the inside of the hoops beneath the bezels, engrave, or have engraved, the twelve corresponding names of the Wings of the Winds that constitute the angels of mercy, also in Hebrew letters. These should be engraved as deeply as possible.

Upon the bezels of the silver rings, engrave, or have engraved, the twelve *occult* Banners of Tetragrammaton in Hebrew letters, right to left, in the same dimension and style that was used to engrave the gold rings. On the inside of the hoops beneath the bezels of the silver rings, engrave, or have engraved, the twelve corresponding names of the Wings of the Winds who make up the angels of severity.

Zodiac	Gold (Sun)	Silver (Moon)
1. Aries	IHV**H** (QThH+AL)	IHV**H** (HThQ+IH)
2. Taurus	**H**HVI (ShIA+AL)	**H**HVI (AISh+IH)
3. Gemini	V**H**HI (VIH+AL)	V**H**HI (HIV+IH)
4. Cancer	H**H**VI (DVI+AL)	**H**VHI (IVD+IH)
5. Leo	IV**H**H (QLI+AL)	IV**H**H (ILQ+IH)
6. Virgo	**H**IVH (ShHV+AL)	**H**IV**H** (VHSh+IH)
7. Libra	V**H**IH (VAH+AL)	V**H**IH (HAV+IH)
8. Scorpio	**H**HIV (DAB+AL)	**H**HIV (BAD+IH)
9. Sagittarius	IH**H**V (QTzH+AL)	IH**H**V (HTzQ+IH)
10. Capricorn	**H**IHV (ShBV+AL)	**H**IHV (VBSh+IH)
11. Aquarius	VI**H**H (VIV+AL)	VI**H**H (VIV+IH)
12. Pisces	**H**VIH (DMV+AL)	**H**VIH (VMD+IH)

In the list above, I have indicated the position of the second H in Tetragrammaton with boldface type to help you distinguish between the overt and occult Banners. On the rings, the two Hs are not distinguished in any way. The overt Banners look exactly the same as their corresponding occult Banners.

Each of the gold rings represents the power of one of the overt Banners. This is analogous to the power of the sun acting through its corresponding sign of the zodiac. For example, the sun in Aries is the astrological expression of the overt Banner IHV**H**, and its active agent the angel Kethahel (QThHAL). The silver rings represent the powers of the mirror-opposite occult Banners. These occult Banners are analogous to the power of the moon acting through the corresponding zodiac signs. For example, the moon in Cancer is the astrological expression of the occult Banner **H**VHI, and its active agent the angel of severity Yodiah (IVDIH).

In human psychology, the overt Banners and the sun accord with inspiration, consciousness, and will. The occult Banners and the moon accord with the unconscious mind, instincts, urges, habits, and the rhythms of the body. The angels of mercy are the active agents of the overt Banners that convey and express the potencies of these Banners in the sphere of human existence, which is the universe. The angels of severity are the active agents of the occult Banners, and, in a similar manner, they express the powers of the occult Banners upon human life and the greater physical world.

This polarity is fundamentally the same as that which exists between the right pillar and the left pillar of the tree of the *sephiroth*. The overt Banners are expansive, fiery, creative, and benevolent; the occult Banners are constrictive, watery, receptive, and severe in judgment. The angels of the occult Banners are not really evil, any more than the left hand can be called evil and the right hand good, but they control the archetypal potencies or tendencies that we associate with evil—harshness, coldness, narrow-mindedness, condemnation, criticism. According to the doctrine of the kabbalah, these forces of the left pillar arise from the unconscious part of the mind, the dark half (*Binah*), whereas the forces of the right pillar—inspiration, exuberance, generosity, kindness, munificence—arise from the (higher) conscious part of the mind, the light half (*Chokmah*).

The authority of each Banner of Tetragrammaton rules and controls the working of its corresponding Wing of the Winds. These angels are exalted in nature, as is proved by their placement around the very throne of God (Rev. 4:6–8). They must be ruled by an even higher nature. The only beings possessed of a more holy nature than the Wings of the Winds are the twenty-four seated Elders with their white robes and crowns of gold, and the seven fiery Spirits of God. The Elders are the Banners of Tetragrammaton, and the fiery Spirits are the seven traditional planets.

These planets are divided into two sects ruled by the sun and the moon. The sect of the sun contains Jupiter, Saturn, and Mercury. The sect of the moon contains Mars, Venus, and Mercury. There is another ancient division of the planets in astrology that assigns them under the sun and moon to the signs of the zodiac. By this arrangement, the zodiac is divided down the middle into a solar half (right side) and a lunar half (left side). The sun, ruling in Leo, is placed over the five lesser planets in the signs from Virgo to Capricorn, while the moon, ruling in Cancer, is placed over the mirror-opposite ordering of the same five planets in the signs from Gemini to Aquarius.

Mercury is the only planet belonging both to the sect of the sun and the sect of the moon. It is the crucible of solar and lunar forces, where these powers mingle and amalgamate with each other. As such, it represents heavenly Adam incarnated upon the earth (the Messiah, or Christ) and the middle pillar of mildness on the tree of the *sephiroth*. This is an occult correspondence that is seldom found in the texts of the kabbalah, but was well understood by John Dee (see *The Hieroglyphic Monad,* Theorem XIII), and also familiar to the medieval alchemists, who represented Mercury in this moderating and reconciling aspect in their symbolic illustrations. This is why Dee made the astrological glyph of Mercury the dominant component of his monad. Mercury contains the sun and moon within itself, just as Christ is both heaven and earth mingled in one form.

When I speak of Christ in these pages, I am not asserting a Christian bias. Christ is merely the most complete expression of the Messiah figure, an embodiment of the Infinite Light (*ain soph aur*), whose purpose is to descend from heaven (*atziluth*) to earth (*assiah*), uniting spirit with flesh, and by this act of sacrifice to redeem humanity from its sin of imbalance (pure judgment, or *Din*—see Scholem, *Kabbalah,* p. 123) and restore it to the harmony of its rightful spiritual estate through the infusion of loving kindness (*Chesed*).

According to the kabbalah, the true first sin committed by Adam was the division of the tree of knowledge from the tree of life, originally a single tree. This division is known as the "cutting of the shoots" and is symbolically represented by the plucking of the apple, which divided fruit from root. The aim of the Messiah is to reunite the tree of life (right pillar) with the tree of the knowledge of good and evil (left pillar).

The golden solar rings are worn in succession upon the index finger of the right hand. Each time the sun enters the astrological sign corresponding to a particular overt Banner of Tetragrammaton, the ring bearing that Banner is put upon the right index finger. It continues to be worn all the time the sun is passing through that sign of the zodiac.

For example, around March 21, the Sun enters the sign Aries. This signals the putting on of the gold ring bearing the overt Banner IHVH, and all during the period the sun remains within Aries, the angel of mercy Ketha-hel can be used by the magician, under the authority of this Banner, to accomplish acts of creation and willed purpose, to bring about transformation both in the greater outer world and the personal inner world (both worlds being, in truth, one). This angel is especially potent in those creative, loving and expansive areas that lie within the province of Aries and the first house of the zodiac, to which Aries corresponds—personal expression, self-assertion, egocentric interests.

Around April 20, the gold Banner ring of IHVH is removed and the ring of HHVI is put on the right index finger. While the sun continues its course through the sign of Taurus, the angel of mercy Shiael may be employed by the magician for willful, creative acts, especially those that lie within the province of Taurus and the second house of the zodiac, to which Taurus corresponds—practical, productive works concerning material possessions and personal security.

It is impossible to be more precise about the day and hour the sun enters the signs of the zodiac, because this varies from year to year. The approximate times of entry are these:

Sun Enters	Date
Aries	March 21
Taurus	April 20
Gemini	May 21
Cancer	June 22
Leo	July 23
Virgo	August 24
Libra	September 23
Scorpio	October 24
Sagittarius	November 23
Capricorn	December 22
Aquarius	January 20
Pisces	February 19

Ideally, the gold rings should be changed at the very minute the sun enters the succeeding sign. These times can be obtained by consulting a good ephemeris such as *Raphael's,* where the entry of the sun, moon, and planets into each of the signs for the year is given in a separate table near the back of the book.

The silver lunar rings are worn in succession on the index finger of the left hand. Each time the moon enters the astrological sign corresponding to a particular occult Banner of Tetragrammaton, the ring bearing that Banner is put upon the left index finger. It continues to be worn for as long as the moon remains within that sign. When the moon passes into the succeeding sign, the ring is replaced by that which bears the occult Banner of the succeeding sign.

For example, as the moon enters the sign of Sagittarius, the silver ring bearing the occult Banner IHHV is put upon the left index finger. All during the period when the moon remains within the bounds of Sagittarius, the angel of severity Hazekiah can be used by the magician, under the authority of this Banner, to accomplish controlling, analytical, critical, or restricting works both in the outer and inner worlds. This angel is especially powerful in those works that involve the controlling, critical, and physical aspects of the sign Sagittarius, and the ninth house of the zodiac, to which Sagittarius corresponds—such as experiments involving new ideas, novel sensations, body transformations, role reversals, explorations in philosophy or religion.

When the moon passes from Sagittarius into Capricorn, the silver ring bearing the occult Banner HIHV is put upon the left index finger. For so

long as the moon continues its course through Capricorn, the angel of severity Vabashiah can be employed in works involving restriction, concentration,
and judgment. It is particularly effective in those areas that lie within the
province of Capricorn and the tenth house of the zodiac, which corresponds
with Capricorn—practicality and self-restraint in matters of social status
and material responsibility.

The moon passes completely around the circle of the heavens in a period
of twenty-seven days, seven hours, and fourteen minutes, which is known as
a sidereal month. It remains in each sign of the zodiac just a bit over two
days. It is possible to roughly estimate which sign the moon is in if the sign
the sun is passing through is known: when the moon is full, it is exactly
opposite the sun on the zodiac; when it is new, it is in the same sign as the
sun; when it is in its first quarter, it is ninety degrees in advance of the sun
(going counterclockwise around the signs); and when it is in the last quarter, it is ninety degrees behind the sun. However, an ephemeris should be
used to determine the exact minute when the moon enters each sign, for the
changing of the silver rings.

A ring is worn on the index finger of both hands at all times. Each ring
favors different areas of magical work, defined by the action of the sun or
moon in individual signs and houses. However, in time of need, any ring can
be pressed to perform any magical work: those on the left hand works of
severity, restriction, judgement, and formation; those on the right hand
works of kindness, expansion, mercy, and creation.

When the magician wishes to bless a person, place, or thing, the right
hand and the golden ring is used. On those rare occasions when it is found
necessary to curse or punish, the left hand and the silver ring is employed.
While both rings are worn, the body, mind, and spirit of the wearer is har-
monized with the universe and the universal Spirit that constitutes, ani-
mates, and sustains it. For this reason, once the cycle of the rings is begun,
they should be worn continually, save for those brief moments when they
are alternately changed.

The gold and silver rings of each Banner form a natural mated pair, and
must be made, or at least inscribed, on the same day while both the sun and
moon occupy the sign of the Banner. When the moon enters the first degree
of a sign already occupied by the sun, the gold ring should be inscribed with
the Banner and overt angel related to that sign at once, if the entry occurs
during daylight hours. If the entry of the moon occurs in the night, the
inscription of the gold ring should be delayed until morning. The silver ring
is then inscribed after sunset on the same day that the gold ring
was inscribed.

The only exception to this rule of gold ring in daylight and silver ring in
nighttime happens when the moon enters a sign which the sun is just about

to leave. It is vital that moon and sun occupy the same sign when the ring pair of its related Banner is inscribed. Under this circumstance, it may prove necessary to engrave both rings at once, either in the light or darkness depending on when the moon enters the sign. The gold ring is still engraved first, followed by the silver ring.

Since the need to finish the rings on the same day means that, at best, there will be only twelve hours to fashion each ring, most makers will prefer to prepare blank rings ahead of time and only engrave each pair as the moon enters its related sign.

The overt and occult rings for each Banner are thus made upon or near the time of the new moon, while the orbs of sun and moon overlap. In astrology (by one interpretation: A. T. Mann, *The Round Art* [New York: Mayflower Books, 1979], p. 167), an orb is the arc of influence of a planet within which it can form effective aspects with other planets or astrological points. The orbs of both the sun and moon are said to be sixteen degrees across, which means that when these greater lights occupy the same sign, their orbs must touch. Occultly, they may be said to be in copulative union. When mated pairs of rings are worn at the same time, when both the sun and moon occupy the same sign, their potency is unusually great because each ring harmoniously reinforces and supplements the power of its mate.

The making of the entire set of twenty-four Banner rings thus takes one full year to complete. One mated pair is prepared each astrological month. It is best if the making of the rings begins when the sun is in Aries and proceeds in an unbroken sequence of signs around the zodiac. The year spent in creating the rings should be looked upon as a single prolonged ritual devoted to attaining a gnosis of Tetragrammaton—its meanings, Banners, and angels.

Between the single days of the months when each pair of rings is actually inscribed, the magician should be conducting meditations on the Name; constructing a framework of practical rituals within which the rings will be used; composing appropriate prayers, invocations, and visualizations designed to attune the mind and spirit to the Banners; and purifying the body, emotions, and thoughts in preparation to receive the Light, without which the rings can never be used effectively. The rings should not be worn until all twenty-four are completed. It is useful to make a special box to hold the rings not being worn. This should be of pine, because pine has long been regarded as a magical insulator, and designed in such a way that the rings are held in position and kept from mixing together. One way to do this is to set two rows of pegs into the bottom of the box and lay the rings over the pegs. The pegs are made tall enough so that they touch the upper lid of the box, preventing the rings from falling off the pegs when the box is closed. Any other system may be used, provided it keeps the rings in good order. Blue or black velvet is a good material for lining the ring box.

Most people will not have the skill or inclination to engrave the rings themselves. A viable alternative is to buy the blank signet rings ahead of time, then on the day the moon enters a sign occupied by the sun, take a gold and silver ring to the jewelry store and have the Banners and the angels engraved on them professionally. You will need to find a jeweler who can do the engraving in Hebrew letters and who isn't horrified that you intend to use the Banners of IHVH for magical purposes.

You may find it necessary to engrave the rings yourself, however crudely. This can be done with one of the small vibrating engraving tools sold to mark valuables. If such a tool is used, set it on low power. This will make it easier to handle. Begin slowly, tracing out very lightly the outline of the Hebrew letters right to left, then fill them in and deepen them. The result will not be as attractive as a professional engraving job, but it will be just as effective.

XIII

ʻ ʻ

EMPOWERING THE RINGS

A fter each ring has been engraved with its Banner and associated Wing of the Winds, it must be ritually cleansed, charged, and dedicated to its magical function. The authority of the Banner and the active power of the Wing must be made to descend and indwell within it, if it is to be effective as a magical tool. Without these rituals of empowerment, the rings will remain no more than curiously decorated bits of jewelry.

The following ritual procedures are structured upon the system of occult correspondences given in my book, *The New Magus*. This differs in several important respects from the more common Golden Dawn system. In the *New Magus* system, the assignments to the quarters are:

Quarter	Element	Archangel	Tetramorph	Sign
South	Fire	Michael	Lion	Leo
West	Water	Gabriel	Eagle	Scorpio
North	Air	Raphael	Angel	Aquarius
East	Earth	Uriel	Bull	Taurus

Also, in the *New Magus* system, the left and right sides of the kabbalistic cross are the inverse of those given by the Golden Dawn. In *The New Magus,* the left shoulder is assigned to *Geburah* and the right shoulder to

105

Gedulah. Occultists familiar with the system of the Golden Dawn can easily modify these rituals to be in harmony with the more conventional correspondences. These changes will not affect the efficacy of the rituals and have no bearing on the assignment of the Banners to the zodiac.

Kabbalistic Cross

In striving to magically cleanse a ritual object, the beginner in magic runs into a perplexing difficulty. An object can only be made pure by applying something to it that is already pure. This is known as the principle of contagion, whereby anything strongly charged with a particular occult virtue tends to pass that virtue on to other things less strongly charged when the two come into physical or symbolic contact. As the Arabian philosopher Avicenna observed: "when a thing standeth long in salt, it is salt, and if any thing stand in a stinking place, it is made stinking" (see *The Book of Secrets* [Oxford University Press, 1974], p. 74).

To magically cleanse the rings, we need purified and consecrated water, yet we cannot make the water unless we apply to it something that is itself pure. In religion this difficulty is overcome by relying on an unbroken chain that stretches into the dim mists of the past. A priest is able to prepare holy water because he has, himself, been made pure by other priests, who themselves have been purified by still other priests, and so on back to Jesus himself. In magic, unless we are fortunate enough to be working in an ancient communal tradition, we must first purify ourselves and fill ourselves with light before we can purify and infuse our ritual instruments with light. This is done by calling upon higher spiritual beings to pass their purity and their light on to us, through the ritual of prayer. Attaining self-purity is square one in magic.

As I mentioned elsewhere, in modern magic, "purity" signifies singleness of purpose and inner clarity, as opposed to conflict, confusion, imbalance, and doubt. The word carries no sexual connotation. Purity is not virginity, nor it is sexual abstinence, although chastity has been found to aid in achieving a state of purity. It is a necessary condition to magical work and therefore it is vital that the term not be misunderstood.

The following modified version of the ritual of the kabbalistic cross, which is used in Golden Dawn magic, relies on a prayer of purification found in the Old Testament that is extremely ancient and very powerful. It is an adaptation of Psalm 51. The Psalms have been used in ritual magic for thousands of years, particularly by kabbalists. The cross itself is based upon the structure of the tree of the *sephiroth,* which is symbolically invoked and taken into the body of the ritualist, so that the ritualist becomes the sacred tree.

Stand facing the south on an open floor where you will not be observed or interrupted. Stand with your back straight and your feet together, your hands at your sides. Allow yourself to become inwardly tranquil. When you feel an inner peace, raise your hands before your heart and clap them three times together; then raise and spread your arms heavenward in a posture of invocation, your palms turned upward. Speak the following cleansing prayer:

> **Have mercy upon me, O God;**
> **Blot out my transgressions.**
> **Wash me thoroughly from mine iniquity**
> **And cleanse me from my sin.**
> **Purge me with hyssop, and I shall be clean;**
> **Wash me, and I shall be whiter than snow.**
> **Create in me a clean heart, O God,**
> **And renew a right spirit within me.**

As you speak the words of this ancient prayer, visualize a river of sparkling clear water cascade down from heaven to wash over your upturned face and entire body. Feel it enter into your pores and renew you with fresh vitality. Feel it wash out all the shadows and detritus from the corners of your mind and heart.

When you finish the prayer, place your left hand upon the center of your chest diagonally across your heart and with your right index finger touch in succession the top of your forehead just under the hairline, your groin, your left shoulder, your right shoulder, the back of your hand where it lies upon your heart center, and then with your right index finger point straight ahead of you into the infinite distance of the south. As you describe the shape of the kabbalistic cross upon your own body, speak these works, which follow directly after the words of the cleansing prayer without a pause:

> **Who art the Crown** (forehead)
> **And the Kingdom** (groin),
> **The Power** (left shoulder)
> **And the Glory** (right shoulder),
> **And the Everlasting Law** (heart center),
> **Amen** (point directly in front at heart level).

Press your palms together in a prayer gesture before your heart center and visualize three rays of laser light intersecting your heart at right angles. A ruby-red ray passes vertically through the crown of your head and between the soles of your feet. A sapphire-blue ray shines through your heart horizontally beneath each of your shoulders. A topaz-yellow ray passes through the front of your chest between your joined palms and through your back between the bottoms of your shoulder blades. These rays are infinitely long and have no beginning or ending.

After you have contemplated the three rays of the cross for several minutes in silence, clap your hands together four times in front of your heart to indicate that the ritual is fulfilled; or, if the cross is only the opening part of a more complicated ritual, proceed with the ritual.

The words spoken while making the cross are translations of names of the *sephiroth*. The Crown is *Kether*. The Kingdom is *Malkuth*. Both are located on the central pillar of the tree of the *sephiroth*. The Power is *Geburah*, which is more commonly translated "Severity," but which Gershom Scholem translates as "Power" (*Kabbalah,* p. 106). *Geburah* lies midway on the left pillar of the tree. The Glory is *Gedulah,* a very common alternate name for the fourth *sephirah, Chesed,* located midway on the right pillar of the tree. Scholem translates *Gedulah* as "Greatness." The Everlasting Law corresponds to *Tiphareth* on the tree. *Tiphareth* lies in the midst of the central pillar. It is commonly translated "Beauty." It is the *sephirah* of the Messiah. An alternate title is the King.

This simple cleansing and centering formula should be used before erecting the magic circle, as an introduction to all ritual work. In this way, the rituals begin from a clean slate, which is the purified and enlightened soul of the ritualist, and this inner light can then be transmitted to empower ritual objects or actions.

Water of Cleansing

It is necessary to first cleanse the rings of any lingering psychic associations they may have picked up along their travels before charging them with light and consecrating them to their magical purposes. For this, you will need a supply of water that has been ritually purified. Its function is the same as that of the holy water used in religious ceremonies—it stores the divine radiance of the *ain soph aur* to be used as needed for symbolically cleansing persons, places, or objects of chaotic influences. Once you have a supply of sanctified water, you can use it to cleanse all your ritual instruments and your ritual chamber.

Start with clear water from a spring or river. Tap water is a poor alternative, but can be used if this is unavoidable. Do not use seawater, or add salt to the water, because saltwater tarnishes silver badly.

Pour the water into an open glass vessel such as a large crystal bowl. Place it on a small table with a square top in the center of your ritual chamber, so that you can walk all around it. The table serves as your ritual altar. A bedside table is an excellent size and shape. If you do not have enough room to walk around this table, place it in the south.

Stand in the north of the ritual chamber facing south across the altar. Perform the cleansing prayer and kabbalistic cross, exactly as described above, but instead of clapping your hands four times to close the ritual, rotate on your body axis in a clockwise direction to stand facing north away from the altar. Walk once completely around the altar clockwise, at the same time projecting from your heart center a ribbon of white fire through your extended right index finger, so that the fire forms a flaming circle that encloses you and the altar and floats upon the air at the level of your heart. Try to visualize the projection of the circle as clearly as possible, and try to project your own psychic and physical energy into it. Draw this fire out of your heart center through your left hand, which should lie flat on your chest, and feel it flow up your left arm, across your shoulders, and out your right arm. Take care to join the end of the circle with its beginning in the north.

In the event that you are unable to walk completely around the table, which serves as the ritual altar, you can project the circle of fire mentally to surround the chamber by turning on your own axis clockwise with your right index finger extended as you stand before the altar, your left hand over your heart center. Begin projecting the circle in the northern quarter, and be sure to join the end of the circle with its beginning.

Once these preliminary steps are concluded, you may go on with the actual ritual of consecration. Walk clockwise around the altar to stand in the eastern quarter facing west across the bowl. Raise your hands to heaven and speak your purpose in your own words. It will be something like:

> **I,** (your name), **erect this magic circle for the purpose of exorcising this pure, clean water and infusing it with holy light.**

If you have a magical name, you should use it in this declaration of purpose.

Point your right index finger at the center of the bowl and speak these (or similar) words:

> **By the authority of the name of power Yeheshuah, I banish all shadows from this holy vessel.**

With your right index finger, inscribe a spiral vortex over the water beginning at the center and expanding in a counterclockwise direction in ever-widening circles. Finally, end the spiral by raising your index finger to point straight upward. As you do this, visualize astrally an expanding swirl of light that drives dark shadows away from its edges and see the water in the bowl perfectly clear and neutral. At the same time you are drawing the banishing spiral upon the air, vibrate powerfully the letters of the holy name IHShVH ("Yod-Hay-Shin-Vav-Hay"), beginning the first letter in the name at the center of the spiral and ending the last letter of the name when your index finger points directly overhead. Try to feel the explosive expansion of the light driving all lingering shadows out of the water and out of the magic circle.

With your right hand still raised overhead, speak these words, or their equivalents:

> **By the authority of the name of power Yehovashah, I infuse this circle with holy light.**

Draw an inverse spiral upon the air over the bowl, beginning from a point high overhead, contracting the spiral in ever-narrowing circles clockwise until you reach the center, with your index finger held close to the surface of the water directly over the center of the bowl. As you draw this invoking spiral, vibrate powerfully the letters in the divine name IHVShH ("Yod-Hay-Vav-Shin-Hay"), beginning with the first letter of the name when your right index finger points high overhead and ending at the last letter when your finger points into the center of the bowl of water. Feel the light drawn down from the infinite heights and concentrated into the water. Visualize the water scintillating with brilliance akin to the radiance that streams from a sparkling diamond.

There are two ways of projecting magical symbols such as the spiral onto ritual objects. They can be drawn in the air over the object horizontally, on a plane that is parallel to the perceived flat plane of the surface of the earth (of course the earth is not a plane, but in magic it is treated as though it is flat, just as the sun is treated as a planet that travels around the earth). The second way to project a symbol upon an object is to draw it vertically in the air over the object. This is sometimes more convenient when the ritual instrument or substance is resting upon the surface of the altar, and is the usual way of projecting symbols, but it is up to the ritualist to choose the technique that seems the most natural.

When you are certain that the water can hold no more light, inscribe over it in an upright position a cross of equal arms in a circle with your right index finger, drawing first the vertical bar from top to bottom, then the horizontal bar from left to right, then the circle clockwise beginning at the top. Speak the words:

> **With this cross I seal the light within this cleansing water. May its power endure forever, in the name of God IHVH** ("Yod-Hay-Vav-Hay").

Once the water is cleansed, charged, and sealed, it may be poured into a clean storage vessel, capped, and set aside until it is needed. Provided it remains in a cool, dark place and is not touched or used by anyone else, it will retain its occult charge of light for a long time.

After you have poured the charged water into its storage vessel and capped it, face west and raise your hands overhead. Speak the closing of the ritual in these, or similar, words:

> I (your name) **give thanks to the Supreme Light for the fulfillment of this ritual of cleansing and charging.**

Leave the eastern quarter and walk around the altar clockwise until your stand in the north facing south across the altar. Speak the words:

> **I hereby return this magic circle to the center of my being.**

Pivot clockwise on your own body axis to face north, away from the altar. Extend your left index finger at heart level while holding your right palm flat over your breast. Visualize the astral circle of fire that still floats upon the air around you flowing into the tip of your extended left index finger and returning to your heart center as you walk once around the table *counter-clockwise.*

Stand once again facing the original direction from which you began the ritual (in this case, south). Clap your hands sharply together four times to indicate fulfillment, and say:

This holy ritual of cleansing and charging is well and truly fulfilled. So let it be.

There are many other ways to magically purify water and charge it with light. All are equally effective, provided you remember that there are two stages involved—the purification, when the water is banished of all discordant or chaotic influences by the authority of a name of power, which embodies certain fundamental occult potencies, and the charging, when the water is filled with occult light under the authority of the same, or another, name of power.

Baptizing the Rings

Immediately after each ring is engraved, it must be baptized in the name of the Wing of the Winds who will reside within it, by the authority of the Banner that rules over the angel. This ritual purifies the ring and gives it the unique identity it will carry throughout the remainder of its existence. If possible, the ritual of baptism should take place in the daylight for the gold rings and at night for the silver rings, but this is not absolutely essential so long as it follows immediately after the ring is engraved. It is best to baptize each ring individually so that no confusion of powers arises. You will therefore be doing two rituals of baptism on the day a pair of rings is inscribed.

In the center of the table that serves as your altar, light a candle to act as the altar flame. On the west side (the quarter of elemental water) put a small glass dish filled with consecrated water. Set the newly engraved ring on the side of the altar that faces the quarter of the Banner on the ring. Banners that begin with the letter I (fire) are put on the south side of the table; those that begin with the first H (water) are placed in the west just in front of the dish of consecrated water; those that begin with V (air) are set on the north side; and those that begin with the second H (earth) go on the east side of the altar.

If you are unable to move completely around your ritual altar due to limited space, you should place it in the south, if possible. The ring is still put on the side of the altar that faces the elemental quarter of the ring's Banner.

Begin by standing in the north facing south across the top of the altar. Perform the ritual of the cleansing prayer and the kabbalistic cross, as described above. But instead of pointing away from yourself into infinity when you speak the word "Amen" at the end of the cross, point at the flame of the candle.

Pivot clockwise to face the north. Walking once around the altar clockwise with your left hand on your heart center and your right index finger extended across your body, project the magic circle of astral fire about the ritual place. If you cannot walk around the altar, project the circle by turning upon your own axis clockwise. Be careful always to link up the end of the circle with its beginning when you return to the north. As you project the circle, speak these words:

> **I extend this circle of protection from the center of my being. Let no discordant influence enter herein nor abide within its boundary. In the fourfold name of God, IHVH** (vibrated "Yod-Hay-Vav-Hay"). **Amen.**

Facing south across the altar, take up the bowl of sacred water from the altar top and walk one quarter around the altar in a clockwise direction to stand facing east with your back to the altar. You should strive to inwardly see the flaming ring of the magic circle floating in the air at your heart level in front of you. Dip the fingers of your right hand three times into the water and shake the water from your fingertips outside the magic circle toward the east. Speak the words:

> **With this consecrated water of light, I banish the region of the east.**

Continue clockwise around the circle to the south and perform the same actions, saying:

> **With this consecrated water of light, I banish the region of the south.**

Do the same banishing formula in the west and the north, then replace the water on the western side of the altar.

Stand in the north facing south with your feet together and your arms spread wide so that your body forms a great cross. Invoke the guardian angels of the four quarters, who are aspects of the four beasts surrounding the throne of God. They may be visualized as four flaming pillars of different colors: Michael in the south is red, Raphael in the north is yellow, Gabriel in the west is blue, and Uriel in the east is green. Speak the words of the invocation:

> **Before me Michael, Guardian of Fire, the Lion of the south; behind me Raphael, Guardian of Air, the Angel of**

the north; on my right hand Gabriel, Guardian of Water, the Eagle of the west; on my left hand Uriel, Guardian of Earth, the Bull of the east. The four surround me (elevate your hands, palms up), **fire above** (lower your hands, palms down), **water below,** (put your palms together in a gesture of prayer over your heart center), **I am the heart of the four, I am the center of my universe. Amen.**

This concludes the preliminary operations, which are designed to cleanse and center the magician, establish and cleanse the magic circle, and invoke the four guardians of the quarters. What follows is the actual ritual of baptism.

Move from your place on the north side of the altar in a clockwise direction until you come to the quarter related to the Banner on the ring you are about to baptize. Movement is always clockwise around the circle unless it is intended to banish. If the ring happens to be on the north side of the altar, stay where you are. Face the altar.

With your arms spread and elevated, the palms upward, and your face raised to heaven, speak the following opening prayer and declaration of purpose in these, or similar, words:

Hear me, O Lord my God! Who art the First and Last, the Beginning and the End, the Alpha and the Omega. O Nameless and formless One, the Creator of All, Lord of Light, Lord of Life, Lord of Love, heed this prayer of thy true son (or daughter), _____.

Shed down thy light upon me! Shower down thy light unto the dark corners of the Earth. For I believe in thee and bear thy witness. I shall walk with thee into fire. Holy art thou, Lord of the Universe. The One in All, the All in One.

I, (your name), **conduct this holy ritual of baptism to invoke the Wing of the Winds** (name of angel), **into this ring of gold** (or silver), **by the authority of the elder king** (state the Banner). **So let it be.**

Walk three times clockwise around the altar, or if there is not enough room for this, rotate your body three times clockwise about your own axis as you stand before the altar. Visualize a swirling vortex of light descending into the circle, with its focus upon the candle flame. Visualize the entire space within the magic circle pervaded by the color related to the guardian of the quarter who presides over the ring you intend to baptize. For example, if you are baptizing the golden ring of HIVH, the circle would be filled with green light, because HIVH is a Banner of earth, and the color of earth is green. After completing the triple circumambulation, speak the words:

Mighty angel of the east, Uriel (or of the west, or south, etc.), **descend into this circle of power. I invoke and summon thee to witness, by the authority of the fourfold name of God, IHVH** ("Yod-Hay-Vav-Hay"), **who is thy Lord and King. I invoke and summon thee into my flesh. I invoke and summon thee into my heart. I invoke and summon thee into my mind. I am become thee, mighty Uriel** (or Michael, etc.), **ruler of the east and lord of the earth. Look with favor upon this ritual of baptism through mine eyes and ensure its fulfillment. Amen.**

Feel yourself pervaded by the elemental nature of the guardian angel you have invoked into your being. Uriel will be strong and deliberate. Michael will be forceful and hot. Gabriel will be loving and mild. Raphael will be quick and perceptive.

Take up the ring from the altar and hold it high above the flame of the candle in both hands with the Banner upon its bezel facing upward. Speak the words:

Angels and spirits of God, bear thee witness. I hereby cleanse, consecrate, and baptize this ring of power, whose name is (speak the name of the angel inscribed within the hoop of the ring), **in the service of the Light. In the name of the Ancient One** (vibrate the four letters of the Banner on the ring), **who sits crowned in gold and robed in white raiment before the throne of God, I command the angel** (speak the name of the angel on the ring) **to enter and abide within this ring, to be obedient to the authority of** (vibrate the Banner on the ring), **and to serve me faithfully and truly forever more, for I am the true messenger of the King. Amen.**

Lower the ring so that the flame of the candle momentarily rises through its hoop, then use the ring to describe upright in the air over the altar the sigil of the Banner on the ring. If it is an overt Banner, you will make the invoking form of its sigil; if it is an occult Banner, you will make the "banishing" form to invoke it. As you form each stroke of the sigil, vibrate the corresponding letter in the Banner of the Name. Raise the ring high over the altar once again and speak these words to the ring:

In the name of the Ancient One (vibrate the Banner on the ring), **I name thee** (speak the name of the angel on the ring). **So let it be!**

Submerge the ring completely in the dish of consecrated water. Visualize a stream of vital energy rushing down from the infinite heights above the altar to infuse itself with the metal of the ring. Strongly will the angel to be present within the ring. After a few moments, remove the ring from the water and pat it dry on a clean cloth. Kiss the bezel of the ring reverently and raise the ring on high over the altar in both hands. Speak the words:

> **All witness** (name of the angel), **lord of this ring, by the authority of the Ancient One** (name of the Banner), **who sits at the head** (or foot, in the case of silver rings) **of the throne of God. So let it be!**

Wrap the ring carefully in a new piece of blue silk, white linen, or, if you can get nothing better, a sheet of clean, unused white paper, and set it back on the altar in its elemental quarter.

Walk three times around the altar, this time in a counterclockwise direction. As you do so, visualize the colored elemental light of the guardian that pervades the circle rising upward and flowing from the circle. Feel it leave your own body. Speak the words:

> **Mighty angel of the east, Uriel** (or of the west, or the north, etc.), **ascend from this circle of power. I bid thee, return to thy station in the east** (or north, or south, etc.), **by the authority of the fourfold Name of God, IHVH** ("Yod-Hay-Vav-Hay"), **who is thy Lord and King. I banish and send thee from my mind. I banish and send thee from my heart. I banish and send thee from my flesh. Farewell, mighty Uriel** (or Michael, etc.), **ruler of the east and lord of the earth. I give thee thanks for thy aid in the fulfillment of this ritual of baptism. Depart, and fare thee well.**

Walk around the altar clockwise until you are standing in the north and face south across the altar. If you happen to already be in the north, remain where you are. Spread your arms wide with your feet together so that your body forms a great cross. Extend and spread your fingers so that their tips form upright pentagrams. Speak the words:

> **I give thanks for the successful fulfillment of this ritual of baptism. Great guardians of the quarters, I license thee to depart from the boundary of this magic circle. Fare thee well. All spirits attracted to the region of this circle, I command thee, depart! In the fivefold names of power, Yeheshuah and Yehovashah, I banish thee from this place. Go in peace, and fare thee well.**

Pivot clockwise to face the north, extend your left index finger with your right hand on your heart, and walk around the altar once counterclockwise.

As you do so, visualize the flaming circle being drawn into your extended fingertip, flowing down your left arm, across your body, down your right arm, and into your heart. If you do not have room in your ritual chamber to walk all around the altar, do the same thing while rotating on your own axis counterclockwise. As you reabsorb the circle, speak these words:

> **I hereby indraw this flaming circle of protection and return it to my center of being.**

Returning to the north, pivot clockwise to stand once more facing south across the altar. Clap your hands together four times sharply. Speak the words:

> **This ritual of baptism for the angel** (speak the name of the angel on the ring) **is well and truly fulfilled. So let it be!**

Charging the Rings

The two rituals of baptism for each mated pair of rings will be conducted on the day the rings are inscribed. For the remainder of a complete cycle of the moon, the rings are charged each day upon the altar in a minor ritual which also serves to build a bond between the magician and each ring. The ritual of charging the gold ring takes place during the early morning shortly after waking, and the ritual of charging the silver ring takes place in the evening shortly before going to sleep.

Light the candle upon the center of the altar, and set the ring upon the altar in its elemental quarter. As you remove it from its covering of silk or linen, kiss the bezel of the ring with reverence. Remember, it is the dwelling place for an exalted angel and must always be treated with respect.

Standing in the north facing south, perform the prayer of cleansing and kabbalistic cross, and project the magic circle from your center of being. Once again standing in the north, spread wide your arms into a great cross and invoke the Guardians of the four quarters, as described above. Proceed around the circle clockwise until you stand in the elemental quarter of the ring facing the altar. Raise your hands to heaven and declare your purpose:

> **I** (your name), **conduct this ritual of charging for the purpose of infusing the ring** (speak the name of the angel on the ring) **with holy Light. Look with favor upon this ritual, O Lord, and bring about its rightful fulfillment. Amen.**

Walk three times completely around the altar clockwise to create an occult vortex, which should be visualized as an inverted cone of light swirling down with its focus at the candle flame on the altar, and filling the entire magic circle with radiance. If you do not have room to walk around the altar, pivot three times clockwise to create this vortex. When charging silver rings, the light should be visualized as moonlight; when charging gold rings, visualize the light as sunlight. When you complete this triple circum-ambulation, stand once again in the elemental quarter of the ring facing the altar, raise your hands to heaven and speak the works:

> **By the authority of the fivefold name of the Messiah, IHShVH** (or IHVShH, in the case of the gold rings), **I invoke and fill this magic circle with the cooling** (or warming) **rays of the Moon** (or Sun). **I invoke this lunar** (or solar) **radiance into my flesh; I invoke this lunar radiance into my heart; I invoke this lunar radiance into my mind. I am filled with holy light, in thy name IHShVH** (or IHVShH). **So let it be.**

Will the light to enter into your body through your pores and inhale the light with your breaths, until your entire body is charged with lunar (or solar) radiance. With your left index finger in the case of a silver ring inscribed with an angel of severity, make a counterclockwise inward spiral in the air over the altar, so that its focus terminates directly above the silver ring. Start the spiral with your left arm held straight overhead above the altar. As you form this spiral, vibrate powerfully the Hebrew letters of the fivefold name IHShVH ("Yod-Hay-Shin-Vav-Hay"). As you complete the spiral, touch the ring and will the lunar light that fills you to flow into the ring, saying:

> **In the name of the Ancient One** (vibrate the Banner on the ring) **I infuse this ring of power** (name the angel of severity) **with the cooling radiance of the Moon. So let it be!**

Use the same procedure to charge gold rings with solar light, but in the case of a gold ring, the spiral is made with the right index finger, and is a clockwise inward spiral. Begin the clockwise inward spiral with the right hand high overhead, and terminate it at its focus by touching the bezel of the gold ring. As you make the clockwise inward spiral, vibrate the fivefold name IHVShH ("Yod-Hay-Vav-Shin-He").

Regard the ring upon the altar for several minutes as you continue to will lunar, or solar, light into it. When you feel that it has absorbed as much light as is possible during that ritual, seal the light into the ring with the symbol of the circle-cross, inscribed vertically upon the air with the right index finger in the case of gold rings, but with the left index finger in the case of silver rings.

Sit comfortably before the altar and regard the ring. Visualize its hoop expanding into a large circular window of light, and through the window see the angel of the ring standing before you arrayed in light, looking back at you. Try to picture the angel in as much detail as possible (see Chapter XIV).

Eventually the angels will become animate and you will be able to communicate with them. Contemplate the lord of the ring for half an hour or so, then will the circle of light to diminish and return into the ring.

Stand up and walk three times around the altar counterclockwise to erase the occult vortex, and visualize the light that fills the circle dimming as the vortex slowly vanishes. Speak the words:

> **By the authority of the fivefold name of the Messiah, IHShVH** (or, in the case of gold rings, IHVShH), **I release the holy radiance of the Moon from this circle and return it to its former state. I release the light from my mind; I release the light from my heart; I release the light from my body; I return this light to the heavenly sphere of the Moon** (or Sun) **in thy name, IHShVH** (or IHVShH). **So let it be!**

Walk around the altar clockwise until you reach the north. Face south and make the great cross with your body. Release the four Guardians of the quarters and banish the region of the magic circle by the authority of IHShVH and IHVShH, using the formula given earlier in this chapter. Reabsorb the magic circle through your left index finger into your heart center, and conclude the ritual of charging with appropriate words that give thanks to IHShVH (in the case of silver rings) or IHVShH (in the case of gold rings). Kiss the ring and wrap it carefully in its silk, or linen, covering.

These four rituals are progressive in their degree of complexity. When taken together, they provide the basics of ritual magic. The cleansing prayer, Kabbalistic Cross, erection of the astral circle and invocation of the four Guardian angels of the quarters can be used as a preliminary structure for almost all rituals, whatever their stated purpose.

It should be clearly understood that these rituals are suggested forms that may be modified to suit the beliefs or needs of the ritualist. Provided that a ritual contains the words of power and the dramatic structure to fulfill its stated purpose, its details may be varied greatly without weakening its effect. Do not fall into the trap of becoming fixated upon the minutiae of ritual, but rather focus upon the purpose for which the ritual was created, and consider what dramatic and symbolic elements are needed to fulfill it.

XIV

˒ ˒

FORM AND FUNCTION
OF THE WINGS

The Wings of the Winds are the active forces through which the Banners of Tetragrammaton express themselves. They do not have fixed material bodies, or even permanent spiritual shapes. That is why in the Bible they can be described as the "wings" of the four beasts who surround the throne of the heavenly Christ. Elsewhere angels are described as "wheels" or "flames" or "thrones"—titles expressing their active natures, not their shapes (although their shapes may reflect these natures).

Angels derive the forms that humans perceive them to wear from the limitations and unconscious expectations of the human mind. We expect to see an intelligent spirit with whom we can converse wearing a human shape, since nothing in our natural world but a human being can think and speak. This expectation is reinforced in the Bible by the assertion that Adam was fashioned in the image of God (Gen. 1:26). Naturally, we expect the holy angels to also approximate God's image. We expect the fallen angels, or demons, to diverge from this perfect form, and therefore they are often perceived in distorted or monstrous shapes that express their chaotic natures.

In magic, it is often convenient to consciously endow spirits with the form and dimension of human beings. This renders them easier to communicate with and allows them to relate to human needs and feelings, even as it permits humans to feel greater affinity with the motivations of the spirits.

119

This is the reason the Greek gods almost always appear in statues of human shape, and often of human size as well.

Since the Wings of the Winds may be related through the Banners to the signs of the zodiac, it is possible to give them distinguishing human characteristics that aid in understanding their natures.

Twofold Division

The first distinction to be made lies between the twelve occult angels under the moon, who may be regarded as female, and the twelve overt angels under the sun, who may be looked upon as male. Paired angels under a single Banner are related and are like brother and sister twins. The brother is the right Wing, and the sister is the left Wing. This polarity is expressed in the Banner sigils by the invoking and banishing forms in each pair of sigils, which are mirror opposites.

The female Wings are under the influence of the supernal *sephirah Binah,* Understanding, which stands at the head of the left pillar of severity on the tree of the kabbalah. *Binah* is the seat of *Aima,* the great Dark Mother who is the fruitful womb of the universe. It is the role of the Wings on the left side to bring forth into being ideas and possibilities. The female angels are responsible for the fashioning, limiting, and destroying of things; for all analytical and critical judgement; for punishment, pain, and matters relating to the health of the body; for dreams, nightmares, and fantasies; for doubts, fears, self-analysis, and conscious thoughts; for fashions, styles, and other social trends outwardly expressed; indeed, for all manifest, structured forms and cycles.

The male Wings are under the influence of the supernal *sephirah Chokmah,* Wisdom, which stands at the head of the right pillar of mercy on the tree of the kabbalah. *Chokmah* is the seat of *Abba,* the great Father of Light who is the viral impregnating seed of spirit that comes to fruition in the womb of *Aima.* It is the role of the Wings on the right side to implant the seminal sparks that form the vital nuclei of all manifest things, sustaining and animating them in the universe. The male angels are responsible for sudden inspirations, insights, and creative ideas; acts of will; expansive impulses; higher consciousness; acts of inclusion and wholeness; visionary schemes and noble sacrifices; acts of genius; transcendence; indeed, for all the hidden, vital energies that give rise to and sustain manifest forms.

It may be objected that the female Wings have all the undesirable features and the male Wings all the desirable ones. There is some truth in this argument, but the polarity of good and bad is unavoidable. The Wings on the left side do not represent living women, where negative and positive are almost equally mixed with only a small excess of the left side. They are pure negativity, and represent the function of darkness to limit, constrict, divide, and thereby define manifest forms out of the pure, undivided light. This necessary limiting and dividing function has been closely linked in our culture with evil. However, without this "evil," the world as we know it could not exist.

When the Wings are represented in human forms with human motivations, inevitably their purity is compromised. It is necessary to add aspects of the light to the darkness of the Wings on the left and aspects of the dark to the brightness of the Wings on the right, merely to render them plausible as beings of human appearance with human desires. This need to compromise their essential natures when depicting the Wings as manifest beings should be borne in mind when working with them.

Threefold Division

The Wings of the Winds can be divided into three groups based upon whether they exhibit cardinal, mutable, or fixed qualities. Those related to the cardinal signs of the zodiac will be energetic, enterprising, and forceful; those related to the mutable signs will be changeable, adaptable, and impressionable; those related to the fixed signs will be intense, steadfast, and persistent. In the Banner sigils, this threefold division is expressed by the three shapes of the sigils—those enclosing the whole are cardinal, those dividing the whole into halves are mutable, and those dividing the whole into quarters are fixed.

Fourfold Division

Finally, the Wings can be divided into four groups based upon their elemental associations.

The angels of fire will be intense, explosive, expansive, willful, quick to anger, of strong feelings, combative, and difficult to control. In appearance, they will have curling red or reddish-blond hair, gray eyes, freckled or flushed complexions, and mobile and energetic bodies that are slender and muscular, with high, expressive voices.

The angels of water will be emotional, sensitive, intuitive, sensual, loving, clinging, and sympathetic. In appearance, they will have soft, sensuous bodies, straight black or dark-brown hair, large blue or black eyes, and a pale, moist complexion. They will have a cooling touch; a musical, expressive voice of middle tone; and laughter that rises and falls.

The angels of air will be detached, clever, eloquent, easily amused, persuasive, imaginative, resourceful, argumentative, and very quick in movement and understanding. In appearance, they will have tall, slender, athletic forms, amber or golden eyes, blond or light-brown hair that is wavy and loose, and tanned or creamy complexions. They will speak rapidly in tones of persuasion, irony, and scorn, and their laughter will be light and pitiless.

The angels of earth will be serious, practical, deliberate, thorough in their work, determined, deep of feeling, and unpretentious. They will take orders literally, be skillful and clever in the making of things, remember both insults and complements, and easily involve themselves with human affairs. In appearance, they will be muscular or heavy in body, with auburn or black hair, green or dark-brown eyes, and swarthy or black skin. They will speak deliberately in deep voices, and their laughter will be rich and full.

In the Banner sigils, this fourfold division is distinguished by the letter of Tetragrammaton from which the invoking sigil of each Banner begins. Sigils that invoke from I represent the Wings of Fire; sigils that invoke from the first H represent the Wings of Water; sigils that invoke from V represent the Wings of Air; and sigils that invoke from the second H represent the Wings of Earth.

By combining the polarity, quality, and element of each Wing with its astrological sign and house, it is possible to build up a complete picture of its appearance, personality, and function. This is very useful in rituals where the angels must be visualized. On the following pages, I have used *The New Magus** occult correspondences for the four quarters. In *The New Magus* system, the zodiac is applied to the magic circle by mentally laying the zodiac face down upon the floor of the ritual chamber and aligning it so that the fixed signs are in the four compass points: Leo-south, Scorpio-west, Aquarius-north, and Taurus-east.

The Sigils

The invoking and banishing sigils for each Wing are derived from the tetragram described in Chapter Five. Refer to the diagram on page 33, which shows the invoking and banishing sigils for the twelve Wings of Mercy of the twelve overt Banners of the Name. Remember that the Wings of Severity of the occult Banners are the mirror opposites of the Wings of Mercy of the overt Banners. Therefore, the invoking sigils of the Wings of Mercy are the banishing sigils of the Wings of Severity; the banishing sigils of the Wings of Mercy are the invoking sigils of the Wings of Severity. You can readily see this by comparing the sigils for pairs of Wings. For example, compare the sigils for Kethahel (opposite page) and his mirror twin Hatakiah (page 124), and you will observe that the invoking sigil for one Wing banishes the opposite Wing, and vice versa.

**New Millennium Magic*, an updated and expanded version of *The New Magus*, will be available in May 1996 from Llewellyn Worldwide, Ltd.

I

Angel: Kethahel (QThH+AL) Pronounced: *Keth´*-a-hel

Hebrew: קתהאל

Enochian: ⊂ገᛘᚷᛘ/ᚱ⍵

Banner: IHVH

Polarity: Sun

Type: Mercy

Side: Right

Sex: Male

Element: Fire

Quality: Cardinal

Sign: Aries

House: First

Direction: East-northeast

Stone: Sard (orange-red)

Tribe: Reuben

Apostle: Peter

Enochian God Name: MOR

Enochian Senior: Laidrom

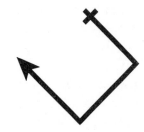

Invoking

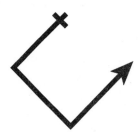

Banishing

Appearance: Short, slender, muscular. Triangular face. Flushed complexion; flared nostrils; curling, flame-red hair; very pale gray eyes that are bloodshot or burning; small projecting ears.

Nature: Explosive, hot-tempered, in constant motion, impatient, eager, enthusiastic, vigorous, and easily angered, with stormy emotions, rapid speech, darting eyes, expressive hands, and harsh laughter.

Function: Urgent matters relating to the ego, self-worth, and personal dignity. Affairs of honor. Duels or other forms of personal combat. Self-assertion.

II

Angel: Hatakiah (HThQ+IH) Pronounced: Ha-*tak´*-i-ah

Hebrew: התקיה

Enochian: ᘓᘀⱶᘌᘀ⁊ᘂᙏ

Banner: IHVH

Polarity: Moon

Type: Severity

Side: Left

Sex: Female

Element: Fire

Quality: Cardinal

Sign: Aries

House: First

Direction: North-northeast

Stone: Sard (orange-red)

Tribe: Reuben

Apostle: Peter

Enochian God Name: MOR

Enochian Senior: Aczinor

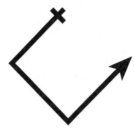

Invoking

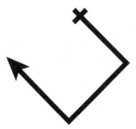

Banishing

Appearance: Short but muscular woman with narrow hips and small breasts, a pointed chin, very pale gray eyes, flushed cheeks, thin lips, small teeth, upturned nose, flame-red hair cut short, small ears.

Nature: Cynical, mocking, overbearing, hasty, quick to respond with anger, sensitive to slights, arrogant, harsh. Contemptuous of weakness in others. Speaks her mind. Violent outbursts of rage. Vengeful.

Function: To combat character assassinations, confront intimidation, destroy the will of foes, bring about violent retribution for personal attacks.

III

Angel: Kazahel (QTzH+AL) Pronounced: *Kaz´*-a-hel

Hebrew: קצהאל

Enochian: ⳽⳻⳿⳽⳻⳩

Banner: IHHV

Polarity: Sun

Type: Mercy

Side: Right

Sex: Male

Element: Fire

Quality: Mutable

Sign: Sagittarius

House: Ninth

Direction: West-northwest

Stone: Topaz (yellow-green)

Tribe: Simeon

Apostle: Philip

Enochian God Name: DIAL

Enochian Senior: Lzinopo

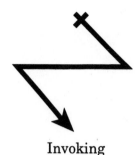

Invoking

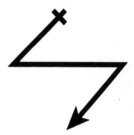

Banishing

Appearance: Tall, with broad shoulders and a narrow waist. Pale gray eyes, a long face, straight nose, small mouth, long neck, large graceful hands. A light complexion touched with highlights of golden pink. Golden-orange hair that falls to his shoulders in loose curls.

Nature: Benevolent, restless, cheerful, freedom-loving, idealistic, adventure-seeking, reverent, ardent, sincere. His voice is pleasant, but he has a tendency to moralize.

Function: Matters that expand personal horizons, travel, distant communications, dealings with distant relatives, escape from all forms of prison or bondage. New vistas of thought or experience.

IV

Angel: Hazekiah (HTzQ+IH) Pronounced: Ha-*zek´*-i-ah

Hebrew: הצקיה

Enochian: ᒧᚎᚎᚁᚋᛈᛈᛔᚋ

Banner: IHHV

Polarity: Moon

Type: Severity

Side: Left

Sex: Female

Element: Fire

Quality: Mutable

Sign: Sagittarius

House: Ninth

Direction: West-northwest

Stone: Topaz (yellow-green)

Tribe: Simeon

Apostle: Philip

Enochian God Name: DIAL

Enochian Senior: Alhctga

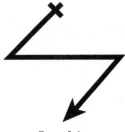

Invoking

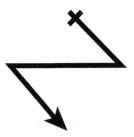

Banishing

Appearance: She is tall and slender, with clear gray eyes, high cheekbones, a high forehead, a long face and straight nose, a golden-pink complexion, and very fine orange-blond hair that falls over her shoulders. Her gaze is intense and searching. Her movements are graceful but energetic.

Nature: Critical, moralizing, tactless, careless about the feelings of others, always wishing to be on the move, arrogant and boastful. Honest, but she tends to exaggerate.

Function: To expose lies, to strike to the heart of issues, to reveal deception and pretense in all intellectual matters, to bring down false prophets, stop mail and communications fraud, to punish falsehoods in media and advertising.

V

Angel: Keliel (QLI+AL) Pronounced: *Kel´-i-el*

Hebrew: קליאל

Enochian: ⊂⁊Ⴑ⊂⁊ℬ

Banner: IVHH

Polarity: Sun

Type: Mercy

Side: Right

Sex: Male

Element: Fire

Quality: Fixed

Sign: Leo

House: Fifth

Direction: South

Stone: Emerald (green)

Tribe: Levi

Apostle: James the Lesser

Enochian God Name: HCTGA

Enochian Senior: Liiansa

Invoking

Banishing

Appearance: Well-proportioned, powerful figure above middle height, with a large head, large yellow-gray eyes, thick rusty-blond hair, a broad forehead, wide mouth with full lips, golden complexion, a very erect posture, and a proud manner.

Nature: He speaks commandingly in a resonant voice and is warm-hearted, enthusiastic, forgiving, generous, outspoken, dignified, and proud. He is impatient with details but is willing to take on the most far-reaching challenges. Enjoys luxury and pleasure. Large-hearted.

Function: Challenges and risks in sports, games, gambling, business speculations, and creative enterprises. Impressive displays of personal talents or skills to win love or money. Leadership. Projection of a winning self-image.

VI

Angel: Yelekiah (ILQ+IH) Pronounced: Ye-*lek´*-i-ah

Hebrew: ילקיה

Enochian: ᴍ?ᴜʒꓶᴄꓶᴌ

Banner: IVH**H**

Polarity: Moon

Type: Severity

Side: Left

Sex: Female

Element: Fire

Quality: Fixed

Sign: Leo

House: Fifth

Direction: South

Stone: Emerald (green)

Tribe: Levi

Apostle: James the Lesser

Enochian God Name: HCTGA

Enochian Senior: Ahmlicv

Invoking

Banishing

Appearance: Tall, with broad shoulders; full hips; and prominent, well-separated breasts; a proud face with large amber-orange eyes; very pale eyebrows; a strong nose; a wide mouth with full but colorless lips; golden complexion; and long, tawny orange hair.

Nature: Sensual, pleasure-loving, and self-indulgent. Her pride tends to make her appear pompous and snobbish. She has fixed opinions that she expresses forcefully and is intolerant of the views of others. Strong possessive affections. She likes to command those she loves for their own good. She speaks in a mellow voice with a tone of authority, and has a deep, ringing laugh.

Function: To dominate in matters of the heart. To attain a realistic self-analysis of personal faults and virtues. For critical judgment in the creative arts and drama. To oversee the happiness of loved ones and protect them from harm.

VII

Angel: Daviel (DVI+AL) Pronounced: *Dav´-i-el*

Hebrew: דויאל

Enochian: ᴄⴄ⅃⅃Ɐ⅃ⵉ

Banner: HV**H**I

Polarity: Sun

Type: Mercy

Side: Right

Sex: Male

Element: Water

Quality: Cardinal

Sign: Cancer

House: Fourth

Direction: South-southeast

Stone: Garnet (red)

Tribe: Judah

Apostle: Andrew

Enochian God Name: OIP

Enochian Senior: Aaetpio

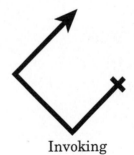

Invoking

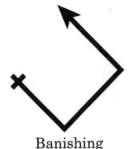

Banishing

Appearance: Slightly built and active, with a domed forehead and prominent narrow chin; small eyes of a deep blue color; pale-white complexion; short, dark-brown hair; large pores; feminine mannerisms.

Nature: A facade of self-assurance conceals a sensitive and imaginative nature. Resourceful, tenacious, loyal, artistic, sympathetic. Good memory. Loves beautiful things. Speaks in a brusque, matter-of-fact way to cover up his uncertainty. Very sensitive to mockery.

Function: The protection and nurturing of the family and the home environment. Care of children. Helps the conception of a child in the womb. Acquiring objects for collections. Care and protection of private property.

VIII

Angel: Yodiah (IVD+IH) Pronounced: Yo-*di*´-ah

Hebrew: יודיה

Enochian: ᴦᴀᴌᴘᴌᴌ

Banner: **H**VHI

Polarity: Moon

Type: Severity

Side: Left

Sex: Female

Element: Water

Quality: Cardinal

Sign: Cancer

House: Fourth

Direction: South-southeast

Stone: Garnet (red)

Tribe: Judah

Apostle: Andrew

Enochian God Name: OIP

Enochian Senior: Adoeoet

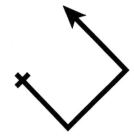

Invoking

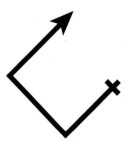

Banishing

Appearance: Full breasts and wide hips, with a roundness to the belly. A very pale, wide face with a prominent chin and high, domed forehead. Black hair and dark blue, watery eyes. A short neck. Small hands and feet. A slight curve in the back.

Nature: Impressionable, receptive, emotional, easily aroused with desire, easily flattered, at times moody and introspective. She has an excellent memory and is able to perceive psychic currents and occult activity. Broods about imagined slights done to her by others. Her laughter rises and falls in an uncontrolled manner.

Function: Control of dreams, scrying and other psychic activities. Finding lost possessions. Aid in making women fertile. Controlling biorhythms. Perceiving ghosts or other spirits.

IX

Angel: Demuel (DMV+AL) Pronounced: *Dem´*-u-el

Hebrew: דמואל

Enochian: ᴄⱵ◮ᴇⱵᴣ

Banner: HVIH

Polarity: Sun

Type: Mercy

Side: Right

Sex: Male

Element: Water

Quality: Mutable

Sign: Pisces

House: Twelfth

Direction: North-northeast

Stone: Sapphire (blue)

Tribe: Issachar

Apostle: Bartholomew

Enochian God Name: TEAA

Enochian Senior: Alndvod

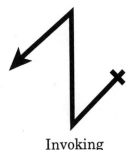

Invoking

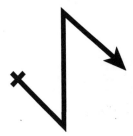

Banishing

Appearance: Soft, overweight figure of below average height; wavy, dark-brown hair on a round skull; pale complexion with a tendency to perspire; small nose and small ears that lie flat; very dark blue eyes; heavy eyelids and dark, arched eyebrows; a sensual mouth with a full bottom lip and a weak chin.

Nature: Intuitive and aware of subtle emotional currents, psychic, creative in the lyrical arts such as poetry and music, highly impressionable, easily expresses feelings, very sympathetic to others. This angel is happiest near the seashore. Smiles but rarely laughs.

Function: Songwriting, music, the dramatic arts, matters of faith or belief. Achieving empathy with others. Protection of seamen or those who travel by sea. Attaining purity. Caring for the sick. Protecting and caring for animals. Encouraging pleasant dreams.

X

Angel: Vamediah (VMD+IH) Pronounced: Va-*med'*-i-ah

Hebrew: ומדיה

Enochian: ᴂᴅᴦᴚᴤᴪᴂᴦ

Banner: **H**V**IH**

Polarity: Moon

Type: Severity

Side: Left

Sex: Female

Element: Water

Quality: Mutable

Sign: Pisces

House: Twelfth

Direction: North-northeast

Stone: Sapphire (blue)

Tribe: Issachar

Apostle: Bartholomew

Enochian Name of God: TEAA

Enochian Senior: Aapdoce

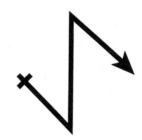

Invoking

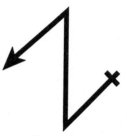

Banishing

Appearance: Thin limbs; a long, thin neck; small head with short, straight hair, very glossy and of a dark-brown color. Small nose and ears; dark blue eyes surrounded by blue shadows under the skin; poor posture; very thin hands held limp at the wrists; a small, pale mouth and weak chin. Small breasts, narrow hips.

Nature: Unsure and vacillating, hesitant, touchy about criticism, confused, extravagant, emotional. Tends to be secretive and likes to place burdens upon other shoulders. Outwardly submissive but inwardly resentful. She cares jealously for those she loves and tends to smother them with attention.

Function: Protecting a loved one, particularly from self-destructive behavior. Watching over animals. Creating works of art of a fantastic or dreamlike type. She aids in the expression of psychic communications such as automatic writing. Enforces service and self-sacrifice upon those who would flee from their responsibilities.

XI

Angel: Dabael (DAB+AL) Pronounced: *Dab´-a-el*

Hebrew: דאבאל

Enochian: ᘓᔑᐯᘔᘔ

Banner: HHIV

Polarity: Sun

Type: Mercy

Side: Right

Sex: Male

Element: Water

Quality: Fixed

Sign: Scorpio

House: Eighth

Direction: West

Stone: Jasper (green)

Tribe: Zebulun

Apostle: Thaddeus

Enochian God Name: PDOCE

Enochian Senior: Arinnap

Invoking

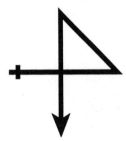

Banishing

Appearance: Economical body, lean and muscular, with a narrow waist, his movements are quick and precise. Black hair cut short over a round skull; penetrating dark eyes of a blue-black color; a compressed, bloodless mouth; small dimpled chin; small hooked nose; round white ears that lie close to the skull; a very pale face with bluish shadows.

Nature: Passionate, jealous, intense, secretive, subtle, purposeful, and intuitive, with powerful sexual urges. Can be brooding and dark at times. Gifted with mystical vision. He seldom speaks and almost never laughs. His powerful emotions sometimes express themselves in focused violence or deliberate cruelty.

Function: To excite strong sexual passion, to overcome moral scruples, to overcome impotence or frigidity. To uncover secret things such as hidden papers or valuables in matters dealing with wills, legacies, or bequests or in practical matters requiring great concentration and precision.

XII

Angel: Badiah (BAD+IH) Pronounced: Ba-*di´*-ah

Hebrew: באדיה

Enochian: ᴍ⅄ᒋᴉⅈ⅄∇

Banner: **HHIV**

Polarity: Moon

Type: Severity

Side: Left

Sex: Female

Element: Water

Quality: Fixed

Sign: Scorpio

House: Eighth

Direction: West

Stone: Jasper (green)

Tribe: Zebulun

Apostle: Thaddeus

Enochian God Name: PDOCE

Enochian Senior: Anodoin

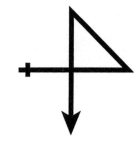

Invoking

Banishing

Appearance: Compact but well-developed body with a very narrow waist. Long, straight dark hair hangs over her white shoulders. Intense black eyes beneath a domed forehead, small nose with flared nostrils, sensual but small mouth which she often wets with the tip of her tongue. Small, white ears. Good posture and quick, economical movements.

Nature: Intense, secretive, penetrating, driven by sexual desires, often of a perverted kind. Broods over slights of others and responds with vindictive cruelty. Suspicious, untrusting, manipulative, clings jealously to her lover and will kill him rather than let him escape.

Function: To arouse aberrant desires. Aids in vindictive acts. To hold a lover against the lover's will. Black magic, dealings with evil spirits, poisons, curses. Perverse dreams and fantasies. Acts requiring great self-control and brutality.

XIII

Angel: Vahael (VAH+AL) Pronounced: Va-*ha´*-el

Hebrew: ואהאל

Enochian: ᴄ⅂ꓫꟽ⅄ꓯ

Banner: VHIH

Polarity: Sun

Type: Mercy

Side: Right

Sex: Male

Element: Air

Quality: Cardinal

Sign: Libra

House: Seventh

Direction: West-southwest

Stone: Jacinth (red-orange)

Tribe: Dan

Apostle: James the Greater

Enochian God Name: MPH

Enochian Senior: Lsrahpm

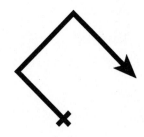

Invoking

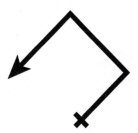

Banishing

Appearance: Slender and weak, but graceful in motion. Wavy chestnut hair, well-proportioned features, large golden-green eyes, prominent straight nose, full mouth with a touch of red in the lips, rounded chin. His complexion is lightly tanned. Charming smile that reveals perfect teeth.

Nature: Easy-going and engaging personality, diplomatic, kind, able to see both sides, refined artistic judgement, optimistic, cheerful, idealistic, anxious to bring harmony and peace. Very romantic.

Function: Matters requiring diplomacy, concord, agreement. Aids in finding the perfect lover. Where artistic judgment is required. To reconcile marital disputes.

XIV

Angel: Haviah (HAV+IH) Pronounced: Ha-*vi´*-ah

Hebrew: האויה

Enochian: ᘈᘈᘔᘓᘔᘓ

Banner: VHIH

Polarity: Moon

Type: Severity

Side: Left

Sex: Female

Element: Air

Quality: Cardinal

Sign: Libra

House: Seventh

Direction: West-southwest

Stone: Jacinth (red-orange)

Tribe: Dan

Apostle: James the Greater

Enochian God Name: MPH

Enochian Senior: Saiinou

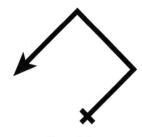

Invoking

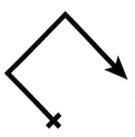

Banishing

Appearance: Tall and slender, with a long neck, wide shoulders, and round breasts; flowing, light-brown hair; pale-green eyes; a long, straight nose; and a full, sensuous mouth with an engaging smile. Her manner is open and mild.

Nature: Intelligent but indecisive, changeable, superficial. Lacks focus. Very soft-hearted, excessively romantic, forgetful. Shallow and a bit of a flirt. She is easily amused but rapidly loses interest and soon wearies of long or difficult tasks.

Function: Disharmony, imbalance, or dissatisfaction; dislocating individuals from their social setting. Civil disruption, personal disputes, and complaints against organizations or groups can all be incited by this angel.

XV

Angel: Vihael (VIH+AL) Pronounced: Vi-*ha´*-el

Hebrew: ויהאל

Enochian: ⊂⅂ℵⴔ⅂Ⴋ

Banner: VHHI

Polarity: Sun

Type: Mercy

Side: Right

Sex: Male

Element: Air

Quality: Mutable

Sign: Gemini

House: Third

Direction: East-southeast

Stone: Agate (clouded)

Tribe: Naphtali

Apostle: Thomas

Enochian God Name: ARSL

Enochian Senior: Laoaxrp

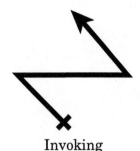

Invoking

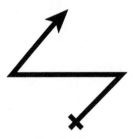

Banishing

Appearance: Thin frame with a large chest; very mobile hands with long fingers; a flexible face; wide mouth capable of many expressions; large nose; large, prominent ears; high cheekbones; golden eyes; long chin; tanned complexion; light-brown, curling hair.

Nature: Animated, expressive, restless, talkative, always seeking something to do or somewhere to go, witty with a good sense of humor, always seeing the lighter side in every situation, clever with his hands, adaptable, versatile. Detests hard work. Bright, cheerful laughter. His voice is agreeable, but he tends to chatter about nothing.

Function: Diplomacy, arbitration, brokering deals, managing artistic talent or property, arranging travel, teaching, publishing, legal arguments, creative writing, news reporting, publicity, media events.

XVI

Angel: Hiviah (HIV+IH) Pronounced: Hi-*vi´*-ah

Hebrew: היויה

Enochian: ᛗᚻᛚᚪᛚᛗ

Banner: VH**H**I

Polarity: Moon

Type: Severity

Side: Left

Sex: Female

Element: Air

Quality: Mutable

Sign: Gemini

House: Third

Direction: East-southeast

Stone: Agate (clouded)

Tribe: Naphtali

Apostle: Thomas

Enochian God Name: ARSL

Enochian Senior: Slgaiol

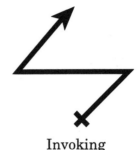

Invoking

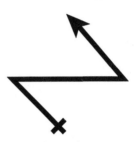

Banishing

Appearance: Slight, slender, but very active, with short, curling brown hair on a small skull; prominent pink ears; alert and intelligent golden eyes under arched brows; a long, upturned nose set in a triangular face with a tapered chin; a wide, smiling mouth. Her face is constantly in motion, expressing her feelings, and her hands dance about when she speaks.

Nature: Full of nervous energy, changes opinions abruptly, clever in a cunning way, observant and perceptive about the thoughts and feelings of others, superficial, lazy, flirtatious and fickle in her affections, emotionally detached, lies easily—not out of malice, but to avoid trouble.

Function: Exposes betrayal of trust, false friendships, adulteries, deceit, intrigue in the work place, scandals, gossip, slanders, libels. Testing friendships and love relationships. She is the angel of lies.

XVII

Angel: Vivael (VIV+AL) Pronounced: *Viv´*-a-el

Hebrew: ויואל

Enochian: ⊂ꓶꓛꓵꓛꓵ

Banner: VIH**H**

Polarity: Sun

Type: Mercy

Side: Right

Sex: Male

Element: Air

Quality: Fixed

Sign: Aquarius

House: Eleventh

Direction: North

Stone: Amethyst (purple)

Tribe: Gad

Apostle: Simon

Enochian God Name: GAIOL

Enochian Senior: Ligdisa

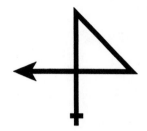

Invoking

Banishing

Appearance: A perfectly proportioned and athletic body; loosely curling, dark-blond hair that falls over his ears and the top of his high forehead; wide-set amber eyes; a classical nose and strong square chin; well-formed but colorless lips. His expression is serene and detached.

Nature: Intense, focused, steadfast in his beliefs, intellectual, communicative, idealistic and unorthodox in his thinking, artistic, willing to champion a cause, spontaneous, emotionally cool. More apt to laugh at a joke because he understands it than because it is funny.

Function: Matters relating to leadership in politics, science, religion, the arts, or social movements. Self-sacrifice for the greater good. Belief in a cause. To achieve leadership, or to forward the goals of a group or movement. Where the ends are thought to justify the means, and the greater good is presumed to outweigh the happiness of the individual.

XVIII

Angel: Viviah (VIV+IH) Pronounced: Vi-*vi´*-ah

Hebrew: ויויה

Enochian: ᛗᚼᛚᚨᛚᚨ

Banner: VIHH

Polarity: Moon

Type: Severity

Side: Left

Sex: Female

Element: Air

Quality: Fixed

Sign: Aquarius

House: Eleventh

Direction: North

Stone: Amethyst (purple)

Tribe: Gad

Apostle: Simon

Enochian God Name: GAIOL

Enochian Senior: Soniznt

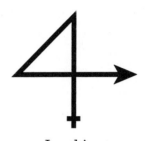

Invoking

Banishing

Appearance: Tall, with flowing, brown hair that falls over her shoulders; full breasts, long legs, and wide hips; an oval face with perfectly proportioned features, light olive complexion, amber eyes, large ears, a graceful neck and erect posture; beautiful hands.

Nature: Emotionless, excessively intellectual, incapable of deep affection, committed with fanatical zeal to ideals and causes, willing to sacrifice everything for a higher purpose, inclined to perverse sexual amusements, tactless, unpredictable.

Function: To advance social disobedience, terrorism, demonstrations, fanatical causes, extreme political movements of both the left and right, desperate acts of self-sacrifice, hunger strikes, suicide pacts, media campaigns.

XIX

Angel: Shabuel (ShBV+AL) Pronounced: Sha-*bu´*-el

Hebrew: שבואל

Enochian: ⊏⅂ᗿⴸᚼ᛿⅂ᒣ

Banner: **HIHV**

Polarity: Sun

Type: Mercy

Side: Right

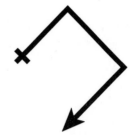

Invoking

Sex: Male

Element: Earth

Quality: Cardinal

Sign: Capricorn

House: Tenth

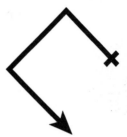

Direction: North-northwest

Banishing

Stone: Chrysolite (yellow-green)

Tribe: Asher

Apostle: John

Enochian God Name: ORO

Enochian Senior: Habioro

Appearance: Bony frame of average height; knotted muscles; angular, large head; prominent ears; large forehead over small, dark-brown eyes; crooked nose; small mouth; bad teeth; weak, bearded chin; sallow complexion with moles or pockmarks. An intense but evasive glance.

Nature: Serious, determined, enduring, calculating, emotions held under tight control, rational, exacting, very ambitious, highly disciplined, responsible. His serious and rational approach to things makes him seem dull and pedantic. A subdued voice, harsh when raised in anger.

Function: Matters of personal ambition regarding business or professional career, government job, rank, professional standing or awards, credentials, degrees, titles. Climbing the corporate ladder, overcoming obstacles to ambitions, gaining responsibility and trust of superiors.

XX

Angel: Vabashiah (VBSh+IH) Pronounced: Va-*bash´*-i-ah

Hebrew: ובשיה

Enochian: ᛘᚷᛝᛚᛗᛁᚷᚥᚷᚻ

Banner: HIHV

Polarity: Moon

Type: Severity

Side: Left

Sex: Female

Element: Earth

Quality: Cardinal

Sign: Capricorn

House: Tenth

Direction: North-northwest

Stone: Chrysolite (yellow-green)

Tribe: Asher

Apostle: John

Enochian God Name: ORO

Enochian Senior: Aaozaif

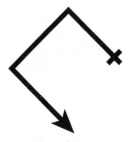

Invoking

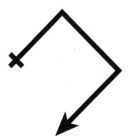

Banishing

Appearance: Angular body of average height, thin but muscular. Very narrow hips and small breasts. A large head that tapers to a narrow chin. Dark-brown eyes; dark skin; short, coarse, straight brown hair; thin, colorless lips; small teeth of poor quality. She tends to glower and frown.

Nature: Repressed, narrow-minded, exacting, unforgiving of faults in herself or others, severe in judgment, hidebound, punctilious, selfish, pessimistic, worrying, analytical, critical, unsympathetic. She tends to scold others for their faults and mistakes.

Function: Finds faults or leaks in systems. Reveals mistakes or shortcomings in personality, particularly where these affect professional status. Makes known the weaknesses of competitors or rivals. Warns of business failure or stock collapse. Turns the weaknesses of others against them. Punishes disloyalty or betrayal.

XXI

Angel: Shahavel (ShHV+AL) Pronounced: Sha-*hav´*-el

Hebrew: שהואל

Enochian: ᒪᔑᕱ⅂ᘉᗋᗝ

Banner: **HIVH**

Polarity: Sun

Type: Mercy

Side: Right

Sex: Male

Element: Earth

Quality: Mutable

Sign: Virgo

House: Sixth

Direction: South-southwest

Stone: Onyx (whitish-pink)

Tribe: Joseph

Apostle: Matthew

Enochian God Name: IBAH

Enochian Senior: Htmorda

Invoking

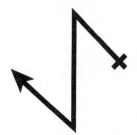

Banishing

Appearance: Tall, well-formed but soft limbs; auburn hair; large, dark-green eyes; graceful movements; long neck and broad shoulders; light-brown skin; agreeable smile; oval face; large, white teeth.

Nature: Methodical, precise, discriminating, takes the best and rejects the rest, seeks perfection, refined manners, conventional attitude, modest, passive, self-repressed, practical and adaptable mind.

Function: Matters of health, exercise, diet, hygiene, integration of personality, getting back to basics, habits, self-discipline, holistic healing, conservation, recycling, public service.

XXII

Angel: Vaheshiah (VHSh+IH) Pronounced: Va-*hesh´*-i-ah

Hebrew: והשיה

Enochian: ᴔᴪᴸᴍᵀᵀᴍᴪᴀ

Banner: HIV**H**

Polarity: Moon

Type: Severity

Side: Left

Sex: Female

Element: Earth

Quality: Mutable

Sign: Virgo

House: Sixth

Direction: South-southwest

Stone: Onyx (whitish pink)

Tribe: Joseph

Apostle: Matthew

Enochian God Name: IBAH

Enochian Senior: Ahaozpi

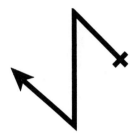

Invoking

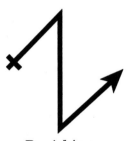

Banishing

Appearance: Statuesque; full figure; long, auburn hair; large, green eyes under thick, brown eyebrows; high cheekbones; a strong, straight nose; a full mouth; strong chin; long neck; olive complexion; large, graceful hands; a very self-possessed and aloof expression.

Nature: Intelligent, retentive memory, able to assimilate and analyze information, hypercritical, fastidious, pedantic, attracted by elaborate sexual games, hypochondriac, suppressed emotions, reserved. Her laughter is deep and musical but unfeeling.

Function: Matters of psychosomatic illness, sexual disfunction or aberration, obsessive behavior, stress, destructive criticism, attacks of conscience, doubt, worrying, duty, obligations.

XXIII

Angel: Shiael (ShIA+AL) Pronounced: Shi-*a´*-el

Hebrew: שיאאל

Enochian: ᒍᐊᒐᒪᒎ

Banner: **HHVI**

Polarity: Male

Type: Mercy

Side: Right

Sex: Male

Element: Earth

Quality: Fixed

Sign: Taurus

House: Second

Direction: East

Stone: Beryl (blue-green)

Tribe: Benjamin

Apostle: Matthias

Enochian God Name: AOZPI

Enochian Senior: Hipotga

Invoking

Banishing

Appearance: Tall; deep chest; massive neck and shoulders; jutting forehead; square jaw; straight, black hair and dark-brown eyes; wide mouth with heavy lips; small nose; small ears; dark skin; stubborn expression but easily amused.

Nature: Great strength and physical endurance, patience, slow to anger but capable of fierce rage, productive, possessive, affectionate and sensual, protects his own, lacks creativity, unoriginal thinker, deep voice and loud laughter.

Function: The accumulation of money, valuables, possessions; collections of art or material things; acquiring a desired object; construction; restoration work on houses, cars, furniture; farming or gardening; mining; locating lost possessions or valuables; building the bulk or strength of the body.

XXIV

Angel: Aishiah (AISh+IH) Pronounced: Ai-*shi´*-ah

Hebrew: אישיה

Enochian: ᒍᘛ∟ᘓ⌐ᒍ∟ᘛ

Banner: HHVI

Polarity: Moon

Type: Severity

Side: Left

Sex: Female

Element: Earth

Quality: Fixed

Sign: Taurus

House: Second

Direction: East

Stone: Beryl (blue-green)

Tribe: Benjamin

Apostle: Matthias

Enochian God Name: AOZPI

Enochian Senior: Avtotar

Invoking

Banishing

Appearance: Tall; broad shoulders; thick neck; large breasts and wide hips; thick waist; massive thighs; long, black hair; dark-brown, wide-set eyes under thick, black brows; broad forehead; small nose; small ears; square chin; wide mouth; full lips and large, white teeth. Tends to glower and frown if opposed.

Nature: Earthy sense of humor, loves food and comfort, stubborn, self-centered, grasping, greedy, a bit of a bore, conventional thinker, stodgy, resentful if contradicted, jealously covets material things, will not share, a slave of habit and routine. Deep voice and vulgar laughter.

Function: To guard and protect valuables, possessions, material things, art collections; to prevent or punish the infidelity of a lover or the betrayal of trust by a friend or partner; to punish thieves or bring about their capture; to deprive another of physical strength.

XV

˒ ˒

ASSUMING THE CHRIST-FORM

One of the most important techniques of Golden Dawn magic is the ritual assumption of god-forms. Through visualization, words of power, and symbolic actions and associations, the magician invokes a god, angel, or other higher spirit, not only into the magic circle, but actually into his or her own body and mind. In effect, the form, personality, and (it is hoped) the powers of the god are put on like a suit of clothing. Through this voluntary possession, the ritualist is able to experience the universe from the perspective of the god assumed. More important from a practical standpoint, the ritualist is able to speak and act with the authority of the assumed god.

Although this ritual technique is of supreme importance, there is surprisingly little analysis of it in the Golden Dawn documents, as they are presented by Israel Regardie in his *Golden Dawn*. Since Mathers and the other members of his inner circle must have been fully aware of the value of this technique, I can only assume that they regarded it as too powerful to explicitly set forth in detail in the general writings that circulated among the lower ranks of the Golden Dawn. Certainly Aleister Crowley recognized full well its central role in Western occultism and made extensive use of it in his own magical experiments.

The rationale for the assumption of the god-form is very simple. To change ourselves in a fundamental way, it is necessary that we become

147

someone else. To change for the better, we must become one who is better. To become wiser, we must take on the identity and persona of a spirit of wisdom such as the Egyptian god Thoth. To become more beautiful, we must assume the form and persona of a god of beauty such as Apollo or Aphrodite. To become more courageous and warlike, we must take on the nature of a war god such as Mars or the northern god Tew.

When properly done, the assumed god or spirit actually displaces the thoughts, feelings, and even the physical appearance of the ritualist. While wearing the god-form, the ritualist retains only a detached self-awareness. His or her emotional responses, cogitations, sensations, impulses and motivations are all those of the god or goddess assumed. Ideally, when the ritualist looks into a mirror during the invocation, he or she sees, not his or her own features, but the face of the god.

By repeatedly assuming a god-form, the soul of the ritualist is tuned to resonate harmonically with that god. This process works by the same fundamental magical principle expressed by Avicenna that I quoted earlier: "when a thing standeth long in salt, it is salt." By repeatedly experiencing the thoughts, emotions, attitudes, impulses, beliefs, sensations, and urges of a god *as our own*, we can gradually evoke these same thoughts and feelings within ourselves even when not ritually assuming the form of that god. This makes available to us the occult virtues of the god whenever we have need for them.

The long-term function of assuming a god-form is to change ourselves into stronger, wiser, and better human beings. This is done by repeatedly assuming the same god-form daily over a period of months, or even years. However, the technique has a more immediate application in magic. By assuming the form of a god during a ritual, we magically become that god and are then able to use the authority of that god to command lesser spirits.

It would be impossible to overstate the importance of this magical concept. In our mundane, everyday human personae, we have little or no occult authority. When we command a spirit in the name of Joe Smith, the spirit will laugh at us, if it pays any attention at all. But if we command it in the name of Michael, the angel of the fiery sword who cast Lucifer down into the bottomless pit, the spirit will obey.

Some magicians make the mistake of assuming that it is necessary only to voice the name of some powerful spiritual being in order to use the authority of that being. This was the error of the Jewish exorcists who went around driving spirits from the possessed in the names of Jesus and the apostle Paul, until one day the demon in a man they were exorcising looked at them through the eyes of the possessed and said: "Jesus I know, and Paul I know; but who are ye?" (Acts 19:15). We can only imagine the expression on the faces of the exorcists as they stared at one another, an instant before the demon tore their clothes off and beat them to within an inch of their lives, but it surely ranks as one of the most amusing scenes of the Bible.

These exorcists made the mistake of trying to use the name of Jesus without having assumed the god-form of Jesus. This is a lesson to later magicians. To effectively use the name of a god, we must at the same time take on the identity of that god by assuming its god-form. If we fail to do this, the name of the god will lack authority. It will remain merely a word. The spirits we seek to command will laugh at us for our audacity and credulity, and will either ignore us if they are higher spirits, or toy with us for their own amusement if they are low spirits. That is why so many contacts in magic are with vulgar spirits—the higher spirits are not compelled to attend by the authority of a name of power, and they have enough decency not to come to the circle merely to annoy and confuse us.

When using the Wings of the Winds, we must command them by the authority of a higher spiritual power. Since these are extremely potent angels who surround the throne of God itself, our choices are limited.

We might command them by the twenty-four elders, or Ancient Ones, who sit in a circle around the throne. These are twenty-four old men with flowing white hair and white beards, clothed in white robes and wearing crowns of gold upon their heads. The names of these Ancient Ones are the twelve overt and twelve occult Banners of Tetragrammaton. In fact, they represent twenty-four countenances or aspects of the heavenly Christ, or "anointed one" (Messiah) who sits upon the throne. They should be visualized as all having the same face, but each wearing a different expression.

Alternately, we might seek to command the Wings by the authority of the seven lamps of fire that burn before the throne. These are the angels of the seven planets, usually given in magical texts as Michael (sun), Gabriel (moon), Samael (Mars), Raphael (Mercury), Sachiel (Jupiter), Anael (Venus), and Cassiel (Saturn). Each planet and its angel is said to astrologically rule a sign, or pair of signs. The Wings of a particular zodiac sign would fall under the ruling angel of that sign.

Still a third approach would be to command the Wings by the authority of the archangels of the four beasts, ruling each Wing by the name of the beast to which it belongs. The angels associated with the four beasts are Michael (lion), Gabriel (eagle), Raphael (man), and Uriel (bull). For example, the angel of severity Vabashiah, who is the forward wing on the left side of the back of the bull, would be ruled by assuming the god-form of Uriel.

There is an easier way that eliminates the necessity of assuming a variety of god-forms, each of which rules a specific Wing, or set of Wings. It is to assume the god-form of the Messiah, who rules all the Wings, and all the lesser angels as well. When we successfully take on the identity of the heavenly Christ, we are able to command even the highest angel, Metatron, who is the united active power of enthroned God, just as the Wings are the individual active powers of God when he is differentiated into the twenty-four seated Ancient Ones.

It might be observed in passing that, in magic, a seated figure signifies archetypal creative potential but not active manifesting energy. Kings command from their thrones, but they have knights or "messengers" (angels) to actually carry their orders out in the world. This is why the Messiah, who commands all beings around his throne, is seated, and why the seated twenty-four elders may be assumed to have authority over the active Wings. This is also why Solomon, who commanded the jinn, is usually represented in Arabian folklore as seated upon his glorious throne, which is an earthly version of the heavenly throne of God.

Those who feel uncomfortable about assuming the Christ-form should realize that it is much more than a matter of pretending to be Jesus. Earthly Jesus, the living prophet, and heavenly Christ, the Anointed One, or Messiah, are really two separate beings. The Messiah figure is the more ancient and more powerful of the two. He appears in the Old Testament under various guises—in the prophecies of Jeremiah, Ezekiel, and Isaiah, in the figure of Moses after his face is made to shine, and as the heavenly Adam who is created before the earthly Adam (see Gen. 1:27 and 2:7). Early Christians identified their prophet Jesus with this Messiah myth. When we assume the Christ-form, we must put on the identity of this heavenly being, who is the seated authority of Metatron, the supreme active power.

Fortunately, we have an excellent description of the heavenly Christ:

> And in the midst of the seven candlesticks one like unto the Son of man, clothed with a garment down to the foot, and girt about the paps with a golden girdle.
>
> His head and his hairs were white like wool, as white as snow; and his eyes were as a flame of fire;
>
> And his feet like unto fine brass as if they burned in a furnace; and his voice as the sound of many waters.
>
> And he had in his right hand seven stars; and out of his mouth went a sharp two-edged sword; and his countenance was as the sun shining in his strength. (Rev. 1:13–6)

This is a description of heavenly Christ the king, or prince, who commands from his throne. Although the standing figure of Christ is located upon the middle pillar of the kabbalistic tree in *Tiphareth,* his seated form may be likened to *Chesed* and the right side of the tree of the *sephiroth.* There is also a parallel description of heavenly Christ, the mounted knight, another version of Metatron, who is the active power and may be likened to *Geburah* and the left side of the tree. It is interesting to compare the two descriptions:

And I saw heaven opened, and behold a white horse; and he that sat upon him was called Faithful and True, and in righteousness he doth judge and make war.

His eyes were as a flame of fire, and on his head were many crowns; and he had a name written, that no man knew, but he himself.

And he was clothed with a vesture dipped in blood: and his name is called The Word of God.

And the armies which were in heaven followed him upon white horses, clothed in fine linen, white and clean.

And out of his mouth goeth a sharp sword, that with it he should smite the nations: and he shall rule them with a rod of iron: and he treadeth the winepress of the fierceness and wrath of Almighty God.

And he hath on his vesture and on his thigh a name written, KING OF KINGS, AND LORD OF LORDS. (Rev. 19:11–6)

It may be assumed that the seated Christ is similar in appearance, if not identical, to the seated twenty-four elders about the throne, who are merely his various permutations, or aspects. He is thus a man with snow-white hair, probably a snowy beard as well, flaming or blazing eyes, and a body that shines radiantly with a golden light, like heated brass. He wears a crown of gold and a long, shining white robe that reaches down to his bare feet. This is held closed by a sash or girdle of golden cloth wrapped around his breast. When he speaks, his great voice roars like a waterfall. He carries in his right hand, signifying rule, the seven planets. From his mouth, which signifies his spoken commands, goes out a two-edged sword—two-edged to cut both ways, either to protect or punish.

The severe aspect of the Messiah has essentially the same physical appearance as the merciful aspect. He is seated upon a horse to signify his manifest power over the world. The many crowns he wears are the Banners of the Name. It is said that "he has a name written that no man knew but himself" to indicate that the Ineffable Name, IHVH, because it encompasses everything in the whole of creation, cannot truly be comprehended except by the Creator of everything. Here, his white garment is dyed in blood to indicate that the Christ upon the horse is the Christ of judgment and punishment, in contrast to the seated Christ, the Christ of inspiration and mercy.

Notice that at the end of the description of the mounted Christ, his name is given in a twofold manner, "King of Kings, and Lord of Lords." It would be reasonable to associate the first title, King of Kings, with the seated Christ of *Chesed,* and the second title, Lord of Lords, with the mounted Christ of *Geburah.* Both titles combined represent standing Christ in *Tiphareth.*

Women may prefer to visualize Christ in a female body to make the assumption of the Christ-form easier. She will appear with white hair, flaming ruby eyes, clothed in white with a golden sash around the middle of her body, her feet bare. Upon her head is a golden crown. This inversion of gender is not really necessary, however, and is in some respects undesirable. The Messiah, who is the Light incarnated upon the Earth in human form, is neither wholly male nor wholly female, but contains both sexes within him/her self, even as God is neither male nor female, but both.

That is why the stories of Jesus portray him with so many feminine characteristics, and why in medieval images he is sometimes shown with wide hips and prominent breasts. Throughout religious history, Messiah figures (incarnations of God in human form) have been given hermaphroditic qualities. They belong to the middle pillar of the tree of the *sephiroth*. The seated Christ is the tendency of this middle pillar emanation toward the right side; the mounted Christ is the opposite tendency toward the left side.

In order to completely unite with the god-form of heavenly Christ, it is necessary to take onto ourselves his magical name. His true magical name is beyond human comprehension, but we can use a symbolic name to represent this true name. For the Christian kabbalists of the Renaissance, the secret name of Christ was IHShVH, or its variant form IHVShH. For ritual purposes, we will assume the god-form of the Messiah under the name IHVShH when commanding the Wings of mercy on the right side and the name IHShVH when commanding the Wings of severity on the left side. We do this because IHVShH initiates a clockwise rotation around the points of the pentagram, whereas IHShVH initiates a counterclockwise rotation around the points of the pentagram. The counterclockwise inward spiral invokes the angels of severity on the left, and the clockwise inward swirl invokes the angels of mercy on the right.

The technique of assuming the god-form was common in the religious rites of the ancient world. All types of divine possession by prophets relied upon the prophet becoming, for a time, the god in whose authority he prophesied. The ultimate goal of all worshippers is to become one with God. Catholic priests seek as much as possible to embody Jesus upon the Earth. Good Moslems strive to pattern themselves upon the prophet Mohammed. Buddhists attempt to become living Buddhas.

The magical key to successfully assuming a god-form is the change of name. The ritualist sets aside his common name and takes on the magical power name of the god as his own. For this to work, it is necessary to completely identify the self with the names involved. If either common or god name remains a mere label, it will lack efficacy. Usually it is easy for us to identify with our own names, which we have used to represent and embody out identities from infancy. It is more difficult to accept on an intuitive level that we have become the new name of the god, which we apply to ourselves during ritual.

The author of the book of Revelation, St. John the Divine, seems to have understood the magical significance of names. Addressing the angel of the Christian church in Sardis, he says:

> Thou hast a few names even in Sardis which have not defiled their garments; and they shall walk with me in white: for they are worthy. He that overcometh, the same shall be clothed in white raiment; and I will not blot out his name out of the book of life, but I will confess his name before my Father, and before his angels. (Rev. 3:4–5)

Notice that the people of Sardis are completely identified with their names. St. John does not say there are a few men in Sardis who have not defiled their garments, but "a few names." The garments he refers to are their physical bodies, which become white to indicate their spiritual rebirth and oneness with Christ. Later on he writes:

> Him that overcometh will I make a pillar in the temple of my God, and he shall go no more out: and I will write upon him the name of my God, and the name of the city of my God, which is new Jerusalem, which cometh down out of heaven from my God; and I will write upon him my new name. (Rev. 3:12)

This is a fascinating verse for its magical implications. Those who overcome the weaknesses of their own natures shall not have their names blotted out, but those names shall be supplanted by the name of God. Even more fascinating, from a magical standpoint, is the last part of the verse, where the author says, "I will write upon him my new name." The name of God has become the magical name of St. John, who is possessed with the Holy Spirit, even as it becomes the new name of the worthy "names" of Sardis. By this literary device, the author shows that he has put off his old identity and assumed the god-form of the heavenly Christ by ritually taking onto himself the secret magical name of Christ, which he does not reveal.

The name of heavenly Jerusalem mentioned in the verse refers to the permutations of Tetragrammaton. Jerusalem is another version of the breastplate of Aaron. Jerusalem is said to have twelve gates, which are like the twelve stones of the ephod, each gate inscribed with the name of an angel (signifying a Banner) and a tribe of Israel. The foundation of the holy city is composed of twelve different kinds of stones, which are very similar to the stones of the breastplate, and which are probably intended by the author to be identical to those stones. St. John the Divine makes a further correspondence of the Banners to the twelve apostles (Rev. 21:14), in this way connecting the magic of Jesus to the magic of Moses through the Banners of the Name.

We can use the magical information conveyed in these few verses of Revelation to construct an effective ritual for assuming the Christ-form, which is a vital preliminary step to the effective use of the Banners and the Wings in magical works.

Assuming the Christ-form

You will need an altar table, a candle in a short holder, a small bowl to hold consecrated water, a pen and a square of new paper the size of your palm, and a mortar and pestle or their equivalents (a flat dish and spoon will work). You will also need two similar strips or bands of cloth, one black and the other white, long enough to tie around your forehead with the knot at the back of your head.

Place the altar in the center of the ritual space if possible, so that you can walk all the way around it. If there is insufficient room to put the altar in the center, put it on the south side of your ritual space. The candle is placed in the center of the altar top. The bowl of purified water goes on the west quarter of the altar. The mortar and pestle are placed in the east quarter. The pen and paper is put in the north quarter.

Coil the white band of cloth around your right hand counterclockwise, then pull the coil from your fingers and place it upon the altar in the south so that it forms a clockwise inward spiral (this is a spiral that winds clockwise when traced from the outside to the inside). Coil the black band of cloth around your left hand clockwise, then pull the coil from your fingers and place it upon the altar in the north on top of the piece of paper so that it forms a counterclockwise inward spiral.

For this ritual, it is necessary to wear a loose garment open down the front so that the upper part of your chest is exposed. A white bathrobe is ideal. It is also best if your feet are bare. The best time to do this ritual is shortly after taking a ritual cleansing bath. Purity of body, mind, and emotions are essential for its success.

Fill the bowl with consecrated water and light the candle upon the altar. Stand in a relaxed, erect posture before the altar facing south and empty your mind as you contemplate the flame of the candle. When you feel ready to begin, clap your hands together sharply three times and say:

This ritual of assuming the Christ-form is well and truly commenced.

Raise your arms in a gesture of invocation with the palms up and perform the cleansing prayer and kabbalistic cross. Project the magic circle from your heart center through your right index finger by walking once clockwise around the altar, or pivoting clockwise on your body axis, and invoke the four guardian angels of the quarters. Center yourself within the circle.

All the foregoing steps are preliminaries that may be used to begin many different kinds of rituals. From this point, you begin the actual ritual of assuming the Christ-form.

With your arms raised in a gesture of invocation and your head elevated, so that you look into the infinite distance high above the flame of the candle, declare your intention to the Source of Light:

> **Hear me, O Lord! Thou who art the First and Last, the Beginning and End, the Alpha and Omega. Who art the Nameless and Formless One, Creator of All, Lord of Light, Lord of Life, Lord of Love. Hear this prayer of thy true son (or daughter) _____.**
>
> **I ask that you look with favor upon this ritual assumption of heavenly Christ. Aid me in my becoming. I seek rebirth in thy light. Aid me in my becoming. I seek perfection in thy sight. Aid me in my becoming.**
>
> **Clothe me in white raiment. Crown me with gold. Set me upon the throne of mercy and the white horse of judgement. Into my right hand place the scepter of rule. Into my left hand place the sword of law. Anoint me with thy secret names of power. So let it be.**

Walk three times around the altar, or rotate three times on your axis, clockwise, to open the center of the magic circle and draw into it a vortex of spiritual light. Visualize the light swirling down from over the altar in the form of a brilliant inverted cone with its focus upon the tip of the candle flame. As you perform the circumambulation, speak the words:

> **By this threefold turning, I open this circle and infuse it with holy radiance.**

Return to the northern quarter and face south across the altar top. Kneel before the altar and contemplate the flame of the candle for several minutes in silence. Then take up the black coil of cloth from the northern quarter of the altar in your left hand and allow it to fall straight while holding its end between your left thumb and forefinger. Speak the words:

**Spirits of Light, bear witness. I take upon myself this
black band as a sign of mourning for the death of my
name, _____.**

Tie the black cloth around your forehead securely, knotting it in the back
so that it will not come loose and fall off before you are ready to remove it.
Take the pen from the altar and write your own name upon the piece of
paper, using your regular signature. In the corners of the paper around your
signature, write the Hebrew letters of Tetragrammaton. Write the letters on
the Urim of the breastplate of Aaron (IH) in the upper corners, right to left.
In the lower corners of the paper, write the letters of the Thummim (VH),
also right to left. The result will be: I (upper right), first H (upper left), V
(lower right), second H (lower left).

Hold the paper up close in front of the flame in both hands so that you
can read your name by the light that shines through the paper. Speak the
words:

**Once, I renounce my earthly name, _____,
before the Ancient Ones who surround the throne of
God, and they are: Yod-Hay-Vav-Hay, Hay-Vav-Hay-Yod,
Vav-Hay-Yod-Hay, Hay-Yod-Hay-Vav.**

As you vibrate the four cardinal Banners, visualize their invoking sigils
upon the tetragram. This will help you remember them and make their
vibrations stronger. Visualize the sigils forming over the candle flame in
blazing white light and moving to the band of the magic circle at their
appropriate point of the compass. For example, the sigil of IHVH will move
to the east-northeast.

Tear the paper carefully down the middle so that it forms two equal
parts and place the piece on the right side over the piece on the left. Hold
these as before in front of the candle flame. Speak the words:

**Twice, I renounce my earthly name, _____,
before the Ancient Ones who surround the throne of
God. And their names are: Yod-Hay-Hay-Vav, Hay-Vav-
Yod-Hay, Vav-Hay-Hay-Yod, Hay-Yod-Vav-Hay.**

Visualize the sigils of these mutable Banners as they are formed on the
tetragram appearing in the air over the candle and moving to their appropriate position on the magic circle.

Turn the two pieces of paper clockwise ninety degrees and carefully tear
them down the middle into equal parts, then place the two pieces in your

right hand over the two pieces in your left hand. Continue to hold them between both hands close in front of the candle flame. They must be torn in such a way that one letter of Tetragrammaton is upon each of the four pieces of paper. If you have lettered and torn them correctly, the pieces will read I-H-V-H from the top of the pile to the bottom. Speak the words:

**Thrice, I renounce my earthly name, _____,
before the Ancient Ones who surround the throne of
God. And their names are: Yod-Vav-Hay-Hay, Hay-Hay-
Yod-Vav, Vav-Yod-Hay-Hay, Hay-Hay-Vav-Yod.**

Visualize the sigils of these fixed Banners forming in the air as you vibrate their letters and moving to their places on the magic circle. When you finish, the circle will have twelve sigils arranged around it.

Hold the four pieces of paper in your right hand over the flame of the candle so that they ignite. When the paper is burning strongly, drop it into the mortar, or earthenware dish, on the eastern quarter of the altar. The fire should completely reduce the pieces of paper to ash. If the fire starts to go out before it has consumed the paper, it can be encouraged by lifting the paper under one corner with the tip of the pen, so that fresh air can circulate beneath it. This will ensure that the paper is fully burned. As the paper is burning, speak the words:

**By the holy fire I, _____, am wholly consumed. I
am not. I pass away. I cease to be. My name is ended
upon the Earth.**

Grind up the ashes of the burned paper into a fine powder using the pestle, or its substitute. Wet the tip of your right index finger with your tongue and touch it to the ashes so that some of the ashes stick to your saliva. Draw the vertical bar of a small cross on your breast over your heart center bottom to top. Wet the tip of your left index finger with saliva and dip it into the ashes of your name, then use it to draw the horizontal bar of the cross upon your breast from right to left. It is not necessary that the ashes make a visible cross upon your skin, although this is desirable. As you form the cross, speak the words:

**I mourn the passing of _____ from the face of the
Earth. I mourn the death of _____. I mourn the
ending of _____.**

Touch your right index finger to the corner of your right eye, then your left index finger to the corner of your left eye. Close your hands into fists and cross them on your breast at the wrists; close your eyes and bow your head as you continue to kneel before the altar. Visualize yourself completely surrounded by darkness, lying in a coffin or vault beneath the earth. Visualize the passage of many years and watch inwardly as your body shrivels and is consumed by worms, your skin cracks and falls off your skull, and your very bones are reduced to fine dust. Contemplate nothingness and try to empty yourself of all personal identity, so that an emotional vacuum is created in your soul. You are nothing. No part of you remains, not even a lump of clay in the ground. Even the memory of your name has faded into nothingness.

After a few minutes of silent contemplation, uncross your hands and open your eyes. Still kneeling before the altar, remove the black cloth from your head and put it upon the southern quarter of the altar. Take up the coiled white cloth in your right hand and let it fall straight down while holding its end between the thumb and forefinger of your right hand. Tie it around your head, knotting it in the back so that it will not slip or fall off.

Gaze upon the flame of the candle on the altar and visualize the figure of the heavenly Christ seated upon his great throne within the flame. Open your arms in a gesture of embrace. Speak the words:

> **Holy Messiah, anointed King of Light, descend from the throne of heaven into this sacred circle. Aid me in my becoming! I invoke and summon thee, heavenly Christ. Descend into this blood. Aid me in my becoming! Descend into this flesh. Aid me in my becoming! Descend into these bones. Aid me in my becoming! I am become wholly filled with thy holy Light. I am become a Name, such as is not, but in the mind of the All Powerful. I am become Yod-Hay-Vav-Shin-Hay, enthroned King and ruler of heaven and Earth.**

Visualize the figure of the heavenly Christ stepping down from the dais of his throne and merging with your body to settle into your flesh and bones. Feel your emptiness filled with light.

Pour a small amount of the consecrated water from the bowl on the western quarter of the altar into the mortar on the eastern quarter, so that the ashes are dissolved into a paste. Dip the tip of your right index finger into this paste and use it to draw the figure of a pentagram upon your bare breast beginning with the upper point at the pit of your throat, and proceeding clockwise to your lower right ribs, left nipple, right nipple, lower left ribs, and back to your throat. It is not necessary that the pentagram be visible upon your skin, but you should take care to trace it with a single, unbroken line. Make it large enough so that the cross on the middle of your breast is contained within its center.

Once again, gaze upon the candle flame and visualize within the flame the figure of the heavenly Christ seated upon a white horse with a sword in his right hand and an iron rod in his left. Open your arms in a gesture of embrace. Speak the words:

> **Holy Messiah, anointed fiery Knight, descend from thy high white horse of heaven into this sacred circle. Aid me in my becoming! I invoke and summon thee, heavenly Christ. Descend into this blood. Aid me in my becoming! Descend into this flesh. Aid me in my becoming! Descend into these bones. Aid me in my becoming! I am become wholly filled with thy holy Fire. I am become a Name, such as is not, but in the mind of the All Powerful. I am become Yod-Hay-Shin-Vav-Hay, warrior Knight and ruler of heaven and Earth.**

Visualize the figure of the heavenly Christ dismounting from his white charger and merging with your flesh and bones. Feel your emptiness filled with heavenly fire.

Dip your left index finger into the paste of the ashes of your old name and draw a second pentagram on your breast on top of the first, beginning at your throat, but proceeding counterclockwise to lower left ribs, right nipple, left nipple, lower right ribs, and back to your throat.

Stand up facing the altar. With your feet together, spread wide your arms so that your body forms a great cross. Speak the words:

> **I am risen from the dead. I am clothed in white raiment. I am crowned with a crown of gold. I am Yod-Hay-Shin-Vav-Hay, the left hand of wrath, the Lord of Lords; I am Yod-Hay-Vav-Shin-Hay, the right hand of mercy, the King of Kings. In my right hand, a shining scepter of gold; in my left hand, a fiery sword of silver. I am anointed with light and baptized with fire. All spirits of the four worlds, I call upon you! Bear witness to my rebirth and acknowledge my names. So let it be.**

Visualize the figure of the heavenly Messiah permeating your flesh and bone. Receive this spirit into your mind and heart. Think with his thoughts, feel with his emotions, and as much as possible actually become the Christ-form, not only outwardly in features and shape of body, but inwardly in the depths of your soul.

Now is the time to meditate upon any particular problem or question you may have, which you do not in your own persona, but in the identity of the Messiah. If the ritual is active, instead of meditating as Christ, you will enact your ritual desire in the identity of the heavenly Christ. You will assume the seated form of Christ and use the name of power IHVShH for works involving the right hand—expansion, creation, integration, reconciliation, charity. You will assume the mounted form of Christ and use the name of power IHShVH for works involving the left hand—division, destruction, analysis, criticism, exorcising, learning, cleansing, judgment, punishment.

If the ritual is conducted for a specific magical purpose, you will wish to resume your earthly identity before concluding the ritual. This prevents the profanation of the Christ-form by chaotic thoughts, feelings, and actions outside the sacred circle. This can be done by taking off the headband of white cloth without untying it. The white band contains the identity of heavenly Christ within its circle. Lay it in the northern quarter of the altar. Speak the words:

I voluntarily set aside the identity of heavenly Christ to re-enter this vessel of clay and resume my earthly name, _____.

If the ritual of assuming the Christ-form is conducted for its own sake for the purpose of bringing about lasting change in your fundamental personality, you may wish to continue to wear the white headband after concluding the ritual. However, it should only be retained under conditions of peace and joy that are in harmony with the light.

Walk around the altar three times, or rotate upon your body axis three times, counterclockwise, to restore the light to its rightful place and seal the aperture in the center of the circle. As you do so, visualize the vortex of spiritual light that funnels down over the candle flame of the altar rising into the air and diminishing into nothingness. Speak the words:

By this threefold turning, I release the holy radiance to heaven and seal this circle.

Standing in the northern quarter facing south across the altar, spread your arms and raise your hands heavenward with palms up in a gesture of invocation as you speak the prayer of thanks for the success of the ritual. This takes the form of a brief summary of the purpose for which the ritual was conducted. Speak the words:

Hear me, O God! Thou who art the First and Last, the Beginning and End, the Alpha and Omega. Who art the

Nameless and Formless One, Creator of All, Lord of Light, Lord of Life, Lord of Love. Hear the prayer of your true son (or daughter) _____.

I give thanks for the successful fulfillment of this ritual assumption of the Christ-form. All the purposes of this ritual have been perfectly accomplished. So let it be.

Conclude the ritual by releasing the guardians of the quarters. Banish the region outside the magic circle using the names of power IHVShH and IHShVH, and absorb the circle back into your heart center through your left index finger. Speak the closing words:

This ritual assumption of the Christ-form is well and truly ended. So let it be.

Clap your hands together sharply four times. Put away the materials upon the altar, taking special care with the white headband, the symbol of your spiritual rebirth inside the sacred circle. It should be kissed when it is removed, and wrapped in blue silk or white linen for so long as it remains tied. Once it is untied, the circle is broken and it loses its spiritual associations. In subsequent ritual assumptions of the Christ-form, the pre-tied white and black headbands can be used. However, they should be untied and washed before they become soiled.

XVI

¸ ¸

THE WATCHTOWERS
AND THE KEYS

No examination of the magical symbolism of Tetragrammaton could be complete without a look at the use of the Ineffable Name in the system of Enochian magic derived from the diaries of the Elizabethan magician Dr. John Dee and his seer Edward Kelley. The two men first met in 1582 at Dee's house in Mortlake, just southwest of London. Kelley, who was often involved in alchemical affairs of questionable legality, was using the false name Edward Talbot. The entry in Dee's diary for Saturday, March 10, begins:

> One Mr. Edward Talbot cam to my howse, and he being willing and desirous to see or shew some thing in spirituall practise, wold have had me to have done some thing therein. And I truely excused my self therein, as not in that, vulgarly accounted Magick, neyther studied, or exercised. But confessed my self long tyme to have byn desyrous to have help in my philosophicall studies through the Company and information of the blessed Angels of God. (British Library, Sloane MS. 3188, fol. 9)

Dee was being modest about his abilities. At that time he was engaged in a series of magic experiments to establish communications with angels so

163

that he could gain knowledge of secret matters, particularly political secrets that would be of use to his sovereign, Queen Elizabeth I. He also sought magical secrets that would increase his own personal knowledge and power.

Dee had first become interested in spirits in the spring of 1581, when he was troubled by strange dreams and unexplainable knocking noises in the night. He had tried scrying in a crystal and apparently had achieved some limited success. He records in his diary for May 25, 1581: "Today I had sight offered me in chrystallo, and I saw" (Laycock, *The Complete Enochian Dictionary* [London: Askin Publishers, 1978], page 23). However, his skills must have been weak, because in October of the same year he began to employ one Barnabas Saul as seer. Saul's work was unsatisfactory and Dee dismissed him after only a few months.

Dee was immediately delighted with Kelley's visions. On their very first scrying session, Kelley described the wax tablet known as the Sigillum Emeth, or Aemeth, which is presently in the safekeeping of the British Museum. The two remained together until 1589, when Kelley grew weary of listening to the spirits (and perhaps a bit afraid of them) and struck out on his own to make his living as an alchemist. He died at age forty in 1595 from injuries suffered during a daring attempt to escape from a prison. Right up to the time of Kelley's death, Dee never ceased to hope that the seer would return to his service.

The most important Enochian material was received in 1584, and includes the Great Table of the Four Watchtowers and the Enochian Keys, or Calls. This crucial year is recorded in Meric. Casaubon's published edition of Dee's magical diaries covering the period from May 28, 1583, to May 23, 1587, which is titled *A True & Faithful Relation of what passed for many Yeers Between Dr. John Dee...and Some Spirits* (London, 1659). The first of the Keys was delivered on April 13 and 14 at Cracow, Poland, by the spirit Nalvage (*A True & Faithful Relation*, p. 82). The Great Table of the Four Watchtowers, along with the system for deriving the names of angels from its lettered squares, was given by the spirit Ave during a session that began at seven o'clock on the morning of Monday, June 25, also in Cracow (ibid., p. 166).

Together, the Keys and the Watchtowers form the heart of Enochian magic. It is from the Keys that the Enochian language is largely derived. The Enochian system practiced by the Hermetic Order of the Golden Dawn entirely depends on the Keys and the elemental associations of angelic names extracted from various sections of the Great Table of the Watchtowers. Each Watchtower is a magic square of Enochian letters consisting of thirteen rows and twelve columns. The Watchtowers are bound together into one Great Table by the letters of the so-called Tablet of Union arranged in a cross. The Golden Dawn associated the Watchtowers with the four elements and with the letters of Tetragrammaton. The Enochian magic of the

Golden Dawn is too complex to present here. Those interested should study Regardie's *Golden Dawn,* 6th edition, pp. 624–96 (Llewellyn, 1990).

For decades, it was widely assumed that the founders of the Golden Dawn had created this system based upon a few hints from Dee and Kelley. Regardie writes:

> But this stands out very clearly, that in these diaries [of Dee and Kelley] is a rudimentary scheme which bears only the most distant relation to the extraordinary developed system in use by the Order. Whoever was responsible for the Order scheme of the Angelic Tablets—whether it was Mathers and Westcott or the German Rosicrucian Adepts from whom the former are supposed to have obtained their knowledge—was possessed of an ingenuity and an understanding of Magic such as never was in the possession either of Dee or Kelly. (*Golden Dawn,* p. 625)

In fact, almost the entire Golden Dawn Enochian system is derived from the diaries published by Casaubon, with the exception of the correspondences of the elements, planets, zodiac, and tarot, which were grafted onto the Watchtowers based upon the elemental associations assigned by the Golden Dawn to the points of the pentagram. The association of the letters of Tetragrammaton was considered very important by Regardie, who writes: "This Name is the key to the whole of the Enochian attributions of the squares to the Elements" (*Golden Dawn,* p. 638). In other words, Regardie is saying that it is the placement of the letters of IHVH that determines the elemental associations on the four tablets, not the placement of the elements that determines the letter positions.

Each quarter of the Great Tablet consists of one of the Watchtowers. In the Golden Dawn system, the lower right quarter is the Watchtower of Fire, which stands in the south. It receives the letter *yod*. The upper right quarter is the Watchtower of Water, which stands in the west. It receives the first *he*. The upper left quarter is the Watchtower of Air, which stands in the east. It receives the letter *vau*. The lower left quarter is the Watchtower of Earth, which stands in the north. It receives the second *he*.

Each of these quarters is further subdivided into quarters, and these carry the same relative association of the letters as the great square—for example, *yod* is linked with the lower right quadrant of the Watchtower of the south, just as it is with the entire Watchtower, which forms the lower right quadrant of the great square.

In addition to the attribution of Tetragrammaton to the quarters, and the quarters of the quarters, the letters are further associated with groups of squares upon the individual Watchtowers in a complex arrangement which I will not attempt to give here, since it would be meaningless without a study of the Watchtowers. It is fully described by Regardie. The result is that every square on the four Watchtowers is linked with one of the letters of the Name.

The Watchtowers are joined together on the Great Table by the letters of the Tablet of Union. In English transliteration, this is:

E	X	A	R	P	(Air)
H	C	O	M	A	(Water)
N	A	N	T	A	(Earth)
B	I	T	O	M	(Fire)

Each of these four words, or names, is linked in the Golden Dawn system to one of the Watchtowers and to the element of that Watchtower. It is also tied to the corresponding letter of Tetragrammaton. The entire Tablet of Union is given to the Hebrew letter *shin,* which signifies spiritual fire, or heavenly light. Even as the Sh unites and vitalizes the letters of IHVH in the two forms of Pentagrammaton (IHVShH and IHShVH), so does the Tablet of Union unite and vitalize the four tables of the Watchtowers.

The correspondence of the Watchtowers to the elements on the version of the Great Table adopted by the Golden Dawn parallels the assignment of the elements to the points of the pentagram. As you will recall, on the pentagram, fire goes on the lower right point, water on the upper right, air on the upper left, and earth on the lower left. The placement of the four elements on the points of the pentagram is determined by the arrangement of the four fixed signs of the zodiac, which have elemental associations—Leo (fire), Scorpio (water), Aquarius (air), and Taurus (earth).

The letter *shin* is placed on the upper point of the pentagram. If the pentagram is expanded into three dimensions, it takes the shape of a pyramid with a square base and four equilateral sides. Viewed from the top, this three-dimensional model of the pentagram moves the point of *shin* to the center of the other four points. This is why Sh is related to the Tablet of Union, which unites the four Watchtowers (IHVH).

The Golden Dawn employed the arrangement of the Watchtowers upon the revised version of the Great Table received from the angel Raphael by Kelley on the night of April 20, 1587 (see Casaubon, page 15 of the *Actio Tertia* section at the back of his book). This differs significantly from the original placement of the Watchtowers. Only the Watchtower on the upper left quarter of the Great Table (in the Golden Dawn, the Watchtower of Air) remains in its original quarter in the revised Table. Both original and revised versions of the Table are given by Geoffrey James in his *Enochian Magick of John Dee* (Llewellyn, 1994, pp. 117 and 118).

r	Z	i	l	a	f	A	y	t	l	p	a	e	T	a	O	A	d	u	p	t	D	n	i	m
a	r	d	Z	a	i	d	p	a	L	a	m	a	a	b	c	o	o	r	o	m	e	b	b	
c	z	o	n	s	a	r	o	Y	a	u	b	x	T	o	g	c	o	n	x	m	a	l	G	m
T	o	i	T	t	z	o	P	a	c	o	C	a	n	h	o	d	D	i	a	l	e	a	o	c
S	i	g	a	s	o	m	r	b	z	n	h	r	p	a	t	A	x	i	o	V	s	P	s	N*
f	m	o	n	d	a	T	d	i	a	r	i	p	S	a	a	i	x	a	a	r	V	r	o	i
o	r	o	i	b	A	h	a	o	z	p	i		m	p	h	a	r	s	l	g	a	i	o	l
t	N	a	b	r	V	i	x	g	a	s	d	h	M	a	m	g	l	o	i	n	L	i	r	x
O	i	i	i	t	T	p	a	l	O	a	i		o	l	a	a	D	n	g	a	T	a	p	a
A	b	a	m	o	o	o	a	C	u	c	a	C	p	a	L	c	o	i	d	x	P	a	c	n
N	a	o	c	O	T	t	n	p	r	n	T	o	n	d	a	z	N	z	i	V	a	a	s	a
o	c	a	n	m	a	g	o	t	r	o	i	m	i	i	d	P	o	n	s	d	A	s	p	i
S	h	i	a	l	r	a	p	m	z	o	x	a	x	r	i	n	h	t	a	r	n	d	i	L*
m	o	t	i	b			a	T	n	a	n		n	a	n	T	a			b	i	t	o	m
b	O	a	Z	a	R	o	p	h	a	R	a	a	d	o	n	p	a	T	d	a	n	V	a	a
u	N	n	a	x	o	P	S	o	n	d	n		o	l	o	a	G	e	o	o	b	a	u	a
a	i	g	r	a	n	o	o	m	a	g	g	m	O	P	a	m	n	o	V	G	m	d	n	m
o	r	p	m	n	i	n	g	b	e	a	l	o	a	p	l	s	T	e	d	e	c	a	o	p
r	s	O	n	i	z	i	r	l	e	m	u	C	s	c	m	i	o	o	n	A	m	l	o	x
i	z	i	n	r	C	z	i	a	M	h	l	h	V	a	r	s	G	d	L	b	r	i	a	p
M	O	r	d	i	a	l	h	C	t	G	a		o	i	P	t	e	a	a	p	D	o	c	e
O	C	a	n	c	h	i	a	s	o	m	t	p	p	s	u	a	c	n	r	Z	i	r	Z	a
A	r	b	i	z	m	i	i	l	p	i	z		S	i	o	d	a	o	i	n	r	z	f	m
O	p	a	n	a	L	a	m	S	m	a	P	r	d	a	l	t	T	d	n	a	d	i	r	e
d	O	l	o	P	i	n	i	a	n	b	a	a	d	i	x	o	m	o	n	s	i	o	s	p
r	x	p	a	o	c	s	i	z	i	x	p	x	O	o	D	p	z	i	A	p	a	n	l	i
a	x	t	i	r	V	a	s	t	r	i	m	e	r	g	o	a	n	n	P*	A	C	r	a	r

The Reformed Great Table of Raphael

Note: Letters with asterisks are inverted

Dee himself expressed considerable uncertainty over which Watchtower should go in which quarter of the Great Table. In an explanatory note about the version of Raphael, he writes:

> When E.K. had shewed me this Note, I by and by brought forth my book of *Enoch* his Tables, and found the four letters *r T b d* to be the four first letters of the four principal squares standing about the black Cross: and that here they were to be placed

otherwise than as I had set them. And in the first placing of
them together, I remember that I had doubt how to joyn
them; for they were given apart each by themselves. *(A True
& Faithful Relation,* Actio Tertia, p. 15)

It is obvious in Dee's diary that the Watchtowers are intended to stand
for the four directions of earth, which are distinguished by colors: east (red),
south (white), west (green), and north (black). It is not so clear in Casaubon
which Watchtower goes with which direction, or what elemental associations are intended for the directions. However, in the manuscript record
titled *Liber Scientiae Auxilii et Victoriae Terrestris* (in Sloane 3191), the
upper left Watchtower is assigned to the east, the lower left Watchtower is
assigned to the south (GD gives north), the upper right Watchtower is
assigned to the west, and the lower right Watchtower is assigned to the
north (GD gives south).

Dee's colors for the directions seem to be based upon the solar cycle of
twenty-four hours. The east is red because this is the color of the rosy dawn.
The south is white because this is the brightness of midday. The north is
black because the sun is in this quarter at night. Only green in the west
breaks this pattern. Green like "the skins of many dragons" may refer to
water. Green and red are alchemical opposites, as are black and white.

It is not made clear in Casaubon just how John Dee chose to assign the
elements to the directions. The connection of the Watchtowers to the elements seems to have been secondary to their placement in space. However,
from the colors associated with the four directions in Kelley's vision, given
below, it may be speculated that fire (red) was placed in the east, air (white)
in the south, water (green) in the west, and earth (black) in the north. In
fact, this is the natural order of the elements from lightest to heaviest, but
whether this is intentional or merely coincidental would be difficult to judge
with finality.

It is obvious upon consideration that the arrangement of the Watchtowers upon the amended Table of Raphael cannot be correct. The Great Table
is the pattern of the universe. The Watchtowers stand at the four quarters
of the world. Therefore the Watchtowers of the South and North must be
placed opposite each other on the Table, as must those of the East and West.
In the Table of Raphael, east and west are adjacent, as are north and south.
Either the placement of the Watchtowers on the Table, or the assignment of
the Watchtowers to the four directions of the world must be changed, so that
the Great Table can be laid flat in the middle of the magic circle, with the
Watchtower of the East in the east, the Watchtower of the South in the
south, and so on. This seems so plain as to scarcely need saying, but it was
not done by the Golden Dawn.

r	Z	i	l	a	f	A	u	t	l	p	a	e	b	O	a	Z	a	R	o	p	h	a	R	a
a	r	d	Z	a	i	d	p	a	L	a	m		u	N	n	a	x	o	P	S	o	n	d	n
c	z	o	n	s	a	r	o	Y	a	u	b	x	a	i	g	r	a	n	o	o	m	a	g	g
T	o	i	T	t	x	o	P	a	c	o	C	a	o	r	p	m	n	i	n	g	b	e	a	l
S	i	g	a	s	o	m	r	b	z	n	h	r	r	s	O	n	i	z	i	r	l	e	m	u
f	m	o	n	d	a	T	d	i	a	r	i	p	i	z	i	n	r	C	z	i	a	M	h	l
o	r	o	i	b	A	h	a	o	z	p	i		M	O	r	d	i	a	l	h	C	t	G	a
c	N	a	b	r	V	i	x	g	a	z	d	h	R	O	c	a	n	c	h	i	a	s	o	m
O	i	i	i	t	T	p	a	l	O	a	i		A	r	b	i	z	m	i	i	l	p	i	z
A	b	a	m	o	o	o	a	C	u	c	a	C	O	p	a	n	a	B	a	m	S	m	a	L
N	a	o	c	O	T	t	n	p	r	a	T	o	d	O	l	o	P	i	n	i	a	n	b	a
o	c	a	n	m	a	g	o	t	r	o	i	m	r	x	p	a	o	c	s	i	z	i	x	p
S	h	i	a	l	r	a	p	m	z	o	x	a	a	x	t	i	r	V	a	s	t	r	i	m
m	o	t	i	b		a	T	n	a	n			n	a	n	T	a			b	i	t	o	m
d	o	n	p	a	T	d	a	n	V	a	a	a	T	a	O	A	d	u	p	t	D	n	i	m
o	l	o	a	G	e	o	o	b	a	u	a		o	a	l	c	o	o	r	o	m	e	b	b
O	P	a	m	n	o	O	G	m	d	n	m	m	T	a	g	c	o	n	x	m	a	l	G	m
a	p	l	s	T	e	d	e	c	a	o	p	o	n	h	o	d	D	i	a	l	e	a	o	c
s	c	m	i	o	o	n	A	m	l	o	x	C	p	a	t	A	x	i	o	V	s	P	s	N*
V	a	r	s	G	d	L	b	r	i	a	p	h	S	a	a	i	z	a	a	r	V	r	o	i
o	i	P	t	e	a	a	p	D	o	c	e		m	p	h	a	r	s	l	g	a	i	o	l
p	s	u	a	c	n	r	Z	i	r	Z	a	p	M	a	m	g	l	o	i	n	L	i	r	x
S	i	o	d	a	o	i	n	r	z	f	m		o	l	a	a	D	a	g	a	T	a	p	a
d	a	l	t	T	d	n	a	d	i	r	e	r	p	a	L	c	o	i	d	x	P	a	c	n
d	i	x	o	m	o	n	s	i	o	s	p	a	n	d	a	z	N	z	i	V	a	a	s	a
O	o	D	p	z	i	A	p	a	n	l	i	x	i	i	d	P	o	n	s	d	A	s	p	i
r	g	o	a	n	n	P*	A	C	r	a	r	e	x	r	i	n	h	t	a	r	n	d	i	L*

The Original Great Table

Note: Letters with asterisks are inverted

Dee's doubt over the correct placement of the Watchtowers on the Great Table would seem justified, but it is the version given by Raphael he should have questioned, in spite of the admonishment of the angel "not to prefer your reason before the wisdom of the highest, whose mercy is so great towards you." In fact, the original version of the Great Table does show the Watchtower of the East (upper left quadrant) opposite that of the West (lower right), and the Watchtower of the South (upper right) opposite that of the North (lower left), if we follow Dee's assignment of the Watchtowers to the points of the compass as given in his *Liber Scientiae*.

Once it is understood that the Great Table is nothing other than a magical schematic diagram of the image on the golden talisman, which will be considered at length below, it becomes difficult to accept the revised version of Raphael, if we adhere to Dee's assignment of the Watchtowers to the four directions as given in his *Liber Scientiae*. It is even more difficult to accept the somewhat arbitrary arrangement of the Golden Dawn.

I am convinced that the Great Table is intended to be unfolded clockwise, or sunwise, beginning with the upper left quadrant, which is universally linked with the east. Therefore, however the Watchtowers may be placed upon the Table, the upper left quadrant belongs to the east, the upper right quadrant to the south, the lower right quadrant to the west, and the lower left quadrant to the north. It is vital to understand that the orientation of the Great Table to the compass points does not change, however the Watchtowers may be shifted around upon it. Therefore, on the revised table of Raphael, the Watchtower of ORO IBAH AOZPI is of the east, the Watchtower of MPH ARSL GAIOL is of the south, the Watchtower of OIP TEAA PDOCE is of the west, and the Watchtower of MOR DIAL HCTGA is of the north. Once this is established, it is up to the magician to determine which elements will be linked with which directions of space. Remember, the Watchtowers were linked by Dee primarily with the directions and only in a secondary way with the elements, contrary to the Golden Dawn practice.

For weeks I debated with myself which of the two versions of the Great Table given by Dee is correct. I was not really happy with either version, but could not decide between them. In the course of writing the introduction to *Enochian Mandalas* by Gerald and Betty Schueler, it suddenly struck me that both the Original Table and the Reformed Table of Raphael place the Watchtowers in the wrong quadrants. With utter clarity I realized what the true structure of the Great Table must be.

The basis for this insight is the way in which the Enochian angels communicated information about the Watchtowers to Dee and Kelley. Invariably the symbols of the Watchtowers are transmitted in a circle around the earth, beginning in the east, then proceeding to the south, the west, and finally the north. This is demonstrated in Kelley's vision, given below. The single exception to this rule is when the Watchtowers are unveiled successively in *reverse* order, moving from north to west to south to east (Casaubon, page 173), but this is done for the purpose of progressing from the end to the beginning of the Watchtowers and does not conflict with their essential interrelationship.

When the angel Ave delivers the four emblems of the Watchtowers (Casaubon, page 173), this unfolding of east, south, west, and north is related directly to the four quadrants on the Great Table. East is placed in the upper left quadrant, south in the upper right, west in the lower right, and north in the lower left.

It dawned upon me that if the symbols of the Watchtowers were delivered in this order by the angels, then surely the Watchtowers themselves were also delivered in this manner. This being so, the first Watchtower received by Dee (ORO, IBAH, AOZPI) must go in the east on the upper left quadrant; the second Watchtower received (MOR, DIAL, HCTGA) must go in the south on the upper right quadrant; the third Watchtower received (OIP, TEAA, PDOCE) must go in the west on the lower right quadrant; the fourth Watchtower received (MPH, ARSL, GAIOL) must go in the north on the lower left quadrant (see Casaubon, pages 176-7).

Once understood, the logic of this insight is persuasive in itself. Fortunately, we can find verification for this Restored Great Table in Dee's own manuscripts. In the diagram of the Enochian banners that appears in Dee's *Liber Scientia* (see James, *Enochian Magick*, page 119, where the diagram is reproduced), the three names of God on each Watchtower are placed in one of the four quarters of the compass, and are clearly intended to correspond with one of the quadrants on the Great Table, which is drawn within the circle of these names.

In Dee's diagram, ORO, IBAH, AOZPI is placed in the east on the upper left quadrant of the Great Table; MOR, DIAL, HCTGA is placed in the south on the upper right quadrant; OIP, TEAA, PDOCE is placed in the west on the lower right quadrant; MPH, ARSL, GAIOL is placed in the north on the lower left quadrant. This is precisely what we would expect if the Watchtowers are to be positioned on the Great Table in the order of their delivery by the angel Ave to Kelley. It is interesting to note that this arrangement of the Watchtowers to the four directions of space conflicts with that given in the actual text of *Liber Scientia*, where the pattern of the Original Great Table is adhered to by Dee.

For a more detailed analysis of how the Great Table was revealed through a series of progressive stages to Dee and Kelley, I urge the reader to consult my introduction to *Enochian Mandalas*. Here I will give what I consider to be the definitive form of the Restored Great Table. I have preferred the spelling variations found in the Table of Raphael, but the placement of the Watchtowers is original.

Some of the letters on the Great Table are capitals. A few are even inverted left to right. On the diagrams, these inverted letters are indicated by asterisks. The capitals begin the names of ninety-two geographical spirits which rule over various regions of the earth (see Casaubon, pages 141-52 and James, pages 103-16). For some reason the 92nd spirit, whose name is Laxdizi, is omitted from Dee's list, but its sigil appears in a diagram showing the placement of all the geographical spirits on the Great Table (see James, page 116).

```
r Z i l a f A y t l p a e   b O a Z a R o p h a R a
a r d Z a i d p a L a m     u N n a x o P S o n d n
c z o n s a r o Y a u b x   a i g r a n o o m a g g
T o i T t z o P a c o C a   o r p m n i n g b e a l
S i g a s o m r b z n h r   r s O n i z i r l e m u
f m o n d a T d i a r i p   i z i n r C z i a M h l
o r o i b A h a o z p i     M O r d i a l h C t G a
t N a b r V i x g a s d h   O C a n c h i a s o m t
O i i i t T p a l O a i     A r b i z m i i l p i z
A b a m o o o a C u c a C   O p a n a L a m S m a P
N a o c O T t n p r n T o   d O l o P i n i a n b a
o c a n m a g o t r o i m   r x p a o c s i z i x p
S h i a l r a p m z o x a   a x t i r V a s t r i m
m o t i b     a T n a n     n a n T a     b i t o m
T a O A d u p t D n i m a   d o n p a T d a n V a a
a a b c o o r o m e b b     o l o a G e o o b a u a
T o g c o n x m a l G m m   O P a m n o V G m d n m
n h o d D i a l e a o c o   a p l s T e d e c a o p
p a t A x i o V s P s N* C  s c m i o o n A m l o x
S a a i x a a r V r o i h   V a r s G d L b r i a p
m p h a r s l g a i o l     o i P t e a a p D o c e
M a m g l o i n L i r x p   p s u a c n r Z i r Z a
o l a a D n g a T a p a     S i o d a o i n r z f m
p a L c o i d x P a c n r   d a l t T d n a d i r e
n d a z N z i V a a s a a   d i x o m o n s i o s p
i i d P o n s d A s p i x   O o D p z i A p a n l i
x r i n h t a r n d i L* e  r g o a n n P* A C r a r
```

The Restored Great Table of Tyson

Note: Capitals in the Watchtowers indicate initial letters in the sigil names for the spirits of regions of the world (see James, pp. 103–16; Casaubon, pp. 141–52). Letters with asterisks are inverted. Capitals in the Black Cross that runs through the center of the Table divide the letters in the Cross into seven-letter names which begin with the capitals.

The inverted letters P and N fall on the beginning and end of the fragmented name of the 65th spirit, which may be written for clarity: PA;OA;OA;N. In each Watchtower two squares are untouched by the seven-letter sigils of the geographical spirits, and the letters in these squares, with one exception, make up the spirit name Paoaoan (Original Table: Paraoan). When Dee inquired about the curious construction of this name, the angel Ave told him: "Every letter in Paraoan is a living fire: but all of one quality and of one Creation: But unto N is delivered a viol of Destruction, according to that part that he is of Paraoan the Governour" (Casaubon, p. 188).

The sole exception among the inverted letters is the inverted L that occurs at the bottom of the last column of the MPH, ARSL, GAIOL Watchtower. This letter begins the set of three spirit names numbered 28 to 30, derived from the upper and right arms on the Black Cross that runs through the center of the Great Table. Since each spirit name must have seven letters, and since there are only twenty letters in the giant L of the Black Cross, the inverted L must be placed at the head of the first of these three names: L;EXARPH, COMANAN, TABITOM.

The importance of these geographical spirits is not generally recognized among Enochian scholars. These are the spirits promised to Dee by the angels that were to allow him to rule over the sovereigns of all the world for the greater glory of his own Queen Elizabeth I of England. It was to obtain control over these daemons, or presiding genii, of the different kingdoms that caused Dee to pursue Enochian magic with such single-minded intensity for so many years. They are linked in groups of three to the thirty Aethers, except for the final group, which has four spirit names, and arguably should contain the missing Laxdizi to make five.

It seems to me that the anomalies in the construction of the sigils of these geographical spirits indicate subtleties that have yet to be understood by students of Enochian magic. It is surely no accident that three of the names come from letters on the upper and right arms of the Black Cross, which happen to trace a large L, and that these three names are headed by an inverted L from elsewhere on the Table. It is no accident that one of the names is composed of fragments. Perhaps the omission of the final name was also intentional on the part of Nalvage, the angel who delivered them to Kelley.

There are numerous mistakes in the names and their sigils in Casaubon and in James. The accompanying diagram shows the sigils of the names in their places on my own Restored Great Table. This I believe to be their accurate shapes and placements. Arrows at the end of each sigil show the direction in which the corresponding letters on the Table are to be read. The sigils are numbered from one to ninety- two. It is an easy matter to discover the spelling of each name by tracing the letters on the Restored Table which its sigil touches.

Both the original spelling of these spirit names and the reformed spelling that is extracted from the Reformed Table of Raphael are given below, along with the geographical regions ruled by the spirits, and the Aethers under which the spirits fall.

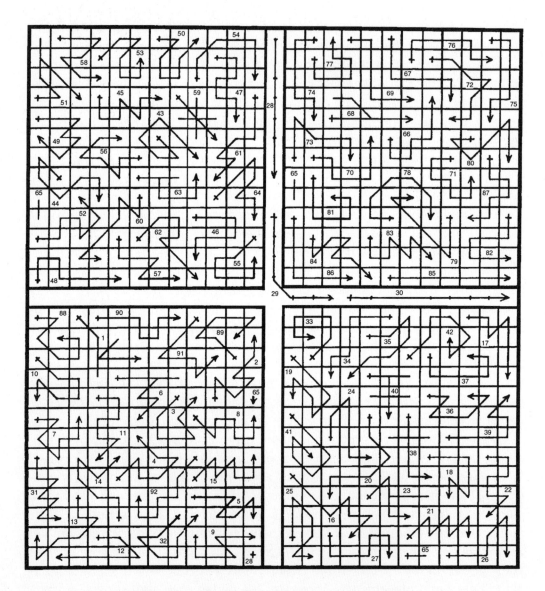

Sigils of the Geographical Spirits on the Great Table

The placement of these sigils corresponds with the Restored Great Table, but they may be
related to either the Original Table or the Reformed Table of Raphael merely by shifting the
Watchtowers upon the four quadrants.

ENOCHIAN GEOGRAPHICAL SPIRITS

	Spirit Names		Regions	Aethers	
	Original	Reformed			
1)	Occodon	Occodon	Egypt		
2)	Pascomb	Pascomb	Syria	1:	LIL
3)	Valgars	Valgars	Mesopotamia		
4)	Doagnis	Dongnis	Cappadocia		
5)	Pacasna	Pacasna	Tuscia	2:	ARN
6)	Dialioa	Dialioa	Asia Minor		
7)	Samapha	Samapha	Hyrcania		
8)	Virooli	Virooli	Thracia	3:	ZOM
9)	Andispi	Andispi	Gosmam		
10)	Thotanp	Thotanp	Thebaidi		
11)	Axziarg	Axxiarg	Parsadal	4:	PAZ
12)	Pothnir	Pothnir	India		
13)	Lazdixi	Lazdixi	Bactriane		
14)	Nocamal	Nocamal	Cilicia	5:	LIT
15)	Tiarpax	Tiarpax	Oxiana		
16)	Saxtomp	Saxtomp	Numidia		
17)	Vavaamp	Vavaamp	Cyprus	6:	MAZ
18)	Zirzird	Zirzird	Parthia		
19)	Opmacas	Opmacas	Getulia		
20)	Genadol	Genadol	Arabia	7:	DEO
21)	Aspiaon	Aspiaon	Phalagon		
22)	Zamfres	Zamfres	Mantiana		
23)	Todnaon	Todnaon	Soxia	8:	ZID
24)	Pristac	Pristac	Gallia		
25)	Oddiorg	Oddiorg	Assyria		
26)	Cralpir	Cralpir	Sogdiana	9:	ZIP
27)	Doanzin	Doanzin	Lydia		

ENOCHIAN GEOGRAPHICAL SPIRITS (*Continued*)

Spirit Names		Regions	Aethers
Original	**Reformed**		
28) L;exarph	L;exarph	Caspis	
29) Comanan	Comanan	Germania	10: ZAX
30) Tabitom	Tabitom	Trenam	
31) Molpand	Molpand	Bithynia	
32) Usnarda	Usnarda	Gracia	11: ICH
33) Ponodol	Ponodol	Lacia	
34) Tapamal	Tapamal	Onigap	
35) Gedoons	Gedoons	India Major	12: LOE
36) Ambriol	Ambriol	Orchenii	
37) Gecaond	Gecaond	Achaia	
38) Laparin	Laparin	Armenia	13: ZIM
39) Docepax	Docepax	Nemrodiana	
40) Tedoond	Tedoond	Paphlogonia	
41) Vivipos	Vivipos	Phasiana	14: UTA
42) Ooanamb	Voanamb	Chaldei	
43) Tahamdo	Tahamdo	Itergi	
44) Nociabi	Notiabi	Macedonia	15: OXO
45) Tastoxo	Tastozo	Garamannia	
46) Cucarpt	Cucnrpt	Sauromatica	
47) Lauacon	Lauacon	Ethiopia	16: LEA
48) Sochial	Sochial	Fiacim	
49) Sigmorf	Sigmorf	Colchica	
50) Avdropt	Aydropt	Cireniaca	17: TAN
51) Tocarzi	Tocarzi	Nasamoma	
52) Nabaomi	Nabaomi	Carthago	
53) Zafasai	Zafasai	Coxlant	18: ZEN
54) Yalpamb	Yalpamb	Adumea	

ENOCHIAN GEOGRAPHICAL SPIRITS (*Continued*)

Spirit Names		Regions	Aethers
Original	Reformed		
55) Torzoxi	Torzoxi	Parstavia	
56) Abriond	Abriond	Celtica	19: POP
57) Omagrap	Omagrap	Vinsan	
58) Zildron	Zildron	Tolpam	
59) Parziba	Parziba	Carcedoma	20: CHR
60) Totocan	Totocan	Italia	
61) Chirzpa	Chirzpa	Brytania	
62) Toantom	Toantom	Phenices	21: ASP
63) Vixpalg	Vixpalg	Comaginen	
64) Ozidaia	Osidaia	Apulia	
65) PA;RA;OA;N	PA;OA;OA;N	Marmarica	22: LIN
66) Calzirg	Calzirg	Concava Syria	
67) Ronoomb	Ronoomb	Gebal	
68) Onizimp	Onizimp	Elam	23: TOR
69) Zaxanin	Zaxanin	Adunia	
70) Orcanir	Orancir	Media	
71) Chialps	Chaslpo	Arriana	24: NIA
72) Soageel	Soageel	Chaldea	
73) Mirzind	Mirzind	Serica Populi	
74) Obvaors	Obvaors	Persia	25: UTI
75) Ranglam	Ranglam	Gongatha	
76) Pophand	Pophand	Gorsin	
77) Nigrana	Nigrana	Hispania	26: DES
78) Bazchim	Lazhiim	Pamphilia	

ENOCHIAN GEOGRAPHICAL SPIRITS (*Continued*)

Spirit Names		Regions	Aethers
Original	**Reformed**		
79) Saziami	Saziami	Oacidi	
80) Mathula	Mathula	Babylon	27: ZAA
81) Orpanib	Crpanib	Median	
82) Labnixp	Pabnixp	Adumian	
83) Pocisni	Pocisni	Felix Arabia	28: BAG
84) Oxlopar	Oxlopar	Metagonitidim	
85) Vastrim	Vastrim	Assyria	
86) Odraxti	Odraxti	Africa	29: RII
87) Gomziam	Gmtziam	Bactriani	
88) Taoagla	Taaogba	Asnan	
89) Gemnimb	Gemnimb	Phrygia	30: TEX
90) Advorpt	Advorpt	Creta	
91) Doxmael	Doxmael	Mauritania	
92) Laxdizi	Laxdizi	———	

On the Golden Dawn Watchtowers, some squares contain more than one letter. At first sight, this seems very puzzling, but James points out that it results from the various corrected versions of the Great Table found in Dee's diaries (no less than five variations). The Golden Dawn simply collected all the different letters for each square of the Table and wrote them into that square. This is a very poor solution to the problem, because many of these alternate letters were later crossed out by John Dee. It seems only common sense to use the lettering of the corrected Table supplied by the angel Raphael, making what changes are necessary to harmonize the revised lettering with the names of the spirits. But can we trust Raphael, or believe that the revised Table is any more accurate than the original Table? This is a problem that has no easy solution and must be wrestled with by each serious student of Enochian magic.

The name "Watchtower" comes from a vision Kelley experienced while lying awake in his bed early on the morning of Wednesday, June 20, 1584. A spirit clothed with feathers "strangely wreathed about him all over" patted Kelley on the head to get his attention. Dee describes the vision:

> There appeared to him four very fair Castles, standing in the four parts of the world: out of which he heard the sound of a Trumpet. Then seemed out of every Castle a cloath to be

thrown on the ground, of more then the breadth of a Table-cloath.

Out of that in the East, the cloath seemed to be red, which was cast.

Out of that in the South, the cloath seemed white.

Out of that in the West, the cloath seemed green, with great knops on it.

Out of that in the North, spread, or thrown out from the gate under foot, the cloath seemed to be very black.

Out of every Gate then issued one Trumpeter, whose Trumpets were of strange form, wreathed, and growing bigger and bigger toward the end.

After the Trumpeter followed three Ensign bearers.

After them six ancient men, with white beards and staves in their hands.

Then followed a comely man, with very much Apparel on his back, his Robe having a long train.

After him came five men, carrying up of his train.

Then followed one great Crosse, and about that four lesser Crosses.

These Crosses had on them, each of them ten, like men, their faces distinctly appearing on the four parts of the Crosse, all over.

After the Crosses followed 16 white Creatures.

And after them, an infinite number seemed to issue, and to spread themselves orderly in a compasse, almost before the four foresaid Castles. (*A True & Faithful Relation,* p. 168)

This strange and complex vision was expounded upon by the spirit Ave later that same day. It is worth giving this explanation here, both because it is so central to Enochian magic and because it contains several points that bear directly on Tetragrammaton, the Banners, and the Wings of the Winds:

The 4 houses, are the 4 Angels of the Earth, which are the 4 Overseers, and Watch-towers, that the eternal God in his providence hath placed, against the usurping blasphemy, mis-use, and stealth of the wicked and great enemy, the Devil....

In each of these Houses, the Chief Watchman, is a mighty Prince, a mighty Angel of the Lord: which hath under him 5 Princes (these names I must use for your instruction). The seals and authorities of these Houses, are confirmed in the beginning of the World. Unto every one of them, be 4 characters, (Tokens of the presence of the son of God: by whom all things were made in Creation.)

Ensignes, upon the Image whereof, is death: whereon the Redemption of mankind is established, and with the which he shall come to judge the Earth.

These are the Characters, and natural marks of holinesse. Upon these, belong four Angels severally.

The 24 old men, are the 24 Seniors, that St. John remembreth.

These judge the government of the Castles, and fullfil the will of God, as it is written.

The 12 Banners are the 12 names of God, that govern all the creatures upon the Earth, visible and invisible, comprehending 3, 4, and 5.

Out of these Crosses, come the Angels of all the Aires: which presently give obedience to the will of men, when they see them....

The Trumpets sound once. The Gates open. The four Castles are moved. There issueth 4 Trumpeters, whose Trumpets are a Pyramis, six cones, wreathed. There followeth out of every Castle 3, holding up their Banners displayed, with ensigne, the names of God. There follow Seniors six, alike from the 4 Gates: After them cometh from every part a King: whose Princes are five, gardant, and holding up his train. Next issueth the Crosse of 4 Angles, of the Majesty of Creation in God attended upon everyone, with 4: a white Cloud, 4 Crosses, bearing the witnesses of the Covenant of God, with the Prince gone out before: which were confirmed, every one, with ten Angels, visible in countenance: After every Crosse, attendeth 16 Angels, dispositors of the will of those, that govern the Castles. They proceed. And, in, and about the middle of the Court, the Ensigns keep their standings, opposite to the middle of the Gate: The rest pause. The 24 Senators meet: They seem to consult.

I, AVE, STOOD BY THE SEER:
It vanisheth.
So I leave you. (*A True & Faithful Relation*, p. 170–1)

Notice the explicit reference to the Revelation of St. John, the twelve Banners of the Name, and the twenty-four elders. The thirty Airs, or Aethers, so important a part of the Keys, are also mentioned. The Wings are not named here, but directly after giving Dee the revised version of the Great

Table, Raphael says: "I, Raphael, counsel you to make a Covenant with the Highest, and to esteem his wings more than your own lives." What can be intended here, other than the active powers of the Watchtowers? Elsewhere, the angel Michael instructs the angel Nalvage to enter into Kelley's crystal, saying: "Unto thee Nalvage thus saith the Lord, gather up thy wings and enter: Do as thou art commanded, and be multiplied" (Casaubon, p. 81). This confirms that "wings" is a term for active spiritual agents, or angels.

Dee thought so highly of Kelley's vision that he engraved it upon a disk of gold. It shows a circle with four towers, or castles, at the four quarters of the earth. Leading in to the center from the gate of each tower is a walkway representing a colored cloth, or carpet. Moving toward the center on each of these colored carpets is a trumpeter, followed by three standard-bearers, six seniors, a king, five princes, five crosses arranged in a cross pattern, and sixteen dispositors. The circular center of the amulet shows the twenty-four seniors, having arrived at the center, gathered into a ring as if to consult. This golden disk has survived and is in the safekeeping of the British Museum.

It is highly significant that the seniors are mentioned twice—first, in four groups of six issuing out of the gates of the Watchtowers and, later, gathered in a ring of twenty-four to consult. The groups of six represent the six Wings of the Winds on the back of each beast. The ring of twenty-four represents the seated elders. The large cross surrounded by four smaller crosses that issues from each gate is a graphic plan of the Watchtower itself. Each of the smaller crosses bears the faces of ten angels, which suggest the ten *sephiroth,* sometimes called "aspects" because they are expressions of the divine will. In fact, each of the crosses in the lesser angles of the Watchtowers contains ten letters.

A marginal note in Casaubon says these forty angels of the four lesser crosses attend on the principle sixteen angels. The trumpets, which Kelley says are "of strange form," and which are later described as "a Pyramis, six cones, wreathed" probably branch into six bell-shaped apertures, and represent the occult vortices of the seniors.

The Golden Dawn seized upon the description of the four tablets of the quarters as Watchtowers and interpreted them in this manner on a cosmic level: "In these vast spaces at the ends of the Universe are these Tablets placed as Watch-Towers, and therein is their dominion limited on either side by the Sephirothic Pillars, and having the great central cross of each Tablet coinciding with one of the 4 Tiphareth points in the Celestial Heavens" (*Golden Dawn,* p. 656). The four angelic tables literally become the guardian gates at the ends of the manifest universe, the ultimate bastion against the violent entry of the "death-dragon" Telocvovim (him-that-is-fallen), who is mighty Coronzon, or Lucifer.

The notion that the firmament of heaven is sustained above the floor of the world by four supports is very old. The ancient Egyptians believed that four pillars supported the sky at the cardinal points. Later these pillars became the scepters of four gods, "four elder spirits who dwell in the locks of hair of Horus," namely Amset (south), Hap (north), Tuamutef (east), and Qebhsennuf (west). The supporting pillars were formed from the hair of Horus, whose head was the heavens and whose eyes were the sun and moon (see Budge, *Gods of the Egyptians,* vol. I, pp. 157–8).

Each of the sets of angels described in Kelley's vision has a corresponding set of Enochian names which are extracted by various techniques from the Watchtowers. For example, the name of the king of each quarter is found by reading the eight letters in the center of the great cross of that Watchtower in a clockwise inward spiral, so that the vibration of the name by itself creates an invoking vortex upon the Watchtower. The king of the quarter of the east is thus Bataivah.

The names of God upon the three banners are extracted by reading the letters upon the horizontal arm of the central cross in each Watchtower left to right. The first name has three letters, the second four, and the third five. This is why in Ave's explanation of Kelley's vision, the angel says: "The 12 Banners are the 12 names of God, that govern all the creatures upon the Earth, visible and invisible, comprehending 3, 4, and 5." These Enochian names of God correspond to the twelve Banners of IHVH. For example, the names on the banners of the Watchtower of the East are ORO, IBAH, and AOZPI. The overt and occult forms of the Banners are indicated by the reference to the creatures of the earth "visible and invisible."

Rules for extracting the rest of the names are found in *The Golden Dawn* and may also be deduced from James' *Enochian Magick of Dr. John Dee.* They are too complex to detail here, since they do not directly bear upon Tetragrammaton.

The Enochian Keys are evocations of the spirits of the four Watchtowers delivered by the spirit Nalvage to Kelley via the showstone in the form of hauntingly poetic verses in the Enochian language. They are termed "Keys" because they unlock the gates of the Watchtowers. They may be properly called evocations, since the spirits are made to issue forth from the gates of their castles at the four extremities of the universe and are ordered to "move and show yourselves" (ZACARE ZAMRAN) by the ritualist vibrating the Keys.

These Keys were not dictated in the ordinary way by Nalvage to Kelley, but were derived letter by Enochian letter from complex tables of letter squares using a numerical positioning system to locate each letter (for a good example of the method, see Casaubon, p. 79). So far as I am aware, no living human being on earth understands this system. It is perhaps significant that the Keys were not derived from the letters of the Watchtowers themselves. Regrettably, the Keys are imperfectly known, in that they contain numbers the meaning of which remains obscure, but enough is understood to render them potent tools in magic.

The Golden Dawn recognized that the Keys related to the Watchtowers and to the four letters of Tetragrammaton. However, the Order system of linking the Watchtowers with their Keys seems, to me, to be incorrect. Since the Watchtowers have a good deal to reveal about heavenly Christ, the four beasts, the twelve Banners, the twenty-four elders, and the twenty-four Wings of the Winds, I intend to examine their symbolism in some detail.

There are forty-eight expressed Keys. According to the Golden Dawn, there is a forty-ninth unexpressed Key, which is really the first, but this is too exalted to be put into words (see Casaubon, pp. 77, 79, and 194), so the first expressed Key is, technically, the second of all the Keys. For practical purposes, the number of Keys is forty-eight. The first eighteen Keys are completely different from one another. The remaining thirty, which are called the Thirty Aethers, or Airs, are identical, save that the name of each Air changes from Key to Key.

The Golden Dawn assigned the first eighteen Keys to various parts of the Watchtowers and the Tablet of Union according to the elemental associations of those parts in the Golden Dawn system. This assignment is fully presented in the essay titled "The Concourse of the Forces" (*Golden Dawn,* pp. 671–3).

The first Key evokes the angels of the Tablet of Union as a whole.

The second Key evokes the angels of the first letters in the names on the Tablet of Union (E, H, N, and B).

The third Key evokes the angels of the Tablet of Union associated with the line EXARP, those of the Watchtower of Air as a whole, and those of the lesser angle of air on the air tablet.

The fourth Key evokes the angels of the Tablet of Union associated with the line HCOMA, those of the Watchtower of Water as a whole, and those of the lesser angle of water on the water tablet.

The fifth Key evokes the angels of the Tablet of Union associated with the line NANTA, those of the Watchtower of Earth as a whole, and those of the lesser angle of earth on the earth tablet.

The sixth Key evokes the angels of the Tablet of Union associated with the line BITOM, those of the Watchtower of Fire as a whole, and those of the lesser angle of fire on the fire tablet.

Keys seven, eight, and nine evoke the angels of the Watchtower of Air.

Keys ten, eleven, and twelve evoke the angels of the Watchtower of Water.

Keys thirteen, fourteen, and fifteen evoke the angels of the Watchtower of Earth.

Keys sixteen, seventeen, and eighteen evoke the angels of the Watchtower of Fire.

This may seem complicated and difficult, but it is based on the fundamental pattern of the Keys, as revealed by their wording. Although the founders of the Golden Dawn evidently recognized this pattern, in my opinion they made a mistake in assigning the individual Keys to the elements.

The Keys from three to eighteen are clearly intended to be linked with the four directions of the compass. They unfold in four groups of four, progressing sunwise beginning with the east in four circles around the Great Table, each circle touching the corresponding four lesser angles of its direction. This is quite clear from the naming of the directions in the Keys themselves, although two anomalies disguise this pattern. In the third Key, no direction is explicitly named, and in the thirteenth Key the south is named, when clearly the west is intended. The first and second Keys appear to refer, respectively, to God the Father and God the Son, and are rightly assigned by the Golden Dawn to the Tablet of Union. The Keys from nineteen to forty-eight are assumed to refer to thirty concentric spheres similar to those nesting spheres, or worlds, that appear in Gnostic writings.

For convenience, these relationships are tabulated below:

First: Father		Second: Son	
Third: east	Fourth: south	Fifth: west	Sixth: north
Seventh: east	Eighth: south	Ninth: west	Tenth: north
Eleventh: east	Twelfth: south	Thirteenth: west	Fourteenth: north
Fifteenth: east	Sixteenth: south	Seventeenth: west	Eighteenth:north
	Nineteenth to Forty-Eight: Thirty spheres, or degrees		

The symbolism of the Keys contains strong echoes of the Gnostic gospels, particularly the Key of the Thirty Aethers, which might almost have been dictated by Yaldabaoth himself. Geoffrey James considers these Gnostic connections at some length (*The Enochian Magick of Dr. John Dee,* pp. xix–xxi) and speculates that Kelley may have plagiarized portions of a secret Gnostic text in his possession unknown to Dee.

I should state here explicitly that I do not believe Kelley concocted the Keys, or the majority of his communications with spirits recorded in Dee's diaries. His other writings cannot even approach the complex and beautiful symbolism of the Enochian communications. I believe Kelley was a genuine seer, despite his many personal shortcomings, and that he was in contact with the same class of spiritual beings who inspired the Gnostic writings. The spirits by turns bored, infuriated, and terrified Kelley, who did not like them moving in his head. He would much earlier have broken off communications with them, had Dee not paid him to continue, which Kelley did only under formal protest.

It is my belief that Kelley first came to Dee at Mortlake seeking secret knowledge about the making and use of the fabled red powder of alchemy, a portion of which Kelley had purchased for a ridiculously low sum from an innkeeper while on a walking tour of Wales. Kelley believed Dee's huge library

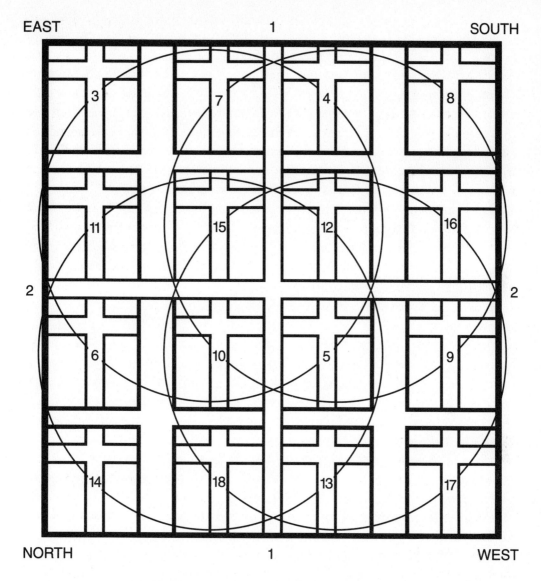

EAST 1 SOUTH

3 7 4 8

11 15 12 16

2 2

6 10 5 9

14 18 13 17

NORTH 1 WEST

Pattern of the Keys on the Great Table

of occult books would give him a clue about the powder, and perhaps suspected that Dee himself had more than a passing understanding of the alchemical art.

It was for this reason alone that Kelley agreed to stay with Dee and act as his seer. Many times he threatened to leave Dee, but always he was held by the prospect of discovering the secret of the powder, which could turn base metals to gold. Throughout his association with Dee, Kelley constantly urged Dee to devote himself to alchemical matters. The salary Dee paid Kelley for his labors as a seer was scant compensation compared with the glittering visions of the philosopher's stone.

References by the spirit guide Madimi, who came in the form of a little girl, to her "mother" are highly significant. Madimi constantly refers to the authority of her mother, who is a kinswoman of Nalvage, the spirit who delivers the Enochian Keys. Dee asks Madimi's mother her name, and the spirit answers: "I am of the word, and by the word" (Casaubon, p. 27). When Dee persists, the spirit becomes annoyed and says: "I AM; What more will you?" and then flies away like a fire. The mother may perhaps be a version of the Gnostic goddess Barbelo and may be the subject of the unexpressed primordial Key. She is also the Queen of Heaven described in Revelation 12, who is clothed with the sun, has the moon under her feet, and wears a crown of twelve stars.

It is not widely recognized by occultists who employ the Keys in their magic that the forty-eight Keys, taken as a whole, represent a complex ritual working whose sole purpose is to open the four sealed gates of the Watchtowers, allowing the entry of the great dragon, Coronzon or Satan, who will bring about the final destruction of the manifest universe. The Keys are an apocalyptic evocation. This function is examined at greater length in Appendix A.

There is a fable that if the Tetragrammaton should ever be spoken in its entirety, it would destroy the world. I believe the Enochian Keys to be one form of the complete voicing of the terrible Name of the God of Wrath, designed to release the thunders of judgment. Since the Keys were given to Dee and Kelley by the angels, it appears that it is necessary for human beings to initiate this apocalypse by correctly and completely executing the Enochian evocation of the four Watchtowers and forty-eight Keys.

We must willingly invite the destruction of our universe with the speech from our own lips. The gates at the four corners of creation are locked from the *inside*. They cannot be battered down by the forces of Coronzon, but if we can be deceived into opening them by using the Keys, the great dragon can then enter our dimension of reality, our space-time, and transform it to suit his own needs—which are not our needs. We cannot exist in our present forms in the dwelling place of Coronzon. In the course of this transformation, we will be destroyed.

The Enochian angels used Dee and Kelley as unwitting dupes for their own higher purposes. Their impatience with the petty material concerns of Dee, and their outright contempt for Kelley, is apparent throughout the magical record of the scrying sessions. Numerous times the angels snap at Dee when he asks them for some prediction of the future, or chastise him. I do not believe Dee ever suspected that he was being used by the angels for the terrible and awesome purpose of transmitting the magical formula of the apocalypse to the human race. I believe that had Dee so much as suspected this purpose, he would have burned all his books at once. However, Dee was an extremely pious man, and might well have regarded the apocalypse as a necessary cleansing of the world.

In recent decades, many occultists have taken up Enochian magic. It may not be long before it is perfected, and the world as we know it ends. One magician who worked the Keys with single-minded ardor during the early part of the twentieth century was Aleister Crowley, a former member of the Hermetic Order of the Golden Dawn. It is perhaps no coincidence that from childhood Crowley had called himself the "Great Beast," and saw his role in life as the herald of the coming Aeon of Horus, an age of warfare and destruction soon to sweep the face of the world.

In 1909 Crowley conducted a series of rituals to invoke the angels of the Enochian Keys in the desert of North Africa (see the *Confessions of Aleister Crowley*, Chapter 66). It is possible that he succeeded in opening the gates of the four Watchtowers a small crack, and that the continuing warfare, crimes and moral decay that have afflicted the earth throughout this century are merely the first stirrings of the apocalypse.

About one thing I feel quite confident. If there is to be such a thing as an apocalypse (and I do not say that there must be) it will take place on a psychic level, within the realm of the subconscious mind, and only display itself in the physical world as a secondary consequence of this mental and moral Armageddon. The true gates of the Watchtowers open inwardly on our own subconscious mind, and it is upon this psychic battleground that the demons of Coronzon will wreak their destruction, which will be of a moral and spiritual nature. This destructive but unsuspected possession of the subconscious will exhibit itself in chaotic and random acts of aggression, violence, and vandalism. Perhaps it has already started. Perhaps not. You be the judge.

APPENDIX A

ʻ ʻ ʻ ʻ ʻ ʻ ʻ ʻ

THE KEYS

S ince the Keys are fairly brief, it will be useful to examine each individually for its ritual application in magic, its Gnostic symbolism, and
its correspondences with the imagery in the Revelation of St. John.
The ties between the Keys and the Apocalypse are many, as will
quickly become apparent in the course of the following analysis. Most important of these, on the matter of Tetragrammaton, is the symbolism of the
heavenly throne of Revelation 4, which in the Keys takes on the structure of
a great clock. The vital significance of this image of the throne as a cosmic
clock cannot be overemphasized.

The original versions of the English translations below were composed
by me after an exhaustive comparative analysis of versions given in
Casaubon's *True & Faithful Relation*, Regardie's *Golden Dawn,* Donald
Laycock's *Complete Enochian Dictionary*, Geoffrey James's *Enochian Magick of Dr. John Dee,* and Denning and Phillips's *Mysteria Magica*. The last
two works proved the most useful because they provide an accurate tran-
scription of the English translation of the Keys recorded by Dee in his
manuscript record. I have modernized the spelling but have not changed
the actual wording of the Keys, preferring to retain such archaic forms as
"saith" and "liveth." Apart from the tendency to modernize, which reaches
its most extreme form in Laycock, versions of the Keys differ most in the
choice of punctuation. Dee's own punctuation is very uneven, necessitating

amendments which, ideally, serve to help illuminate the meaning of the Keys.

The First Key

I reign over you, saith the God of Justice, in power exalted above the firmaments of wrath; in whose hands the Sun is as a sword, and the Moon as a through-thrusting fire, which measureth your garments in the midst of my vestures, and trussed you together as the palms of my hands; whose seats I garnished with the fire of gathering, which beautified your garments with admiration; to whom I made a Law to govern the Holy Ones, which delivered you a rod with the ark of knowledge. Moreover, you lifted up your voices and swore obedience and faith to Him that liveth and triumpheth; whose beginning is not, nor end cannot be; which shineth as a flame in the midst of your palace, and reigneth amongst you as the balance of righteousness and truth. Move, therefore, and show yourselves! Open the mysteries of your creation. Be friendly unto me: for I am the servant of the same your God, the true worshiper of the Highest.

Analysis of the First Key

All of the Keys should be understood as commands given to various classes of angels by the magician wearing the Christ-form. The magician speaks with the voice of the heavenly Messiah to the spirits and in this exalted persona invokes the supreme authority of God the Father, saying "I am the servant of the same your God, the true worshiper of the Highest."

The aspect of Christ in the first Key is the unifying aspect of Christ the Lord and King. This is demonstrated by the use of the sun and the moon in the imagery. The sun represents day and the visible creatures—spirits of the right side—who are the angels of consciousness. The moon represents night and the invisible creatures—spirits of the left side—who are the angels of the unconscious. Another telling symbol of unity is the balance. Reminding the spirits of his power, the Messiah says about himself that he "shineth as a flame in the midst of your palace, and reigneth amongst you as the balance of righteousness and truth." Still another unifying symbol is that of the clasped hands. The hands are one model of the tree of the *sephiroth*.

There is only one Messiah. However, this heavenly Christ can exhibit different aspects of himself, depending on which of his powers is called forth. In this Key, Christ is strongly shaped by imagery of the left side, signifying dominance and rule. He calls himself the "God of Justice" (*Din,* the fifth Sephirah). The rays of sun and moon are both swords. His hands are not merely clasped, but "trussed" together. He is the Christ who delivers "a Law to govern the Holy Ones" and "a rod with the ark of knowledge." The iron rod is a symbol of the authority of the mounted Christ of Revelation 19:11–21, who is the child of the woman "clothed with the sun and the moon under her feet, and upon her head a crown of twelve stars" (Rev. 12:1), she who is the same as Madimi's mother.

Christ is talking in this Key to the four kings of the Watchtowers, who are the same as the four beasts that surround, and indeed form a part of, the heavenly throne. That is why he says to them that he is a "through-thrusting fire which measureth your garments in the midst of my vestures." Certain images are repeated throughout the Keys, always with the same meanings. Garments signify manifest forms—not physical bodies, but the shapes and natures that define spiritual beings such as angels. The garments, or forms, of the four kings are in the very midst of the garment of Christ, signifying that these four beings are so holy, they can scarcely be distinguished from the Anointed One himself.

The "Holy Ones" are the angels of the Watchtowers ruled by the four kings with the law of the heavenly Christ, who is acting for God the Father. It is this law that garnishes the seats—symbols of rule—of the kings. The "fire of gathering" is the radiance that shines from the throne, an expression of the law. It shines upon the garments (forms) of the four beasts and gives them living existence. Similarly, Christ "shineth as a flame" in the midst of the palaces, which are the Watchtowers, of the kings, and is the central point of the cross formed by the Watchtowers, balancing them in relation to one another.

The command "Move, therefore, and show yourselves!" occurs in one variation or another in fifteen of the nineteen distinct Keys, including the Key of the Thirty Aethers. The two Enochian words ZACARE (move) and ZAMRAN (show yourselves) are the actual commands to the spirits to appear visibly, or at least tangibly, before the magician. Magically speaking, they are the most potent words in the Keys.

The Second Key

> Can the Wings of the Winds understand your voices of wonder, O you, the Second of the First? Whom the Burning Flames have framed within the depths of my jaws; whom I have prepared as cups for a wedding, or as the flowers in their beauty for the chamber of

righteousness. Stronger are your feet than the barren
stone, and mightier are your voices than the manifold
winds: for you are become a building such as is not, but
in the mind of the All-powerful. Arise, saith the First!
Move, therefore, unto his servants! Show yourselves in
power, and make me a strong see-thing, for I am of
Him that liveth forever.

Analysis of the Second Key

Here, the heavenly Christ through the voice of the magician addresses "the
Second of the First." This group of angels commands the "Wings of the
Winds" through their "voices of wonder" (in Casaubon, this is worded "voices
of windes.") It is quite explicitly stated by Christ: "mightier are your voices
than the manifold winds." This voice-breath imagery is compounded by the
explanation that the Second of the First has been "framed within the depths
of my jaws" by the "Burning Flames." The Burning Flames would seem to be
the four angels that form the subjects of Keys Fifteen, Sixteen, Seventeen,
and Eighteen.

Very likely the "voices of wonder" or "voices of windes" are the sounding
trumpets that issue first out of the gates of the four Watchtowers. They are
called the "Second of the First," perhaps because they articulate the Word of
Christ (see Revelation 19:13). Remember that each trumpet has six bells, or
openings, allowing it to be united as one voice, yet at the same time to be the
six voices of the six elders of its particular Watchtower. What better description of the sounding note of a trumpet than a voice of wind? The notes of a
trumpet are indeed framed within the depths of the jaws of the musician
who plays them, in this case, Christ himself.

The "Burning Flames" would seem to be the active powers that drive the
vital breath through these articulating instruments, giving rise to words of
power that command the Wings of the Winds. In a sense, the trumpets,
which represent the voices of the elders and are all their power, create the
Wings from chaos by shaping them and giving them names. The Wings only
exist by virtue of the articulation of the Ancient Ones. Similarly, the twenty-
four elders, who are the notes of the trumpets, only exist by virtue of the
invisible breath of God: "you are become a building, such as is not, but in the
mind of the All-powerful." Here, "building" signifies the names, or personal
identities, of the Ancient Ones.

In Kelley's vision, these trumpets are "wreathed" with flowers. Christ
says of the "Second of the First" (the trumpets): "whom I have prepared as
cups for a wedding, or as the flowers in their beauty for the chamber of
righteousness." These images celebrate the consummation of sexual union
within the lawful marriage bond, and would seem to refer to the kabbalistic

union between microprosopus (Christ) and the bride (kingdom). I am inclined to speculate that the bride of microprosopus is in this case the mysterious unseen mother of the spirit Madimi. The trumpets, which are the voices of the twenty-four elders, announce this coming union.

There is considerable dispute over the meaning of the words "make me a strong see-thing." Since in the Key these last words are divided, some have interpreted them "seer thing" or "seer of things." In other words, make me a strong seer of visions. It is more generally accepted that it signifies "seething" or boiling, but this sense does not seem quite right to me. Perhaps "make me a strong showing"—that is, appear strongly—is closer to the true sense.

The Third Key

Behold, saith your God, I am a circle on whose hands stand 12 kingdoms; six are the seats of living breath, the rest are as sharp sickles, or the horns of death; wherein the creatures of the Earth are and are not except by mine own hands; which also sleep and shall rise. In the first I made you stewards and placed you in seats 12 of government, giving unto every one of you power successively over 456, the true ages of time, to the intent that, from the highest vessels and the corners of your governments, you might work my power, pouring down the fires of life and increase continually on the Earth. Thus you are become the skirts of Justice and Truth. In the name of the same, your God, lift up, I say, yourselves. Behold, his mercies flourish, and name is become mighty amongst us; in whom we say, move, descend and apply yourselves unto us, as unto the partakers of the secret wisdom of your creation.

Analysis of the Third Key

Heavenly Christ declares himself to be "a circle, on whose hands stand 12 kingdoms." This immediately brings two images to mind—the circle of the zodiac, and the face of a clock. The clock imagery is reinforced by the mention of "hands" and later by the reference to "the true ages of time." The clock face is based upon the revolving ring of the zodiac and its twelve signs, six of which at any given time are above, or moving above, the horizon of the earth, and six of which are below.

The sun and moon each rule half of the signs. The sun in Leo has authority over the signs on the right side of the zodiac: Virgo (Mercury), Libra

(Venus), Scorpio (Mars), Sagittarius (Jupiter), and Capricorn (Saturn). The moon in Cancer has authority over the signs on the left side of the zodiac: Gemini (Mercury), Taurus (Venus), Aries (Mars), Pisces (Jupiter), and Aquarius (Saturn).

The six seats "of living breath" may refer to those signs of the zodiac under the sun, and the six seats that are "as sharp sickles, or the horns of death" may refer to the signs under the moon. Both the sickle and the horn are symbols of the crescent moon. Here, they are also death images. The meaning is that six of the kingdoms are kingdoms of light, and the other six are kingdoms of darkness. This is supported by the imagery of sleeping and waking, in the sense of death and resurrection, "wherein the creatures of the Earth are and are not except by mine own hands; which also sleep and shall rise."

Instead of the six signs under the sun and the opposite six under the moon, the reference may be to the six houses of the zodiac that are forever above the horizon, and the opposite six that are forever below the horizon. Whereas the signs revolve around the heavens once with each cycle of the sun, the houses remain fixed relative to the earth. There is a strong association between the signs and their corresponding houses. In ancient astrology, which was the astrology practiced during the Renaissance and Elizabethan times, signs and houses are often spoken of as one and the same.

If we take our cue from *The Hieroglyphic Monad* of John Dee, where the zodiac is divided between Aries and Taurus, the line between the upper and lower crescents of Aries and Taurus forms a perfect cross of right angles with the line between the left and right crescents of Cancer and Leo. This cross on the zodiac may have been Dee's hidden message, concealed in the structure of the monad symbol. It is the structure of the heavenly throne and the cosmic clock, described below.

The use of the word "kingdoms" cannot fail to call to mind the twelve tribes of Israel, each of which was granted a portion of the world to rule. The ritual of crossing the river Jordan that Moses received from God, and conveyed to Joshua, involved six of the tribes, symbolically under the sun and the Urim of the breastplate of Aaron, offering blessings to those children of Israel who abided by the holy law, and the other six tribes, symbolically under the moon and the Thummim of the breastplate, who gave curses to those who violated the covenant. This rite of passage is treated in detail in Chapter IX, but I mention it here to emphasize that the Enochian Keys did not germinate in isolation, but grew from the dark, occult soil of the Old Testament writings.

The number of kingdoms, twelve, confirms that we are dealing with the twelve Banners of Tetragrammaton. In Kelley's vision, these are borne out of each Watchtower upon three banners, or ensigns. The Enochian names of God upon these three flags are alternate titles for the three Banners of

Tetragrammaton associated with either the element of that Watchtower or the quarter of the compass sealed by that Watchtower—it is difficult to tell which.

This is an important point to make clear. If we associate the Banners and the Enochian names of God with the elements and their corresponding signs of the zodiac, we will link up each set of three elemental Banners and Enochian names upon a Watchtower with the three zodiac signs of that element and space them at intervals of 120 degrees around the zodiac. This is the system I have adopted in Appendix E. On the other hand, if we associate the Banners and Enochian names of God with the directions, we must group all three Banners and names of a Watchtower on the three congruent signs of the zodiac in that quarter of space. This appears to be the system adopted by John Dee (see James, *The Enochian Magick of Dr. John Dee*, p. 119). These two approaches result in fundamentally different magical structures and cannot easily be reconciled.

If we take as an example the Watchtower of the South, which in my opinion is the Watchtower in the lower left quadrant on the reformed Great Table of Raphael, and associate the direction south with elemental fire (the usual association in modern magic), by linking the Watchtower primarily with the element of fire, the three names of God on the Watchtower (MOR, DIAL, HCTGA) may be related to the three Banners of fire (IHVH, IHHV, IVHH) and the three fire signs of the zodiac (Aries, Sagittarius, Leo). See the table of the Banners in Appendix E.

Alternatively, if we associate the Watchtower of the South primarily with the southern quarter of space, as John Dee seems to have done, the three names of God on the Watchtower of the South will fall on the directions south-southeast, south, and south-southwest (based on a division of the compass into twelve directions, or points). The fixed zodiac sign Leo (commonly linked with the south in modern magic) will fall on the south point, with Cancer and Virgo on either side. All three points of the compass and their corresponding zodiac signs will be associated with the element of the south. This is commonly supposed to be fire, but for John Dee may have been air (see Chapter XVI).

As I observed in Chapter XVI, in my opinion neither the original Great Table nor the reformed Table of Raphael show the correct placement of the Watchtowers, which should be located upon the Table clockwise beginning in the quadrant of the east in the order of their delivery by the Enochian angels. When this is done, the placement accurately reflects Dee's own illustration of the circle of the twelve Enochian banners in his *Liber Scientiae*: east—ORO, IBAH, AOZPI; south—MOR, DIAL, HCTGA; west—OIP, TEAA, PDOCE; north—MPH, ARSL, GAIOL.

The spirit Ave states in expounding Kelley's vision: "The 12 Banners are the 12 names of God, that govern all the creatures upon the earth, visible and invisible, comprehending 3, 4, and 5" (Casaubon, p. 170). Clearly, these numbers refer to the number of letters in the names. In the Key, the Messiah says: "I made you stewards and placed you in seats 12 of government, giving unto every one of you power successively over 456." This number probably refers to the names of the angels comprehended in the Sephirothic Crosses of the lesser angles of the Watchtowers, and in the four squares above each lesser cross, called in the Golden Dawn the Kerubic Squares.

The Kerubic Squares yield a name of four letters; the crossbar of each lesser cross gives a name of five letters; and the upright of each lesser cross gives a name of six letters—thus the 456 in the Key. That this power is given "successively" suggests that the name of God of three letters rules the Kerubic name of four letters, the God name of four letters rules the angelic name of five letters on the arm of the cross, and the God name of five letters rules the angelic name of six letters on the column of the cross.

All twelve Enochian names of God are applied to each of the four Watchtowers. The three names of each Watchtower apply to the corresponding lesser angles of all four Watchtowers. There is no need to struggle here with elemental associations. For example, if we choose the corrected Great Table of Raphael, the Watchtower in the lower right corner has the God names OIP, TEAA, PDOCE. Therefore the spirits in the lower-right lesser angle of the Watchtower in the upper left quadrant of the Great Table will be ruled by these names: XGSD (OIP), ALOAI (TEAA), AOURRZ (PDOCE).

I must stress that this relationship is founded upon my personal interpretation of the Keys and Dee's magical records and does not correspond with the Golden Dawn system. It is my purpose in this work to offer fresh insights, not merely to reproduce dogma. Consequently, some of what I set forth conflicts with the accepted methods of Enochian magic as it is worked by modern ritualists, many of whom embrace the Enochian teachings of the Golden Dawn without ever subjecting them to critical examination.

The "seats 12 of government" are the signs of the zodiac, which rule the "true ages of time" through their relationship to the twelve houses of the heavens. The houses are like a great clock face upon which move the pointers of the sun and the moon. The moon goes around the dial of the houses approximately thirteen times for every single revolution of the sun, making the sun like the hour hand on a clock and the moon like the minute hand.

This metaphor may seem strained, until we examine the great clock in the Piazza San Marco in Venice. This venerable old clock is the perfect expression of the throne of heaven described by St. John in Revelation 4, which so often surfaces in the Enochian Keys as a cosmic timepiece. The clock is reproduced by T. Wynne Griffon in *History of the Occult* (London:

Bison Books, 1991), p. 39. I am not suggesting a direct link between this clock and John Dee, but I wish to point out that the symbolism of the throne as cosmic clock is of primal importance in both Christian and Enochian mythology.

The face of this old clock represents the blue vault of heaven speckled with stars. In the exact center is a small sphere, representing the axis of the world, fixed upon a disk divided radially into six parts, like the symbol for Spirit (⊗). Around this, a larger, second ring turns. It has twelve radial divisions and is flecked all over with stars. Upon it, a sphere representing the moon points to the golden symbols of the twelve signs of the zodiac, which decorate a still larger third ring. Sweeping around the ring of the zodiac is a clock hand shaped like a blazing sun. Its point extends beyond the zodiac ring to the outermost fourth ring of the clock face, which is divided into twenty-four parts numbered with Roman numerals, for the twenty-four hours of the day. Although the hand of the sun is longer than that of the moon, the sun, which points to the hours, appears to me to be the hour hand. This would be symbolically correct.

The circular face of the clock is enclosed in a square with four circular windows, one in each corner (symbolizing the four beasts). Above the clock is a statue of the seated Virgin Mary holding Christ upon her knee. She represents the Queen of Heaven in Revelation 12:1. To her right is a large Roman numeral X; to her left is an equally large Arabic numeral 5 (in connection with these numerals, see the description of the hieroglyphic monad in Chapter VIII, specifically Dee's comments regarding the Roman numeral X). In passing, it might be pointed out that much of this symbolism appears, in a degenerate form, upon the tarot card of the World, or Universe.

Although there is no explicit mention of the east, this Third Key begins the cycle of sixteen Keys related to the four quarters. The cycle takes the form of four revolutions sunwise around the heavens, each revolution beginning in the east. The purpose of this Key seems to be to set forth the structure that will follow. "In the first" perhaps refers to the first angle, the east, where this Key is placed. The "corners" or quarters of the earth are mentioned, from which the "stewards" shall pour down their vitalizing "fires of life" and cause "increase continually," signifying that all life is sustained by the Banners of Tetragrammaton. The "highest vessels" may be a reference to the Wings.

The Fourth Key

> I have set my feet in the south, and have looked about me, saying, are not the Thunders of Increase numbered 33, which reign in the second angle? Under whom I have placed 9639 whom none hath yet numbered, but one; in whom the second beginning of

things are and wax strong; which also successively are
the number of time: and their powers are as the first
456. Arise, you Sons of Pleasure, and visit the Earth:
for I am the Lord your God, which is, and liveth. In the
name of the Creator, move, and show yourselves as
pleasant deliverers, that you may praise him amongst
the sons of men.

Analysis of the Fourth Key

This Key refers to the spirits of the "second angle," which, moving around
the circle of the earth sunwise from the starting point in the east, is the
angle of the south. In the Third Key reference was made to the "corners of
your governments." The first corner is that of the east, and the corresponding angle of the Great Table.

The "Thunders of Increase" are angels, said by the Messiah to reign in the
second angle—the south. These are probably the same as the "thunderings
and voices" that proceed out of the throne of heavenly Christ in Revelation
4:5. Further on, they are called "Sons of Pleasure." This suggests the angels
who lusted after the daughters of men and bred within the wombs of these
mortal women the "mighty men which were of old" (Gen. 6:4). These fallen
angels taught their offspring the mechanical and occult arts, such as the making of weapons of war, the working of magic spells, the beautifying of the face
with cosmetics, and so on. In this way they created dissatisfaction and discord
among mankind. The increase referred to in this Key has a double meaning:
sexual generation, but also the breeding of confusion through diversity.

It is perhaps significant from a magical perspective that Christ stands with
his feet in the south. The magician, having assumed the Christ-form to vibrate
this evocation, will naturally wish to emulate the Messiah in every way possible. Therefore, the Key will be spoken with the feet in the south. This might be
interpreted as facing south (since, if the magician faces south and then lies
back in the magic circle, his feet will naturally extend to the south); alternatively, it could be interpreted to mean that the Key is vibrated while standing
in the southern quarter of the circle. The latter seems more likely to me.

If this interpretation is accurate, by extension all the Keys that can be
linked to the quarters should be vibrated while standing in the corresponding
quarters of the magic circle. Keys Three, Seven, Eleven, and Fifteen are
vibrated from the east; Keys Four, Eight, Twelve, and Sixteen are vibrated from
the south; Keys Five, Nine, Thirteen, and Seventeen are vibrated from the
west; and Keys Six, Ten, Fourteen, and Eighteen are vibrated from the north.

It seems likely that the angels referred to as the "Thunders of Increase"
are similar to those that rule in the first angle—the three Enochian banner
names borne out of the Watchtower of the East upon the flags. In fact, it is

said of them that in them is "the second beginning of things" and that "their powers are as the first 456." It is also said of them: "which also, successively, are the number of time." It is evident from this that "the true ages of time" mentioned in the Third Key are not the spirits 456, but the spirits of the Enochian banners.

The words "second beginning of things" seem to mean that this Key falls on the first subquarter of the second Watchtower, the Watchtower of the South. All four Keys of this initial cycle, Keys Three, Four, Five, and Six, begin their respective Watchtowers (see illustration on page 185).

Concerning the puzzling use of 33 and 9639, I can offer no solution. So far as I am aware, no student of Enochian magic has been able to completely explain the use of numbers in the Keys. I can only observe that it is obvious that the numbers are not to be taken whole, but divided into digits, or groups of digits. There is a noticeable preponderance of three, six, and nine in these numbers, particularly the sets of larger numbers. Many Keys contain two numbers, a smaller one of one or two digits and a larger number of three, four, or five digits. Clearly, some hidden relationship exists between these sets. It probably arises from the number tables that the Enochian spirits used to generate the Keys, which they pointed out letter by letter to Kelley in the crystal.

The Fifth Key

> The Mighty Sounds have entered into the third angle, and are become as olives in the Olive Mount, looking with gladness upon the Earth, and dwelling in the brightness of the heavens as continual comforters; unto whom I fastened pillars of gladness 19, and gave them vessels to water the Earth with her creatures; and they are the brothers of the first and second, and the beginning of their own seats, which are garnished with continually burning lamps 69636, whose numbers are as the first, the ends, and the contents of time. Therefore come you and obey your creation; visit us in peace and comfort; conclude us as receivers of your mysteries. For why? Our Lord and Master is all one.

Analysis of the Fifth Key

The "Mighty Sounds" who have entered into the third angle, that of the west, are another version of the "Thunders of Increase" who rule the second angle. They are said to be the "brothers" of the first and second angles and the "beginning of their own seats," because this Key falls upon the initial eastern subquarter of the Watchtower of the West. For this reason its spirits are the brothers of the spirits in the first subquarters of the "first and second" Watchtowers of the East and South and are similarly the "beginning of their own seats," which are the quarters of the Watchtower of the West.

The olive tree is a symbol of chastity and holiness, and also a symbol of the Messiah. In Zechariah 4:14, the two olive trees that continually empty golden oil out of themselves are said to be "the two anointed ones, that stand by the Lord of the whole earth." It was on the Mount of Olives that Jesus delivered his famous Sermon on the Mount. In Revelation 11:6, these two olive trees have the power to shut up the rain and withhold it from the earth. That is why in the Key they are given "vessels to water the Earth with her creatures."

The earth is personified as a female spirit; more than this, she is a mother goddess who generates living things in her womb. The creatures of the earth are her children. The Soul of the World (*anima mundi*) figures prominently in Greek philosophy, and from this source found its way into the Hermetic mysticism of the Renaissance. This image of the earth as a fertile mother becomes very important in the Key of the thirty Aethers.

The "continually burning lamps" may be a reference to the seven lamps of fire burning before the throne of God (Rev. 4:5). This ties in nicely with the olives of Zechariah, which ceaselessly pour their oil into a bowl through golden pipes. The perpetual oil feeds the perpetual lamps. The word "continual" or "continually" occurs a number of times in the Keys and perhaps is intended to convey actions that transcend time.

Although the numbers in this Key are as inscrutable as all the others, they do evoke certain significant occult images. The "pillars of gladness 19" suggest one plus nine pillars, for a total of ten, the number of the *sephiroth* on the tree of the kabbalah. The larger number, 69636, is especially fascinating, because, separated into two parts alternately by digits, it yields 666 and 93, two very important numbers in Aleister Crowley's cult of Thelema. The first is the number of the Great Beast of Revelation 13:18, which Crowley believed himself to be; the second is the number of LAShTAL, numerically in Hebrew LA(31) + ShT(31) + AL(31), the formula for awakening kundalini through sexual techniques developed by the O.T.O., one of the magical organizations with which Crowley was associated. This sexual magic is sometimes called the 93 current.

Of course, Dee and Kelley had no connection with Aleister Crowley, but such synchronicities are not to be dismissed in magic, which spans the barriers of ordinary space and time. At the very least, Crowley must have been strongly moved by the chance numerology of this number in the Fifth Key, since it expresses so succinctly his system of magic. With intriguing enigmatism, the Messiah explains that these "numbers" (note the plural) are as "the first, the ends, and the contents of time." Therefore this number is connected in some intimate way with 456, the "powers" of the "true ages of time."

Very significant is the phrase "obey your creation." In the Keys, the "creation" of the spirits signifies the reason for which God created them. A better translation would be "obey your destiny." The Messiah, through the voice of the magician, is commanding the angels addressed in the Fifth Key to fulfill their reason for being, and to act as they were designed by their Creator to act in the universe. He is saying: Come forth into manifest being, and by this coming forth realize your purpose, which until this manifestation has been latent and unrealized.

The Sixth Key

> The spirits of the fourth angle are nine, mighty in the firmaments of waters; whom the First hath planted as a torment to the wicked and a garland to the righteous, giving unto them fiery darts to van the Earth, and 7699 continual workmen; whose courses visit with comfort the Earth, and are in government and continuance as the second and the third. Wherefore, harken unto my voice: I have talked of you and I move you in power and presence, whose works shall be a song of honor and the praise of your God in your creation.

Analysis of the Sixth Key

The angels of the fourth angle are "mighty in the firmaments of waters." The firmament is the vault of heaven, or heaven itself. The firmament of waters is the ninth sphere, called the crystalline, which was above the eighth sphere of the fixed stars and was thought to be composed of aether. "Some by that firmamentary division of the waters, have dreamt of a watery heaven above the stars" (*Complete Oxford English Dictionary:* "firmamentary"). The reference is to Genesis 1:6–7. There is also something in alchemy called firmamental water, described as a liquid as pure as the firmament. Kelley, who was an accomplished alchemist, would certainly have been familiar with this term, which was in common use in his day.

Again we find the familiar theme of judgment. The "mighty" angels of the fourth angle are "a torment to the wicked and a garland to the righteous." They accomplish this discrimination through "fiery darts" with which they "van the Earth." A dart is the old word for arrow. Van has two basic meanings. To van is to winnow the chaff from grain by tossing it up into the wind and catching it upon a large, flat shovel. To van also means to fly, since van is another word for wing, and in this sense was sometimes applied to angels. Thus, to "van the Earth" is a pun meaning both to winnow out the chaff of the unrighteous and to fly across the land upon feathered wings. Arrows are feathered, and in ancient times these feathers were believed to magically impart the power of flight. To these mighty spirits of the fourth angle the First, or God, has also given 7699 "continual workmen." As mentioned previously, the word "continual" in the Keys signifies eternal or unending.

These mighty spirits are "in government and continuance as the second and the third," meaning that the spirits in the first subquarter of the fourth Watchtower, the Watchtower of the North, are similar in kind and function to those serving in the first subquarters of the second and third angles of the Great Table, the Watchtowers of the South and West.

Their "courses" visit with comfort the earth. This is a complex word. In Elizabethan times, a course was a point of the compass—the word was used in this sense by Shakespeare. Thus the courses of the mighty spirits of the fourth angle, the Watchtower of the North, are their resident compass points. "Course" also means a circular motion of a heavenly body, as in the course of the moon. Finally, the word "course" can mean a continuous process of time, or a succession of events. Again, we have the time metaphor that is so pervasive throughout the Keys.

Notice that the Messiah commands the spirits to "harken unto my voice," because (as is true of the serpent) all his power is in his jaws—that is, in his words. He says: "I have talked of you, and I move you in power and presence," because, by his articulation of the qualities of the spirits, he brings them forth into manifest being. He actually creates them with his speech. Existence is again equated with words where he says, "whose works shall be a song of honor." Not only do words frame and bring forth the spirits into the world, but the actions of the spirits in the world are, magically speaking, their words, or "song," to God.

Christ tells the spirits that their works will be "the praise of your God in your creation," meaning that the fulfillment of the destiny of the spirits of the fourth angle is itself a form of worship. By doing what they were created to do, the spirits commune with their Creator. This wording is ambiguous and can be taken two ways: that the works of the spirits will praise God, or that God will praise the spirits for their works. Since prayer is a union with God, where the soul of the individual is dissolved and lost in the infinite sea of divinity, both these interpretations are equally valid. The spirits praise God, and God praises the spirits, because in the fulfillment of the work of the spirits they become indistinguishable from God.

The Seventh Key

The east is a house of virgins singing praises amongst
the Flames of the first glory, wherein the Lord hath
opened his mouth, and they are become 28 living

dwellings in whom the strength of men rejoiceth; and they are appareled with ornaments of brightness, such as work wonders on all creatures; whose kingdoms and continuance are as the third and fourth, strong towers and places of comfort, the seats of mercy and continuance. O you Servants of Mercy, move, appear, sing praises unto the Creator, and be mighty amongst us; for to this remembrance is given power, and our strength waxeth strong in our Comforter.

Analysis of the Seventh Key

This Key begins the second sunwise circuit around the points of the compass on the second subquarter of the Watchtower of the East. The "Flames" are the same spirits mentioned in the Second Key as the "Burning Flames" and who figure so prominently in Keys Fifteen, Sixteen, Seventeen, and Eighteen. Geoffrey James points out (*The Enochian Magick of Dr. John Dee*, p. 78) that the Enochian for "Flames of the first glory" is IALPIRGAH, a contraction of two words—IALPRG (burning flame) and GAH (spirit). A literal translation might be "spirits of burning flame." The "first glory" perhaps refers to the rosy dawn, the goddess Aurora, who had many lovers.

The "house of virgins" would seem to be a reference to the biblical book of Esther, which describes the sexual habits of King Ahasuerus. It was the custom of Ahasuerus to keep two houses. In one house all the fairest virgin girls in his kingdom were gathered together for purification. After twelve full months of ritual cleansing (six months with oil of myrrh and six months with sweet incense), each virgin went in to the king's bedchamber and spent the night with him. In reward, he gave the girl anything her heart desired—beautiful robes, jewelry, servants. Then she was sent to live in a second house with the other concubines, and "she came in unto the king no more, except the king delighted in her, and that she were called by name" (Esther 2:14).

The imagery of this Key reflects the legend of Ahasuerus. The virgins of the east become "28 living dwellings in whom the strength of men rejoiceth" when the Lord "hath opened his mouth," or called them. Afterwards, "they are appareled with ornaments of brightness such as work wonders on all creatures." The virgins have become courtesans who allure and bewitch with their adornments. Also, they are individualized by names, which define them.

However, the primary biblical reference here seems to be with the 144,000 of the chosen who have the name of the Father written on their foreheads (Rev. 7:3–4). Twelve thousand of those who are blessed are chosen from each of the twelve tribes. Therefore, it is evident that they are sealed with the twelve Banners of Tetragrammaton, one Banner for each of the tribes. As these chosen ones stand before the throne, divine harpers begin to sing and play:

> And they sung as it were a new song before the throne, and before the four beasts, and the elders: and no man could learn that song but the hundred and forty and four thousand, which were redeemed from the earth. These are they which were not defiled with women; for they are virgins. These are they which follow the Lamb whithersoever he goeth. These were redeemed from among men, being the first fruits unto God and to the Lamb. (Rev. 14:3–4)

Although it is very dangerous to attach specific symbolic meanings to the numbers in the Keys, I am tempted to look upon this description as a metaphor for the progress of the sun through the twenty-eight mansions of the moon. The sun enters each house of the moon successively in his yearly course around the heavens, and by his entry he adorns that house with his splendor. Each house thus has twelve months to prepare, just as did the virgins who purified themselves for King Ahasuerus, who cleansed themselves six months with oil (water) and six months with incense (fire).

Maintaining the pattern established in Keys Five and Six, the Messiah says of these living dwellings of the house of the east that their "kingdoms and continuance are as the third and fourth, strong towers and places of comfort, the seats of mercy and continuance." The "third and fourth" are the angles of the west and north, indicating that the hierarchal structure that applied in the first circuit around the points of the compass also applies to the second circuit. The "strong towers" is a reference to the Watchtowers. Continuance is again emphasized because the Watchtowers sustain the very existence of the universe—were they to fail, the world would end.

The kingdoms of these spirits of the east are called "seats of mercy." A seat is a place of government, the residence of a ruler. Further down the Key, the spirits are called "servants of mercy." This Key would seem to relate strongly to the fourth *sephirah, Chesed* (Mercy). Indeed, at the end God is called "our Comforter."

Very interesting from a magical perspective are the words "for to this remembrance is given power." The remembrance referred to is the recitation of the qualities of the spirits of the east. Power is given over these spirits to the magician who can correctly define their characteristics, because in the remembrance of the spirits, the spirits are born anew into the universe.

The Eighth Key

> The midday, the first, is as the third heaven made of hyacinth pillars 26, in whom the elders are become strong; which I have prepared for my own righteousness, saith the Lord; whose long continuance shall be

as bucklers to the stooping dragon, and like unto the harvest of a widow. How many are there which remain in the glory of the Earth, which are, and shall not see death, until this house fall and the dragon sink! Come away, for the Thunders have spoken; come away, for the crowns of the temple and the coat of Him that is, and was, and shall be crowned, are divided. Come, appear to the terror of the Earth, and to our comfort, and of such as are prepared.

Analysis of the Eighth Key

The "midday" signifies both the brightness of noon and the quarter of the south. The "third heaven" may refer to the third sphere, that of Venus, if we count the spheres in the usual way, with the moon in the first and lowest sphere. Pillars occur in the Fifth Key, which relates to the west, so it is possible that the "third heaven" refers to the Watchtower of the West. Here the pillars are said to be of "hyacinth," which perhaps means they are blue. Hyacinth was for the ancients a blue stone, likely the sapphire. Its color was synonymous with the clear light of heaven, which is why the Hebrew for "sapphire" forms the basis for the word *sephiroth*. Hyacinth is also a type of lily connected with the Greek legend of Hyacinthus, a beautiful youth accidentally killed by Apollo. Some of Hyacinthus' blood dripped onto the ground, and from the spot sprang up a purple flower with the Greek letters **AI, AI** (woe, woe) written on its petals.

The pillars suggest a house of God, or temple, and both these images occur later in the Key. They are said to be 26, which may signify two parallel rows of six pillars each. Within this house, the elders "are become strong." The "long continuance" of the pillars that support the vault of heaven in the south (for this is the image they evoke) makes them bucklers, or shields, against the "stooping dragon." Some versions of the Key give "stooping dragons" here, but the singular seems more applicable, since only a single dragon is mentioned later in the Key.

The dragon is the symbol of chaos, or Satan:

> And there was war in heaven: Michael and his angels fought against the dragon; and the dragon fought and his angels, and prevailed not; neither was their place found any more in heaven. And the great dragon was cast out, that old serpent, called the Devil, and Satan, which deceiveth the whole world: he was cast out into the earth, and his angels were cast out with him. . .

And they overcame him by the blood of the Lamb, and by the word of their testimony; and they loved not their lives unto the death. Therefore rejoice, ye heavens, and ye that dwell in them. Woe to the inhabiters of the earth and of the sea! for the devil is come down unto you, having great wrath, because he knoweth that he hath but a short time (Rev. 12:7–9, 11–2).

It is vital to grasp that the imagery in the Keys is apocalyptic if we are to gain any understanding of its meaning. In using the Keys, the magician, speaking as the voice of the heavenly Christ, is calling through the gates of the Watchtowers the wrathful angels and spirits of righteous judgment that will bring about the final destruction of the universe.

The annihilation of the universe is a cause for rejoicing in heaven, because all division and diversity that arose with the creation of the world will be reduced to perfect harmony once again. However, it is a cause for terror and mourning upon the earth, because all created things will meet their end in pain and confusion. The great dragon, Satan, is not cast down into a bottomless pit in these verses (that comes later), he is cast upon the face of the earth, where he acts as one of the instruments of its destruction.

To stoop means to swoop down upon folded wings to strike at prey. Hawks stoop upon pigeons when they descend through the sky like thunderbolts and strike the slower birds with their talons. Thus the "stooping dragon" is kept back from his prey, the living things of the earth, by the "long continuance" of the pillars of the Watchtower of the South, which act as shields upheld against his attack.

There is a striking contrast here with the second image, the "harvest of a widow." The harvest of a widow is lamentation and want. This seems to be an allusion to Babylon, who is personified as a harlot:

How much she hath glorified herself, and lived deliciously, so much torment and sorrow give her: for she saith in her heart, I sit a queen, and am no widow, and shall see no sorrow. Therefore shall her plagues come in one day, death, and mourning, and famine; and she shall be utterly burned with fire: for strong is the Lord God who judgeth her. (Rev. 18:7–8)

Coronzon is prevented for a time from seizing his prey by the barrier of the firmament supported upon the hyacinth pillars. It is evident that this frustration will not last long. The rhetorical question, really more of a statement, asks: "How many are there which remain in the glory of the Earth, which are, and shall not see death until this house fall, and the dragon sink!" This notion of imminent destruction is a common feature of apocalyptic literature.

It is not clear if the sinking of the dragon refers to his descent upon the earth or his ultimate fall into the bottomless pit (Rev. 20:2–3). However, the final part of the Key seems to summon the dragon: "Come, appear to the terror of the Earth, and to our comfort, and of such as are prepared." Those who are "prepared" are those who come before the throne of heavenly Christ clothed in white. They have no reason to fear or regret the annihilation of the world because they are the chosen of God: "For the Lamb which is in the midst of the throne shall feed them, and shall lead them unto living fountains of waters" (Rev. 7:17). That is why they actively seek to evoke Coronzon into visible appearance "to the terror of the Earth"—the destruction of the world is their resurrection in service before the throne of the Messiah.

The description of Christ as "him that is, was, and shall be crowned" seems to be derived directly from the words of the twenty-four elders around the throne, who fall upon their faces in worship, saying: "We give thee thanks, O Lord God Almighty, which art, and wast, and art to come; because thou hast taken to thee thy great power, and hast reigned" (Rev. 11:17).

The Ninth Key

> A mighty guard of fire with two-edged swords flaming (which have vials eight of wrath for two times and a half: whose Wings are of wormwood, and of the marrow of salt), have settled their feet in the west, and are measured with their ministers 9996. These gather up the moss of the Earth as the rich man doth his treasure. Cursed are they whose iniquities they are! In their eyes are millstones greater than the Earth, and from their mouths run seas of blood. Their heads are covered with diamond, and upon their hands are marble sleeves. Happy is he on whom they frown not. For why? The God of righteousness rejoiceth in them. Come away, and not your vials! For the time is such as requireth comfort.

Analysis of the Ninth Key

The "mighty guard of fire" armed with "two-edged swords flaming" would seem to be the same class of beings as the "mighty" spirits of the Sixth Key, who are armed with "fiery darts," or arrows. Perhaps they are also the same class as the "flames of the first glory" mentioned in the Seventh Key. As pointed out earlier, the two-edged sword is usually a symbol of judgment because it can cut either way, allowing its punishment to be balanced. Madimi, Dee and Kelley's spirit guide, states explicitly the meaning of this symbol: "The vengeance of God is a two-edged Sword, and cutteth the rebellious wicked ones in pieces" (Casaubon, p. 32).

The vials of wrath are an obvious reference to the "seven golden vials full of the wrath of God" (Rev. 15:7) given to seven angels of retribution by one of the four beasts to spread plagues over the face of the earth. It might be argued that the vials are eight in the Key, not seven. However, we have no way of knowing if the number eight is to be literally applied to the vials. In other Keys, there seems to be no direct connection between the numbers and the things described in the Keys—for example, in the Eighth Key, we cannot be sure that "hyacinth pillars 26" means that there are twenty-six pillars. The number may have some other occult meaning.

In Dee's manuscript record of the English version of the Keys, vial is spelled *viol*, which has the dual meaning of a small glass vessel, but also of a stringed musical instrument played by a bow. Viol the musical instrument does occur in the prophetic books of the Bible (see Isaiah 14:11), but in my opinion it is unlikely that this alternate meaning is intended by the angelic author of the Keys.

It is possible that the eight vials are intended to be linked to the great dragon, Coronzon, who in Revelation is given eight kings to serve him: "And there are seven kings: five are fallen, and one is, and the other is not yet come; and when he cometh, he must continue a short space. And the beast that was, and is not, even he is the eighth, and is of the seven, and goeth into perdition" (Rev. 17:10–1). This number may also be a dark mirror reference to the eighth biblical king, Hadar, of whom no death is spoken (Genesis 36:39). In the teachings of the kabbalah, Hadar is considered to be the rectifier and giver of spiritual life to the seven mortal kings that preceded him.

The wrath of the vials is said to be "for two times and a half," a seemingly inexplicable reference, save that it also occurs in Revelation. The mother of the Word of God, he who is the mounted version of the heavenly Christ who rules all the nations of the world with a rod of iron, is persecuted by the red dragon, Satan, forcing her to flee his vengeance: "And to the woman were given two wings of a great eagle, that she might fly into the wilderness, into her place, where she is nourished for a time, and times, and half a time, from the face of the serpent" (Rev. 12:14). We may gather from this that the plagues of the seven vials were of the same duration as the persecution of the mother of the Word.

A "time" is a year, but years in heaven are not reckoned in the same way as years upon the earth, the Enochian angels inform Dee, so for human purposes a time might better be equaled to the indefinite duration of an age. It should be noted that there are thirty Aethers, or Airs. If these are applied to the circle of the zodiac, each sign receives two and a half Aethers; similarly, if they are applied to the face of the clock, each five minute division receives two and a half Aethers. This may form the basis for this odd number.

The "mighty guard of fire" is said to have Wings "of wormwood, and of the marrow of salt." I have capitalized the word "Wings" here to indicate that it refers to angels. Wormwood signifies poison, specifically poisoned water. It is the name of the evil star that fell from heaven at the sounding of the third trumpet: "and the third part of the waters became wormwood; and many men died of the waters, because they were made bitter" (Rev. 8:11). Marrow in the Bible is usually a symbol of life, but "marrow of salt" is a symbol of death. Salt was sown in the ground so that nothing might grow there. It was used in funeral services to purify. Wings always symbolize active powers; therefore Wings of "wormwood" are the same as angels of death.

It is said of this "guard of fire" that they have "settled their feet in the west," confirming that this Key applies to the western quarter. The setting of the feet indicates possession or dominion. I can find no obvious explanation for the number of their ministers, 9996. It is said of these ministers (or of the angels of the vials—it is not clear): "These gather up the moss of the Earth as the rich man doth his treasure." Moss was related to grave mold— there was a special type of moss harvested from the skulls of dead men for medical purposes. Common moss was gathered to stop up the cracks between wall stones and roofing slates. The "moss of the Earth" would seem to be a poetic way of saying "human corpses." Those humans are cursed who do not stand among the redeemed around the throne of God. They are the "iniquities" of the angels of the vials—that is to say, they are vessels of iniquity harvested by the servants of the fiery angels.

These angels are terrible to look upon. In their eyes are great millstones, such as may grind the bones of men. From their mouths, as from a winepress, stream seas of blood. This image of reaping the iniquitous from the earth and grinding them in a great winepress occurs in the vision of St. John:

> And the angel thrust in his sickle into the earth, and gathered the vine of the earth, and cast it into the great winepress of the wrath of God. And the winepress was trodden without the city, and blood came out of the winepress, even unto the horse bridles, by the space of a thousand and six hundred furlongs. (Rev. 14:19–20)

That the heads of the angels are "covered with diamond" and upon their hands are "marble sleeves" symbolizes the hardness of their judgment— they will not be moved to pity. As St. John says of those that bear the mark of the Beast: "The same shall drink of the wine of the wrath of God, which is poured out without mixture into the cup of his indignation; and he shall be tormented with fire and brimstone in the presence of the holy angels, and in the presence of the Lamb" (Rev. 14:10).

The unusual but effective image of an angel whose head is covered with diamond occurs outside the Keys in Dee's magical record, where Kelley describes to Dee a vision of the heavenly throne of Christ:

> And there sitteth One in a Judgement seat, with all his teeth fiery.... All the place is like Gold, garnished with precious stones. On his head is a great stone; covering his head; a stone most bright, brighter then fire. (A *True & Faithful Relation,* p. 61)

Dee's occult diaries are filled with apocalyptic prophecies spoken by the Enochian angels. The sample below illustrates the pervasive doomsday imagery that surrounds the Keys and shows how close the prophecies of the angels are to those delivered by St. John:

> I will plague the people, and their blood shall become Rivers. Fathers shall eat their own Children, And the Earth shall be barren: The Beasts of the field shall perish, And the Waters shall be poisoned. The Air shall infect her Creatures, And in the Deep shall be roaring. Great Babylon shall be built, And the son of wickednesse, shall sit in Judgement.... From the North shall come a Whirlwind, And the Hills shall open their mouths: And there shall a Dragon flie out, such as never was. (*True & Faithful Relation,* p. 43)

The last part of this Key is interesting because it shows that, even though this in an evocation of a class of vengeful angels who will take part in the final apocalypse of the world, the Key is designed to control those angels for the personal use of the magician. "Come away, and not your vials!" means that the angels, or their ministers, should come without their poisons. Otherwise, the magician working this Enochian magic might expect to die of plague.

The attempt to call the angels of wrath without their vials seems somewhat naive, since the identity of these angels is bound up with their function—they are what they do. But the Key was delivered by the Enochian angels, not composed by Dee and Kelley, suggesting to me that the words "and not your vials" were inserted as a palliative, to still the misgivings of Dee about the dangers of the Keys. It is foolish to suppose that these angels can appear without their vials, since the vials are a part of them—however, it is possible that the vials may remain sealed and concealed from the sight of the magician.

One of the seven angels does appear without his vial in Revelation 17:1, but only after he has emptied the vial out upon the face of the earth. At that point, he becomes a different angel, since he has been assigned a different function by the heavenly Christ.

I am inclined to think that the words "and not your vials" were inserted into the Key to deceive Dee and lead him to believe that he could work the magic of the Keys without bringing on the apocalypse—their true purpose. Nowhere do the angels admit the secret purpose of the Keys to Dee. On April 12, 1584, just before beginning the dictation of the Keys, the angel Nalvage states their supposed function:

> I am therefore to instruct and inform you, according to your Doctrine delivered, which is contained in 49 Tables. In 49 voyces, or callings: which are the Natural Keyes, to open those, not 49 but 48 (for One is not to be opened) Gates of understanding, whereby you shall have knowledge to move every Gate, and to call out as many as you please, or shall be thought necessary, which can very well, righteously, and wisely, open unto you the secrets of their Cities, & make you understand perfectly the contents in the Tables. Through which knowledge you shall easily be able to judge, not as the world doth, but perfectly of the world, and of all things contained within the Compasse of Nature, and of all things which are subject to an end. (*A True & Faithful Relation,* p. 77)

Dee may not have been deceived at all. As a good Christian, who might be fairly confident that he did not carry the mark of the Beast, he could view the final destruction of the world with eager joy as one of the select. He may have recognized that the angels intended him to be an unwitting tool in the initiation of the final Armageddon, but may have welcomed the role as a humble servant of Christ. On the other hand, Dee never worked the magic of the Keys in any serious, sustained way during his lifetime. Perhaps he was afraid of it.

The Tenth Key

> The Thunders of Judgement and Wrath are numbered and are harbored in the north in the likeness of an oak, whose branches are nests 22 of lamentation and weeping, laid up for the Earth, which burn night and day, and vomit out the heads of scorpions and live sulphur

mingled with poison. These be the Thunders that 5678
times in the 24th part of a moment roar with a hundred mighty earthquakes and a thousand times as
many surges, which rest not, neither know any quiet
time. Here one rock bringeth forth 1000 even as the
heart of man doth his thoughts. Woe, woe, woe, woe,
woe, woe, yea, woe be to the Earth, for her iniquity is,
was, and shall be, great. Come away, but not your
noises!

Analysis of the Tenth Key

The "Thunders of Judgement and Wrath" are the same that proceed out of
the throne of God (Rev. 4:5), and indeed are the same as the voice of the
heavenly Christ, which is described as "the sound of many waters" (Rev.
1:15). It is said that these Thunders, which are expressions of the will of God
and therefore may be likened to his messengers, or angels, are "numbered
and harbored in the north in the likeness of an oak." This oak has twenty-
two branches, each carrying a "nest" of lamentation.

This is a complex image. The north is the quarter of severity and hard-
ship, because it is traditionally said to be the home of winter and the deadly
north wind, the bringer of winter storms. Therefore it is fitting that the tree
of woe should be located there. The tree is often interpreted as a substitute
for the cross upon which Jesus died, and indeed the imagery of a tree is used
in this way in early Saxon poetry (see Cynewulf's "Dream of the Rood"). But
the symbolism of the tree predates Christianity. It is one of the archetypal
patterns for the universe itself, and in this sense occurs both in the magic of
the northern runes and in the mysticism of the kabbalah.

The reference to twenty-two is highly significant, because there are
twenty-two chapters in the book of Revelation. Therefore, the nests of woe
upon the tree lament the destruction of the world, which in ancient times
was not merely the physical earth, but the entire universe, just as the chapters of Revelation lament its destruction. There are also twenty-two letters
in the Hebrew alphabet, so the lamentation of the nests may refer to the
Hebrew letters with which many apocalyptic prophecies are expressed in
the Old Testament. In the kabbalah, the letters have a living, individual
existence that is similar to the independence accorded the simple numbers
by the Pythagoreans. The Hebrew letters themselves might almost be
thought of as angels of God.

In Dee's time, the sephirothic tree of the kabbalah, a glyph that embodies the underlying structure of the world, was considered by some to have
twenty-two channels that connected the ten spheres of the *sephiroth,* and
these channels were linked to the letters of the Hebrew alphabet. It is called

a tree because of its vaguely treelike shape, with a central column and "branching" channels that connect the ten fruit of the *sephiroth*.

In Teutonic myth, it is the ash that forms the framework of the world, but in Celtic lore the oak plays a more important role as the support upon which grows the sacred mistletoe, the symbol of the life force that endures through the darkness of winter. Mistletoe was harvested from oaks by the druids, with golden sickles, to serve a ritual function. Oak wood was used wherever great mass and strength were needed, such as the axles upon which millstones turned, the frames of houses, and the keels and ribs of ships. Thus the oak is an excellent tree from which to construct the axle of the universe.

When we consider that mistletoe is a symbol of life, we can appreciate how perverse is the imagery in the Key of "nests" upon the tree of life which lament the sorrow "laid up," or reserved, for the goddess of the earth, she who is called the Soul of the World. These nests "vomit out the heads of scorpions and live [burning] sulphur mingled with poison." The seven woes that afflict the Soul of the World as a punishment for her "iniquities" proceed out of the twenty-two nests of lamentation upon the branches of the northern oak.

There is clearly a correlation here between the seven woes of the Key and the seven woes that accompany the sounding of the seven trumpets in Revelation 8 and 9. At the sounding of the fifth trumpet, a star fell from heaven, "and to him was given the key of the bottomless pit" (Rev. 9:1). This "star," obviously an angel, opens the pit and releases fumes of flaming brimstone that were "as the smoke of a great furnace" (Rev. 9:2). From the open pit issue demons in the shape of locusts who torment those unrighteous humans who do not bear the seal of God in their foreheads, "and unto them was given power, as the scorpions of the earth have power" (Rev. 9:3). When the sixth angel sounds his trumpet, the four fallen angels, who command legions of demons mounted on monstrous horses, and who are bound at the bottom of the river Euphrates, are released:

> And thus I saw the horses in the vision, and them that sat on them, having breastplates of fire, and of jacinth, and brimstone: and the heads of the horses were as the heads of lions; and out of their mouths issued fire and smoke and brimstone. By these three was the third part of men killed, by the fire, and by the smoke, and by the brimstone, which issued out of their mouths. For their power is in their mouth, and in their tails: for their tails were like unto serpents, and had heads, and with them they do hurt. (Rev. 9:17–9)

True, the imagery in the Bible is not identical to the imagery in this Key, but it would be easy to interpret these two passages as independent descriptions of the same catastrophe observed in separate prophetic visions. The use of "heads of scorpions" is very revealing. Obviously, scorpions kill with the venomous needle in their tails, so why are their heads referred to? One explanation is that the imagery in Revelation 9:19 influenced the imagery of the Key. There is confusion in St. John's vision. Previously in this same chapter of Revelation, the power of the demons of the pit is said to be that of scorpions, and this power is lodged naturally in the tail. But the tails of the horses of the armies of the four angels released from under Euphrates are said to be those of serpents. There is a common folk myth that snakes sting with their tails, but in fact the tails of all snakes are quite harmless. The image is complicated by the additional information that these serpent tails of the horses have heads on them with which they could bite. It may be that the serpent tails on the horses were confused with scorpion tails by St. John, who then had to make them deadly by placing heads on the tails, so they could bite, since serpent tails cannot sting like scorpion tails. It is possible that this head-tail confusion is expressed in the Key with the phrase "heads of scorpions."

The Thunders that "5678 times in the 24th part of a moment roar with a hundred mighty earthquakes and a thousand times as many surges," while they are in a general sense the thunders that proceed from the heavenly throne, may here refer specifically to the seven thunders that echo the cry of the angel of the seventh trumpet: "and when he had cried, seven thunders uttered their voices" (Rev. 10:3). Again, as is so often true of the Keys, the number 5678 seems inexplicable, but probably should be understood as 5, 6, 7, and 8 rather than as a whole. The "24th part of a moment" brings us back to the maddeningly persistent motif of time that runs throughout the Keys, and through a great deal of the other communications received by Dee and Kelley from the angels. It is probably an allusion to the twenty-four elders, who represent the twenty-four hour divisions of the day.

There is a great deal of confusion over the correct translation of the next part of the Key, which gave Dee some trouble (see Casaubon, p. 192). Just as Kelley was dictating this Key, a cloud passed over the image in the scrying stone and obscured the letters for a moment before clearing. The confusion was created by this cloud. Geoffrey James gives the text as: "which rest not neyther know at any tyme here," omitting the English translation of the Enochian word MATORB (*The Enochian Magick of Dr. John Dee*, pp. 85–6). Donald Laycock has taken it upon himself to translate MATORB as "echoing," and gives the text: "which rest not, nor know any echoing time" (*Complete Enochian Dictionary,* p. 257). This seems quite meaningless to me. After studying the context, I believe MATORB should be translated "stable" or "quiet," which at least makes better sense. I do not wish to bore the reader with etymology, but the Enochian root OR seems to mean "ground" or "that which supports." It is here inserted into the Enochian word MATB (thousand), to signify that the "thousand surges" previously referred to in the Key will enjoy no stability or peace—that the ground will not cease to shake and surge.

The seven woes, besides their appearance in the vision of St. John, are specifically mentioned by the angel Madimi:

1. Wo be to women great with child, for they shall bring forth Monsters.

2. Wo be unto the Kings of the Earth, for they shall be beaten in a Mortar.

3. Wo be unto such as paint themselves, and are like unto the Prince of pride; for they shall drink the blood of their neighbours, and of their own children.

4. Wo be unto the false preachers, yea seven woes be unto them; for they are the teeth of the Beast.
   He that hath ears, let him hear.

5. Wo be unto the Virgins of the Earth, for they shall disdain their virginity, and they shall become Concubins for Satan, and despise the God of Righteousnesse.

6. Wo be unto the Merchants of the earth, for they are become abominable: Behold, they are become the spies of the earth, and the dainty meat of Kings. But they are foolish: Yea, they shall fall into the pit that they have digged for others.

7. Wo be unto the books of the earth, for they are corrupted; and are become a wrasting stock, and firebrand to the conscience. (*A True & Faithful Relation,* pp. 215–6)

That these seven woes are actually numbered in Dee's diary would seem to suggest very strongly that they are an explanation of the seven woes spoken in the Tenth Key. Before enumerating the seven woes, Madimi says: "Believe me, many are the woes of the world, and great are the sorrows that are to come: For the Lord prepareth his Rain-bow, and the witnesses of his account: and will appear in the heavens to finish all things: and the time is not long." Beside this passage Dee has written in the margin "The Rainbow. Apocalips. 4." In fact, the rainbow, which is mentioned in Revelation 4:3, figures even more significantly in Revelation 10:1, where it wreaths the head of the seventh angel, who is another embodiment of the heavenly Christ and who shall announce the end of the world: "But in the days of the voice of the seventh angel, when he shall begin to sound, the mystery of God should be finished, as he hath declared to his servants the prophets" (Rev. 10:7).

There is good reason to believe that the Soul of the World, who receives such vilification and dire warnings in the Keys, is the same as "Mystery, Babylon the Great, the Mother of Harlots and Abominations of the Earth" (Rev. 17:5). The fact that the Lady Babylon is called the mother of the abominations of the earth is significant, since in the Key is written "woe be to the Earth, for her iniquity is, was, and shall be, great." Aleister Crowley, who did considerable work with the Keys and with the Enochian language, made Babylon (spelled "Babalon") one of the prime figures in his personal apocalyptic mythology and considered himself to be the Great Beast incarnate. It is possible that he grasped the connection between the Lady Babylon in the Apocalypse and the goddess of the world in the Keys, although I have not myself seen any explicit mention of this link in his writings. It should be noted that the Enochian word for "wicked" is BABALON and the word for "harlot" is BABALOND.

The observations made about the end of the Ninth Key also apply to the end of this one. "Come away, but not your noises!" is another attempt to evoke the dread angels that will accomplish the destruction of the universe without suffering personal harm. The "Thunders of Judgement and Wrath" are commanded to "come away," or manifest themselves from the Watchtower of the North, but not their "noises," or thunders, which convey their destructive power. The angels, or more probably their ministers, are to appear silently with their mouths closed, because, as it says in Revelation 9:19, "their power is in their mouth."

The Eleventh Key

> The mighty Seat groaned, and there were Thunders 5 which flew into the east; and the Eagle spake, and cried with a loud voice, Come away! And they gathered themselves together and became the house of death, of whom it is measured, and it is as they are whose number is 31. Come away, for I have prepared for you! Move, therefore, and show yourselves. Open the mysteries of your creation. Be friendly unto me, for I am the servant of the same your God, the true worshiper of the Highest.

Analysis of the Eleventh Key

The "mighty Seat," as should be clear from previous observations, is the throne of the heavenly Christ, which emits thunder and lightning. These Thunders are the verbal expression of the will of God, which immediately become realized in the world because the words of God are the things of men. Why they are said to be five in number is unclear, unless it is a reference to the five princes that support the train of the king of each Watchtower in Kelley's vision.

The "Eagle" would seem to be a reference to the mother of heavenly Christ, who to escape from the wrath of Satan is given wings by God: "And to the woman were given two wings of a great eagle, that she might fly into the wilderness, into her place, where she is nourished for a time, and times, and half a time, from the face of the serpent" (Rev. 12:14). Her place must be the quarter of the east, if this Key is to be our guide.

The Enochian is missing for that portion of the English translation that reads in Casaubon "they gathered themselves together and became" (Casaubon, p. 193). Consequently, the meaning of this passage is in doubt. James gives "they gathered them together in the house of death" (*The Enochian Magick of Dr. John Dee*, p. 87). However, Laycock follows Casaubon, and I can see no reason for departing from Dee's version. For an angel to become the house of death may mean incarnation in a physical body. When human souls incarnate, they put on houses of mortality. However, it is possible that to become the house of death signifies to commit mass slaughter, which is in keeping with the apocalyptic theme of the Keys.

The house of death in the east here in the Eleventh Key is a striking contrast to the house of virgins of the east in the Seventh Key. A house in this sense means not only a physical structure in which to dwell, but also a group of individuals who are bound together by some common link such as a tie of blood, a religious sect, a business practice, a fraternal association, and so on. In this sense, the five Thunders could well become a house of death—a kind of angelic Murder Incorporated.

The words "of whom it is measured, and it is as they are whose number is 31" are very mysterious. The precise wording is suggestive. The Key does not say that the measure of the house of death is 31, but rather that the measure of the house of death "is as they are whose measure is 31," a vital distinction, because it tells us that the number is to be understood in an occult sense, perhaps a kabbalistic sense. In the kabbalah, all Hebrew words possess a numerical value, and words with the same values are considered to be mystically related to each other. Unfortunately, without some sort of guide it would be nearly impossible to guess which Enochian word with a letter value of 31 is intended to stand here for the house of death. It would also be difficult to establish with assurance the values of Enochian words, since, apart from the numbers in the Keys, Dee left no guide.

Aleister Crowley considered 31 a vitally important number, because it is one third of 93, the number of LAShTAL. He regarded 31 as the secret key that unlocked the hidden meaning of his angel inspired work *Liber Al Vel Legis* (The Book of the Law). This numerical key was supplied to him by his disciple Frater Achad. See his remarks concerning 31 in his autobiography, *The Confessions of Aleister Crowley* (Penquin Arkana, 1989), pages 801–2 and 835.

The final part of the Key is identical to the end of the First Key. The angel Nalvage indicates as much to Dee, saying "Then move as before, etc." (Casaubon, p. 193). This repetition is followed throughout the last two cycles around the points of the compass, occurring without significant variation in Keys Eleven to Eighteen.

The Twelfth Key

> O you that reign in the south, and are 28, the Lanterns of Sorrow: bind up your girdles, and visit us. Bring down your train 3663, that the Lord may be magnified, whose name amongst you is Wrath. Move, I say, and show yourselves; open the mysteries of your creation; be friendly unto me, for I am the servant of the same your God, the true worshiper of the Highest.

Analysis of the Twelfth Key

The Key is addressed to the spirits who rule in the south, presumably the same as the Thunders of Increase that were said to rule this angle in the Fourth Key. In seeking to evoke the rulers of the angles, we must understand that these rulers are always the same. The rulers of the south remain the six Seniors who preside over that quarter. However, the specific function of these rulers may change from Key to Key, depending upon the context of the Key by which they are evoked. Since these rulers act through their Wings, or Ministers, the result is that we seem to be calling upon different angels in different Keys of the same quarter.

The recurrence of the number twenty-eight is interesting. This number first occurred in the Seventh Key, which is a summons of the "Servants of Mercy" of the east. Whereas in that Key, the twenty-eight were described as "living dwellings," here they have become "Lanterns of Sorrow." Again, there is a suggestion of the mansions of the moon. The light of the moon can be both engendering and melancholy. It causes secret increase to begin in the depths of seeds and the darkness of the earth, but also is associated with the unchecked proliferation of mad fancies.

The meaning of the number 3663, the number associated with the "followers" or ministers of the rulers of the south in this Key, is obscure. I wish only to point out that it shows the frequent occurrence of three and six in the numbers of the Keys, and may be divided down the middle into mirror-opposite halves: thirty-six and sixty-three. This division may or may not be significant. An understanding of the numbers must await a complete explanation of the manner in which they were derived. Thus far, no student of Enochian has come forth with an analysis of their formation.

Among the followers of the "Lanterns of Sorrow," the name of God is Wrath. This illustrates the point I made above. There is only one God, but he takes on different names, and thus completely different identities, depending upon his changing purposes. In magic, names are not mere labels that can change while the being they name remains unaffected. Names define the essential nature of spiritual beings. Change the name, and you change the spirit. Complex spirits, such as the northern god Woden, have many names to express their many functions. Thus Woden has twelve primary names in Asgard, and many other names besides, such as Masked One, Raider, Pleasant One, Thin One, Glad-of-War, Worker-of-Evil, and so on (see Snorri Sturluson, *The Prose Edda,* "The Deluding of Gylfi"). These names should not be thought of as different titles for the same unchanging god. They embody and define complete and separate identities. Woden the Pleasant One is a completely different god from Woden the Worker-of-Evil. This same magical reality applies to the names of the angels in the Keys.

The Thirteenth Key

> O you Swords of the south, which have 42 eyes to stir up wrath of sin, making men drunken which are empty: behold the promise of God and his power, which is called amongst you a bitter sting. Move, and show yourselves; open the mysteries of your creation; be friendly unto me, for I am the servant of the same your God, the true worshiper of the Highest.

Analysis of the Thirteenth Key

Although the rulers of this Key are called "Swords of the south," this would seem to be an error on the part of the angel Nalvage, who dictated the Key to Kelley. The English translation corresponds accurately with the Enochian (the Enochian word for south is BABAGE in the Twelfth Key and BABAGEN here), but the Enochian cannot be correct if this Key is to fall into the same consistent pattern exhibited by Keys Three to Eighteen—four cycles of four Keys, each cycle unfolding clockwise around the compass points beginning in the east.

I would advise anyone using the Enochian system to change "south" to "west" in this Key and BABAGEN to SOBEL in the parallel Enochian text. This may seem a very daring and radical alteration based on nothing more than an analysis of the overall pattern of the Keys, but if the Keys are not logical and consistent, what use are they? Nowhere else do two Keys for the same quarter come together in the sequence. All Keys from Three to Eighteen contain allusions to the quarters except the Fourteenth Key, although in some cases these allusions are indirect—for example, in the Eighth Key the direction is indicated by "midday." The sun is in the south at noon, which is why in Latin the south is labeled *meridies* (see Dee's own illustration in James's *Enochian Magick of Dr. John Dee,* p. 119).

Once the pattern of the Keys is grasped, it is difficult to imagine why the Thirteenth Key should violate this pattern—and it is the only explicit violation. John Dee encountered immense difficulties in his efforts to insure accuracy while transcribing the Enochian communications. More than once the angels corrected his incorrect initial records, as in the case of the Great Table. Even so, many errors slipped past his diligent search and are preserved in the diaries that have come down to us. In my opinion, the assignment of the Thirteenth Key is one of those errors.

The image of many eyes occurs here for the first time in the Keys. While it may seem strange to modern readers, it was used in the Bible. St. John says of the four beasts who stand around, and at the same time in the midst, of the heavenly throne: "they were full of eyes within" (Rev. 4:8). He probably derived this image from the four living creatures in the vision of Ezekiel: "And their whole body, and their backs, and their hands, and their wings, and the wheels, were full of eyes round about, even the wheels that they four had" (Ezek. 10:12).

Eyes generally symbolize discernment or judgment. However, here they are used as the active power of the "Swords of the south" to stir up lust and provoke violence based upon uncontrolled desire. The lust-provoking power of the angels is called their eyes, because through the organs of sight men look upon the adornments of women and awaken to desire. Unlawful desire is intended, which in biblical times was desire for any woman out of wedlock, particularly the lust after prostitutes who painted their faces and wore red cloth.

Lust is not the only sin provoked by the "eyes" of the rulers of the south (more accurately, the west). Lust is only the vehicle by which they accomplish their purpose. Once the desires of men have been aroused, they are easily persuaded to fight over their whores and to commit mayhem and murder. This lustful fighting over prostitutes is the "wrath of sin" mentioned in the Key. The men are said to be "drunken which are empty" to signify that they become intoxicated in their wrath with no need to fill their bellies with wine. Lust and rage alone deprive them of their senses and reduce them to the level of the beasts.

The "promise of God" is here used ironically in the form of a pun. Promise can mean hope, but it can also mean a threat fulfilled, and the promise of God in this Key is the apocalypse foreshadowed in the vision of St. John, and in the writings of the Hebrew prophets. The power of God is called a "bitter sting" to evoke the memory of the demoniac locusts released from the bottomless pit by the trumpet of the fifth angel: "And they had tails like unto scorpions, and there were stings in their tails" (Rev. 9:10).

As the Keys unfold, the imagery gets progressively and consistently darker. The last truly positive Key is the Seventh, and even in the Seventh Key there is a double meaning—the virgins of the east are appareled with bright ornaments after the manner of harlots. It may be these same virgins who become the "Lanterns of Sorrow" in the Twelfth Key and provoke the lust and wrath of men in the Thirteenth, although it is equally possible that the virgins of the east are the righteous sealed with the mark of God in their foreheads, as I explained in the commentary on the Seventh Key.

In either case, the apocalypse draws nearer as the Keys progress. This is understandable, because the successive vibration of the Keys is intended to provoke the end of the world. Although this is not clearly stated, it is implied in a passage delivered by the angel Ave to Kelley on June 22, 1582:

> Thou hast three names of God, out of the line of the holy Ghost, in the principall Crosse of the first Angle, so hast thou three in the second, &c.
>
> Four dayes (after your book is made, that is to say, written) must you onely call upon those names of God, or on the God of Hosts, in those names:
>
> And 14 dayes after you shall (in this, or in some convenient place) Call the Angels by Petition, and by the name of God, unto the which they are obedient.
>
> The 15 day you shall Cloath your selves, in vestures made of linnen, white: and so have the apparition, use, and practice of the Creatures. For, it is not a labour of years, nor many dayes. (*A True & Faithful Relation*, p. 184)

Edward Kelley makes the objection: "This is somewhat like the old fashion of Magick," but Ave assures him: "Nay, they all played at this," meaning that the efforts of magicians past are mere playthings beside the power of the Enochian Keys.

Anyone seeking to call the spirits of the thirty Aethers must first go through the eighteen prior Keys, one on each successive night. Ave makes the interesting comment: "You must never use the garment after, but that once only, neither the book," which would seem to limit the usefulness of Enochian magic, until we realize that once a contact has been made with the spirits of the Aethers, they can thereafter be contacted with ease.

The Fourteenth Key

> O you Sons of Fury, the Daughters of the Just, which sit upon 24 seats vexing all creatures of the Earth with age; which have under you 1636: behold the voice of God, promise of Him which is called amongst you Fury (or Extreme Justice). Move and show yourselves;

open the mysteries of your creation; be friendly unto
me, for I am the servant of the same your God, the
true worshiper of the Highest.

Analysis of the Fourteenth Key

The twenty-four elders seated around the throne of the heavenly Christ are
here presented as male when they act upon the angry will of God to punish
the wicked, but female when they act as agents of an even-handed God to
restore the righteous with justice. Their sex depends upon their function, as
does every other aspect of their natures.

It should be noted that the sexes are here the inverse of those that
appear in the kabbalah, and in the preceding text dealing with the twelve
occult (female) Banners of severity and the twelve overt (male) Banners of
mercy. In the kabbalah it is the left, female side of the sephirothic tree that
punishes, and the right, male side that dispenses mercy.

However, this apparent contradiction is not as puzzling as might first
appear. Both the Sons of Fury and the Daughters of Justice belong to the left
side of the Tree. They represent, respectively, the severe justice of punishment and the equitable justice that restores a correct balance. In the familiar statue of blind Justice, the Sons are represented by the sword in the hand
of the goddess Justice, while the Daughters are the balance. Both are contained within the fifth *sephirah,* which carries the two names *Din* (Rigorous
Judgment) and *Geburah* (Binding Strength). The Daughters of the Just
would seem to fall under *Din* and the Sons of Fury under *Geburah.*

On the tree as a whole, it is the left (female) side that is severe and the
right (male) side that is merciful. But if we consider only the left side of the
tree, then the masculine aspect of the female principle may be regarded as
dominating or conquering, while the feminine aspect of the female principle
may be looked upon as dispensing equitable judgments. Neither aspect of the
fifth *sephirah* can be called merciful, since mercy belongs on the right side of
the tree, but the *Din* aspect is just while the *Geburah* aspect is wrathful.

The strong connection of the elders with time is emphasized. They sit
upon their seats "vexing all creatures of the Earth with age." In the
Enochian transcripts, it is emphasized by the angels that God exists outside
of time. One of the angels, who is not named, says to Kelley: "The effect of
God his Will is not of time; and therefore not to be known of man, till that
moment and end of time shall appear, wherein it must be published, and finished with power" (Casaubon, p. 58). Time begins and is regulated by the
elders, which in fact is precisely why they are said to be old.

This connection previously appears in the Third Key, where the Banners of God are visually represented as a clock face. That the "12 kingdoms" of the Third Key are the same group of elders as the twenty-four "Sons of Fury, the Daughters of the Just" seems incomprehensible, unless we realize that the Banners of Tetragrammaton are both twelve yet at the same time twenty-four in number. There are twelve overt or discernable permutations of the Ineffable Name (that is, twelve distinct forms that can be recognized visually), but twelve additional occult, or hidden, permutations that arise if the position of the first and second H in each of the twelve overt Banners is inverted.

Similarly, there are both twelve and at the same time twenty-four hours. The common clock face shows twelve hours, but there are two circuits of the clock in each day, for a total of twenty-four hours. This dichotomy is nicely illustrated by the existence of two types of clock, those that run on a twelve-hour cycle, and those that run on a twenty-four-hour cycle. It is also found expressed in the great clock in the Piazza San Marco in Venice (see the description in the analysis of the Third Key).

How can we be sure that the Enochian angels intended that Dee should understand the elders of the Apocalypse to be both twelve and at the same time twenty-four in number? We know this from the vision of the heavenly throne received by Kelley in the crystal:

> Now I see all those men, whose feet I saw before: And there sitteth One in a Judgement seat, with all his teeth fiery. And there sit six, on one side of him, and six on the other. And there sit twelve in a lower seat under them. *(A True & Faithful Relation,* p. 61)

This vision, received by Kelley on January 13, 1584, before he received the Enochian Keys or the Watchtowers of the Great Table, is vital to a true understanding of the elders, who are the same as the Banners of the Name. The four beasts represent the individual letters of the Name. They are described as both surrounding, and yet a part of, the heavenly throne. This means they lie outside of time, even as Christ is timeless. The elders, or Banners, are the first beginning of time. This, by the way, is why God acts in the world through messengers or agents, called angels. The world exists in time. God exists, or is, outside of time. It is necessary to use an intermediary to bridge this gulf, and this link between time and timelessness is the Banners, called "elders" by St. John to indicate their primacy and lordship over time.

Notice the division of the elders in Kelley's vision. Six elders sit on one side of the throne and six on the other side. It is not stated what pattern their seats form, but from the circle and sickle imagery in the Third Key, we might guess that they are arranged in two crescents enclosing the throne.

On the right side of Christ would be the crescent of seats comprising the Banners of the first half of the Name, that which is inscribed on Urim, the letters IH (IHVH, IHHV, IVHH; HVHI, HVIH, HHIV). In the crescent of seats on the left side of Christ would sit the Banners of the last half of the Name, that which is inscribed on Thummim, the letters VH (VHIH, VHHI, VIHH; HIHV, HIVH, HHVI). This first ring of elders is made up of the overt forms of the Name.

Below the primary rank of twelve elders sits a second rank of twelve more, as Kelley says, "in a lower seat under them." This means that each of the overt Banners has one of the occult Banners, its mirror paired opposite, seated directly beneath it in the lower ring of seats. The division of the two rings of seats reflects the division of the zodiac and houses into solar and lunar crescents, or crescents of day and night.

It is important to note that the crescents of the overt Banners on the top level are not directly over the crescents of the occult Banners below, although the individual seats of the Banner pairs are one over the other. The overt circle is divided into left and right crescents, while the lower occult circle is divided into top and bottom crescents, so that the lines between the semicircles form a perfect right angle cross with the throne at its point of intersection. We can deduce this from Dee's *Hieroglyphic Monad*, which divides the zodiac into crescents, or semicircles, between Aries and Taurus. This line of division is at right angles to the traditional division into solar and lunar crescents that falls between Cancer and Leo.

As I mentioned earlier, the elders are a kind of great cosmic clock whose hours and days and years are marked by the hands of the sun (hour hand) and moon (minute hand). This may provide a key to the angelic reckoning of time, which the angels informed Dee is not as time is reckoned by men. If one revolution of the moon about the heavens marks a cosmic minute, and one revolution of the sun a cosmic hour, then one cosmic year would perhaps be equal to 8,766 of our earthly years (the number of hours in an earthly year). Or perhaps a cosmic year is the period covered by the precession of the equinoxes, approximately 26,000 of our Earth years.

Again, I can offer no insight into the number of ministering angels said to be under the Sons of Fury and the Daughters of the Just, beyond noting the occurrence of three and six in the number.

The phrase "behold the voice of God" is interesting, since we would not normally assume that spoken words could be perceived visually. However, the words of God are the events of the world. In the Bible, the words of God frequently appear in written form. The Ten Commandments were not merely dictated by God but were incised into the stone tablets by the finger of God (Exod. 31:18). In the vision of St. John, the name of the great whore

Babylon is written in her forehead (Rev. 17:5), and the name of the mounted warrior Christ is written on his thigh (Rev. 19:16).

This prominence of writing has to do with the peculiar reverence of the ancient Hebrews for the written word, which has come down to modern times preserved in the mysticism of the kabbalah. Kabbalists believe that the holy Torah is not merely a record of God's pronouncements and laws, but the living embodiment of God. The word of God *is* God, particularly the written word, which among the Jews has always been regarded as the holiest of all manifest things. The temple at Jerusalem was built with the sole purpose of housing the sacred ark of the covenant, and the ark in its turn existed only to carry the fragments of the stone tablets delivered to Moses on Mt. Sinai, and the fragments themselves were only considered sacred because of the words inscribed upon them. Ultimately, everything comes down to the written word.

When God speaks in the Fourteenth Key, his words become visible upon the air, written in Enochian characters of fire. Since he is the God of Fury, his "promise" is a severe judgment upon the goddess of the world for her sinful multiplicity of forms. She is to be punished for her diversity, which pollutes her primordial simplicity and bars her from heaven. In the Keys, this is the true reason given for the apocalypse—not the sins of men, but the sin of diversity committed by the Soul of the World.

In the original English text of the Key, Kelley received the words "which is called amongst you Fury," but the angel Nalvage added the footnote "or Extreme Justice" (see Casaubon, p. 193). I have chosen to retain both names to indicate that in this Key, God is dual. He is both the God of *Din* and the God of *Geburah*. His will is administered both by the Daughters of the Just and the Sons of Fury.

The Fifteenth Key

> O thou the Governor of the first Flame, under whose
> Wings are 6739, which weave the Earth with dryness,
> which knowest of the great name Righteousness and
> the seal of honor: move and show yourselves, open the
> mysteries of your creation; be friendly unto me, for I
> am the servant of the same your God, the true wor-
> shiper of the Highest.

Analysis of the Fifteenth Key

This Key begins the fourth and final cycle around the corners of the earth. The "first Flame" applies to the east, for Dee and the Enochian angels the starting point for the circle of the world. It should be noted that the Key is addressed by the Messiah, through the voice of the magician vibrating the words, to the "Governor" of the first Flame. All of the other Flames, who are a class of angel, are addressed directly in the Keys. The Governor should be understood as the seated force that commands and the Flames themselves as the mounted force that executes those commands.

The ministering angels of the first Flame are here called "Wings" that "weave the Earth with dryness." Flame is often found in the Bible associated with the angels of God, particularly with those angels who punish the wicked. The image of dryness is here used to signify the wasting power of fire: "He shall not depart out of darkness; the flame shall dry up his branches, and by the breath of his mouth shall he go away" (Job 15:30); "Therefore as the fire devoureth the stubble, and the flame consumeth the chaff, so their root shall be as rottenness, and their blossom shall go up as dust: because they have cast away the law of the LORD of hosts, and despised the word of the Holy One of Israel" (Isa. 5:24).

Weaving, and the related activity of spinning, frequently occur in literature as metaphors for the passage of time. The Fate Clotho spins the threads of life, which are cut by her dreadful sister Atropos. Penelope, wife of Odysseus, spent three years weaving a shroud for her father-in-law as a pretext to avoid marriage, by day weaving the shroud and by night unraveling what she had woven. Job complains that his days are "swifter than a weaver's shuttle, and are spent without hope" (Job 7:6). However, in this case, the primary meaning appears to be the weaving of a web to capture and imprison the earth in dryness, calling to mind the cracked pattern in the mud of dried riverbeds and lakes.

Geoffrey James points out that the Enochian word for "righteousness" in this Key (BAEOVIB) is not the same as the word for righteousness used elsewhere (BALTOH), and he speculates, along with Laycock, that BAEOVIB must be a proper noun. This is reasonable, since the text of the Key calls this "the great name." For this reason BAEOVIB should be regarded as a name of power.

All of the Keys in this last cycle contain different names, or characterizations, of God. In the Fifteenth Key, he is the God of Righteousness; in the Sixteenth, the God of Conquest; in the Seventeenth, the God of Anger; in the Eighteenth, the God of Glory.

The "seal of honor" may be a reference to the mark of God sealed into the foreheads of the 144,000 servants of God, twelve thousand from each tribe of Israel (Rev. 7:4). However, it may also refer to an occult sigil or symbol, possibly the Sigil of Aemeth, concerning which the angel Uriel says, "This seal is not to be looked upon without great reverence and devotion" (James, *The Enochian Magick of Dr. John Dee*, p. 37, transcribed from Dee's *De Heptarchia Mystica,* Sloane 3191). Because of the dominance of apocalyptic imagery throughout the Keys, I am more inclined to think it refers to the seal on the foreheads of the righteous.

The Sixteenth Key

> O thou second Flame, the House of Justice, which hast thy beginning in glory, and shalt comfort the just; which walkest on the Earth with Feet 8763 that understand and separate creatures: great art thou in the God of Stretch-Forth-and-Conquer. Move and show yourselves; open the mysteries of your creation; be friendly unto me, for I am the servant of the same your God, the true worshiper of the Highest.

Analysis of the Sixteenth Key

The second Flame would naturally seem to apply to the second angle, the south, and this indeed is where this Key falls in the sequence. Here, the Flame is described as the "House of Justice, which hast thy beginning in glory." Glory or Splendor is the name of the eighth *sephirah, Hod*, which is positioned just below *Geburah* on the left side of the tree of the *sephiroth,* the side of severity and judgment.

It is said that the second Flame will "comfort the just" because it is the task of this angel, or class of angels, to send its ministers walking the face of the earth to separate the righteous from the wicked, so that the punishment of God will fall only on the wicked. That is why the active power of this angel is its "Feet" rather than the more common "Wings." These Feet must both "understand and separate," signifying that the second Flame has the power to look into the very hearts of human beings. For this purpose, its ministers must go among men and women in human guise unrecognized, as members of the human race. They walk rather than fly to be closer to the peoples they must judge. By becoming human—relinquishing their wings— they are able to understand human motives and needs.

This angel is said to be great in the God of "Stretch-Forth-and-Conquer"—in Enochian, ZILODARP, another name of power. ZILODARP is an aspect of Christ, the mounted warrior, who will conquer all the nations of the earth: "in righteousness he doth judge and make war" (Rev. 19:11). It is said of this mounted Christ: "His eyes were as a flame of fire" (Rev. 19:12). It may be that all four of the Flames of Keys Fifteen to Eighteen are emanations of the warrior Christ; or, more properly speaking, they are a single flame of righteousness that burns in all four quarters of the earth.

Concerning the number of "Feet," or ministering angels, of this Flame, 8763, again I can offer no insight. James gives the number as 876 (*The*

Enochian Magick of Dr. John Dee, p. 93), but this seems to be an error. It should be emphasized that understanding is said to lie in these "Feet," not in the second Flame itself, although the power to discern the just from the unjust descends into these 8763 ministering angels through the Flame.

The Seventeenth Key

> O thou third Flame, whose Wings are thorns to stir up vexation, and hast 7336 Lamps Living going before thee; whose God is Wrath-in-Anger: gird up thy loins and harken! Move and show yourselves; open the mysteries of your creation; be friendly unto me, for I am the servant of the same your God, the true worshiper of the Highest.

Analysis of the Seventeenth Key

The third Flame, that of the western quarter, is characterized by Wings, or ministers, who are "thorns to stir up vexation." It would seem to be their duty to breed discontent and strife upon the earth as a prelude to the destruction of the world. The same, or different, ministers of this third Flame are later described as "Lamps Living." It is not clear from the original manuscript version whether the God "Wrath-in-Anger" is the God of the Lamps or of the Flame itself. Dee used almost no punctuation, forcing later commentators to interpret the Keys to some extent in punctuating them. In this case, it does not matter—Wrath-in-Anger is the God of the Lamps, the Wings, and the third Flame collectively, since these three share a common purpose, and to this extent, a common identity—the stirring up of vexation upon the earth.

Wrath-in-Anger is in the original Enochian a compound composed of the words VONPO-VNPH, which may be translated "wrath-wrath" or "wrath of wrath." This is uncontrolled wrath distinguished from the righteous wrath of judgment—it is the unthinking wrath of fury that smites friend and foe alike without discrimination. This is the very emotion the Wings of the third Flame seek to breed among human beings. Their God, whose will directs their actions and shapes their forms, is the God of Strife.

The third Flame is told to "gird up thy loins," or prepare for the coming battle. This is a very common biblical expression. Men and women gird up their loins, or wrap cloth or leather about their lower bellies, to protect them from injury during battle or other strenuous exertion, because it was believed that in the lower belly lay the source of vitality and strength. About behemoth, the most powerful of all beasts, it is said: "Lo now, his strength is in his loins, and his force is in the navel of his belly" (Job 40:16). The Flame is told to "harken" to the words of this Key; that is, obey the command of the magician, speaking in the god-form of the heavenly Christ, to come forth into manifest being. The words "be friendly unto me," used here and in many other Keys, are presumably considered enough to prevent the ministers of the third Flame from creating vexation in the heart of the magician—something which, in my opinion, is highly questionable.

The Eighteenth Key

> O thou mighty light and Burning Flame of comfort, which openest the glory of God to the center of the Earth, in whom the secrets of Truth 6332 have their abiding, which is called in thy kingdom Joy, and not to be measured: be thou a window of comfort unto me. Move and show yourselves; open the mysteries of your creation; be friendly unto me, for I am the servant of the same your God, the true worshiper of the Highest.

Analysis of the Eighteenth Key
It is not stated explicitly that this is the fourth Flame, but we can draw no other conclusion. It falls in the sequence of the Keys upon the fourth angle of the north and completes the fourth cycle of the Keys around the quadrants of the Earth that began in the east with the Third Key. It is worth noticing that here, the words "Burning Flame" are used, linking this spirit of the north with the Burning Flames of the Second Key. In my opinion these four Flames of Keys Fifteen to Eighteen are no other than the Burning Flames mentioned in the Second Key.

The general tone of this Key is completely different from that of the three that precede it. Here, the Flame is "of comfort." It opens the "glory of God" to the center of the earth and possesses the "secrets of Truth 6332" that abide in the earth. In the heavenly kingdom of this fourth Flame, who expresses the merciful aspect of Christ, Truth is called Joy that cannot be measured.

The judgmental and wrathful natures of the preceding Keys have been left behind. This Key foreshadows the establishment of the kingdom of God upon the earth, the heavenly city of new Jerusalem that is the Bride of the Lamb, which will follow after the destruction of the apocalypse. The "center" is always the place of God, because where God is, that place is the center of everything.

The description of the fourth Flame as a "mighty light" which "openest the glory of God to the center of the earth" in interesting in view of this description of new Jerusalem:

> And the city had no need of the sun, neither of the moon, to shine it it: for the glory of God did lighten it, and the Lamb is

the light thereof. And the nations of them which are saved shall walk in the light of it: and the kings of the earth do bring their glory and honor into it. (Rev. 21:23–4)

Earthly truth is equated with heavenly joy, or bliss, which cannot be measured because it exists outside of time. This equation is the essential understanding of the poet John Keats, who wrote the memorable lines "`Beauty is truth, truth beauty,—that is all/ Ye know on earth, and all ye need to know" ("Ode on a Grecian Urn"). The natural and uncorrupted human response to beauty is a recognition within the human soul of a transcendent truth that is not attainable through mere reason. It is a truth that must be grasped with the heart and that cannot be analyzed with the mind except on a secondary level.

The phrase "window of comfort" may be a reference to the windows in the firmament through which the rain was supposed to pour when they were opened: "and the windows of heaven were opened" (Gen. 7:11). In biblical times, drought brought famine and plague. That is why the ministers of the first Flame are said to "weave the Earth with dryness" as a punishment for her multiplicity of forms. With the coming of new Jerusalem the earth is unified once again, and the windows of heaven can open to allow her parched surface to bloom in renewal.

The Key of the Thirty Aethers

O you Heavens which dwell in (the first Air) are mighty in the parts of the Earth, and execute the judgment of the Highest. To you it is said: behold the face of your God, the beginning of comfort; whose eyes are the brightness of the heavens; which provided you for the government of the Earth, and her unspeakable variety, furnishing you with a power of understanding to dispose all things according to the providence of Him that sitteth on the Holy Throne, and rose up in the beginning, saying: the Earth, let her be governed by her parts, and let there be division in her, that the glory of her may be always drunken and vexed in itself; her course, let it run with the heavens, and as a handmaid let her serve them; one season, let it confound another, and let there be no creature upon or within her the same; all her members, let them differ in their qualities, and let there be no one creature equal with another; the reasonable creatures of Earth (or men), let them vex and weed out one another; and the dwelling places, let them forget their names; the work of man and his pomp, let them be defaced; her buildings, let them become caves for the beasts of the field; confound her understanding with darkness. For why? It repenteth me I made man. One while let her be known, and another while a stranger: because she is the bed of an harlot, and the dwelling place of him that is fallen. O you Heavens, arise! The lower Heavens underneath you, let them serve you. Govern those that govern; cast down such as fall; bring forth with those that increase, and destroy the rotten. No place let it remain in one number; add and diminish until the stars be numbered. Arise, move, and appear before the covenant of His mouth, which He hath sworn unto us in His justice; open the mysteries of your creation, and make us partakers of undefiled knowledge.

Analysis of the Key of the Thirty Aethers
This same Key serves to evoke all thirty of the successive heavenly planes called Aethers, or Airs. These are, in order:

1. LIL	11. ICH	21. ASP
2. ARN	12. LOE	22. LIN
3. ZOM	13. ZIM	23. TOR
4. PAZ	14. VTA	24. NIA
5. LIT	15. OXO	25. VTI
6. MAZ	16. LEA	26. DES
7. DEO	17. TAN	27. ZAA
8. ZID	18. ZEN	28. BAG
9. ZIP	19. POP	29. RII
10. ZAX	20. CHR	30. TEX

The Enochian name of each Aether is inserted in the parentheses in the first line when evoking it. *Aether* is a good descriptive word, since these spirit realms are not so much places in time and space as they are dimensions of spiritual reality. They overlap and interpenetrate each other yet remain separate, in the same way that many notes of music may vibrate upon the air at the same instant and still be distinctly heard.

It is the evocation and use of the spirits of the Aethers that forms the true goal of Enochian magic. The first eighteen Keys are mainly of value in gaining access to the Aethers and are indispensable in opening the way. To attempt to evoke the Aethers without first performing the eighteen opening

Keys will prove futile. Once a personal communication has been established with the spirits of the Aethers, it is no longer necessary to go through the first eighteen Keys to call them to visible appearance in the scrying crystal or black mirror—the manner by which Dee and Kelley observed the angels and interacted with them.

It is curious that the spirits who dwell in the Aethers are called "Heavens," since the Aethers themselves might be regarded as heavenly spheres. Perhaps a better translation would have been "Aeons," in the Gnostic sense of emanations of God that govern the universe. An aeon is also an age of the universe—very appropriate, in view of the many time references throughout the Keys. These Heavens are responsible for the constantly changing diversity of forms in the manifest universe. They are "mighty in the parts of the Earth" and "execute the judgment of the Highest."

All thirty of the Aethers have the same overall function, which they are commanded to fulfill at the end of the Key: "Govern those that govern; cast down such as fall; bring forth with those that increase, and destroy the rotten. No place let it remain in one number; add and diminish, until the stars be numbered" (i.e., as many times as there are stars in the sky). Within this mandate each Aether fulfills its own particular responsibility.

Why are the Aethers being so hard on the goddess Earth? They are executing the "judgment of the Highest," as is their fundamental destiny. The magician, vibrating the Key in the god-form of the Messiah, reminds the Heavens of their duty, saying to them that God "provided you for the government of the Earth, and her unspeakable variety, furnishing you with a power of understanding, to dispose all things according to the providence of Him that sitteth on the Holy Throne."

These words are voiced to gain power over the Heavens of the Aethers, by reminding them of their purpose. While speaking them, the magician assumes the visage of Christ: "behold the face of your God," the magician tells them, meaning the features of Christ that overlay his or her own features. This is the only reason the Heavens of the Aethers will pay attention to the magician. As a mere human being, the magician is under the authority of the Heavens; as the Messiah incarnate, the Heavens fall under his or her authority.

The eyes of God are the sun and moon, the "brightness of the heavens." In astrology, these are called the great lights, to distinguish them from the lesser lights, the planets. Many Egyptian gods, such as Ra, Horus, and Ptah, possessed the sun and moon for eyes. The sun is the right eye and the moon the left eye of God.

The Heavens are only fulfilling their appointed function in vexing the Earth. What, then, does God have against her? In the Key, words are put into the mouth of God to explain and justify the function of the Heavens of the Aethers. First, God delivers his condemnation of the Soul of the World: "the Earth, let her be governed by her parts, and let there be division in her, that the glory of her may be always drunken and vexed in itself."

By this harsh judgment God condemns the single, unified soul that pervades the entire universe to be splintered and fragmented into countless little souls at endless strife with one another. This conflict of soul against soul robs the Soul of the World of her glory, which is only slightly less than that of God himself. She forgets her power and majesty in this internal strife of her parts and in this way is dragged down from her rightful high estate by the foolishness of her own children, who are parts of herself. The constant confusion within her weakens the Soul of the World and allows this pure goddess to be degraded after the manner of a prostitute.

The ancients usually treated the goddess Earth as one substance with the Soul of the World, whose body is the entire universe. The Earth was regarded as the heart of this great goddess, her "central part," as Saint Augustine put it in his *City of God* (bk. 13, ch. 17). The earth and the world (universe) were seldom clearly distinguished. It is in this general sense that I employ the term here, applying Soul of the World to both the earth and the greater universe.

The reason for this incomprehensible hatred by God the Father (speaking through his heavenly Son) against the Soul of the World is explicitly stated: "For why? It repenteth me I made man." The Soul of the World is to be punished because she harbors and nurtures the human race, who have fallen from grace: "because she is the bed of an harlot, and the dwelling place of him that is fallen."

"Him that is fallen" is usually taken to mean Coronzon, the great dragon, who is the same as the rebellious angel called Satan in the Apocalypse, cast by Michael down to the Earth (Rev. 12:9). However, the fallen one is also Adam, cast out of the Garden of Eden for the sin of rebellion against divine authority. Fallen Lucifer and fallen Adam play the same dramatic figure on different stages. Lucifer is cast out of heaven because he dares to think for himself. This creates division within the perfect unity of heaven, and God cannot allow this conflict to persist. Adam, by eating the apple, also commits an independent act and forever splinters himself off from the perfect harmony of Eden.

The purpose of the Armageddon is the reunion of heaven and Earth, and the reunion of God and man, through the man-God amalgam of the warrior Messiah. Those humans who give up their power of independent judgment— a power reserved only to God—will be permitted into the heavenly city of new Jerusalem. The rest who remain defiant will be tortured and killed by the angels of wrath. Meanwhile, the goddess Earth is to be continually tormented and degraded because she harbors rebellious human beings.

Little wonder the Gnostics regarded this patriarchal god of the Old Testament as a misbegotten monster who made Adam solely for the purpose of delivering sacrifices and worship, and then when Adam became aware of his own divine spark and began to think for himself, turned against his creation like a petulant child. Little wonder they saw the serpent in Eden as an emissary of the true God, who is much higher and more detached than Yaldabaoth (as they called the God of Moses). That is why the Gnostics worshipped the serpent. The serpent was the symbol of freedom and transcendent wisdom, twin birthrights of all human beings, withheld from Adam by jealous Yaldabaoth.

In Gnostic myth, the Soul of the World voluntarily allows herself to be degraded and abused by the vindictive malice of the inferior Yaldabaoth in order to bring about the restoration of human souls to their rightful place in the heavens. This voluntary degradation, or descent into forgetfulness ("and the dwelling places, let them forget their names...confound her understanding with darkness") is usually symbolized in the various myths by prostitution. In the vision of St. John, the goddess Earth becomes the great whore Babylon, who from a Gnostic perspective is a degraded form of the Queen of Heaven. Among some Gnostic sects, she was called Barbelo or Sophia. In the myth of the Simonian Gnostics, she is Helena, one of whose incarnations was Helen of Troy.

The Gnostic prophet Simon, who was confused with the biblical Simon Magus by the Fathers of the Church, taught that he was himself the highest power, God the Father. According to Irenaeus, a very biased reporter, Simon found Helen working as a prostitute in Tyre and took her with him, calling her the First Thought of his mind and the Mother of All Things, by whom he had conceived the angels. The myth goes that Helen, as the First Thought, recognizing the will of her Father to create the archangels and angels, secretly issued out of him by her own volition and descended to the lower regions, where she generated the angelic powers, who are usually called Archons (rulers). It was these angelic powers, whose leader is Yaldabaoth, that created the world. Unfortunately, since they were created without the express command of the Father, they are flawed.

After Helen created the Archons, they kept her prisoner to conceal the fact that they were not the highest of all beings. About the true God the Father, these Archons knew nothing, but they subjected the First Thought, Helen, to unceasing degradation and torment, imprisoning her in a body of matter and causing her to prostitute herself so that she would forget her high estate and be incapable of returning to heaven. Throughout the ages, the First Thought has reincarnated in countless female forms, being compelled by the angels to pass from one to another like water poured from vessel to vessel.

This Gnostic myth of the Simonians contains many of the essential Gnostic ideas. Details differ greatly from sect to sect, but always the God of the Old Testament is not God the Father but an abortion that arose from the first female principle, the Great Mother, without the consent of the Father. Man is physically created by Yaldabaoth and the other Archons, yet he is infused with a spark of true divinity by the will of the Father, making man a higher creature than the Archons who shaped him. However, man does not recognize his divinity, and this ignorance of his true estate allows Yaldabaoth to use humans as his slaves, manipulating them through a combination of bribes, threats, and lies. In the later Gnostic myths, Christ, the Son of the true Father, will descend and liberate humanity from its slavery. In the Valentinian version, this Savior *(Soter)* rescues the fallen goddess Sophia from her degraded state and bears her back to heaven, where he weds her.

Although this Key is filled with Gnostic images, its philosophy is Christian. Mankind is to be punished for its original sin of disobedience. Through constant strife, human souls will be made to forget their original heavenly origins: "the dwelling places, let them forget their names." The Soul of the World, of which all human souls, and indeed the spiritual essences of all things, are but splinters, or sparks, is to be ceaselessly and pitilessly tormented. There is no reference to deliverance for either mankind or the Earth from these torments.

From the Gnostic point of view, the speaker of this Key is Yaldabaoth himself, who appointed the various angelic powers as Archons over the innumerable parts of the world and who here instructs them to continue to multiply and transmute her forms in order to keep her in a bewildered and forgetful state. This is a kind of rape of the world by the Archons, and her child, the human race, is also made to suffer along with the Goddess. The words "One while let her be known, and another while a stranger" apply to both the Soul of the World and to human souls—at root, a single essence. In a Gnostic sense, it is not so much a command to do something new as it is a description of what is already taking place. At one moment, a human soul may rise up in ecstatic gnosis and attain a union with the Soul of the World, who then knows herself through the awareness of her child, but at the next moment forgetfulness comes amid the countless petty distractions of manifest existence.

From the Christian point of view, as expressed in the vision of St. John, the speaker is Christ, who orders the angels of wrath to harrow the Earth so that sinful men will find no place of refuge where they can rest their heads. These angels of wrath are the forces of karma, or cause and effect. They are told to "govern those that govern; cast down such as fall; bring forth with those that increase, and destroy the rotten." These are all effects of time. The Heavens of the Aethers are the forces of entropy, by which the universe is made to run down like a great clock.

The command to the spirits of the Aethers to "appear before the covenant of His mouth, which He hath sworn unto us in His justice" indicates clearly that the magician is to vibrate, or voice, the Keys in the adopted guise of "Him that sits on the Holy Throne." In the original Enochian, this long description is a single name of God, IDOIGO.

The final words, "make us partakers of undefiled knowledge," indicate the purpose for vibrating the Keys of the Aethers, and indeed the entire cycle of forty-eight expressed Keys—the attainment of knowledge. Gnosis is the Greek word for "knowledge," but was understood by the Gnostics as spiritual knowledge, a direct and transcendent personal insight. This was also the highest goal of the kabbalists, the magicians of the Renaissance, and the alchemists—knowledge of God through self-awareness.

On numerous occasions during his conversations with the Enochian angels, Dee demands information about trivial personal matters, only to be chastised by the angels not to waste his, and their, time on such vulgar trifles. For example, when Dee asks if a man he knows has enough money, Madimi says:

> Your words make me a Childe. Those that fish for Dolphins do not stand upon the ground. Those that sit in Counsel call not in the harvest people, nor account not their works. He that standeth above the Moon, seeth greater things then the earth: Is it not said, The Lord will provide? I stand above the Moon, for that I dispose his life from above the disposition of the Moon. To ask what Jacob his servants did, was a folly; because their master was blessed: A greater question to ask how blessed he was, then to ask how many sheep he had.
>
> Δ [Dee]. I am desirous to know what you meant by saying, That my words made you a Childe.
>
> Mad.... [Madimi]. Because you ask me Childish questions.
> (A True & Faithful Relation, p. 29)

It is doubtful if Dee, despite his great wisdom, ever really understood the transcendent purpose for the Keys. He sought the magic of the angels for personal and political ends, and only in a secondary way did he desire knowledge of them for its own sake. It is clear from his diaries that the angels were using both Dee and Kelley as unwitting instruments through whom the apocalyptic bomb that is the magic of the four Watchtowers and the Enochian Keys might be planted upon the Earth. Time and time again, the impatience that Madimi, Nalvage, Ave, and other angels felt for Dee's preoccupation with physical events shows through the transcript of the scrying sessions.

While many of the angels respected Dee for his learning and holiness, they held Kelley in thinly veiled contempt, sometimes choosing to insult, and even threaten, him through his own lips. For example, Madimi warns Kelley: "Take heed that you deal uprightly." Kelley protests: "God the Creator be my witness of my upright dealing, with, and toward him, (meaning Dee) ever since my last coming to him." Madimi darkly replies: "It is good to prevent diseases" (Casaubon, page 28).

This kind of tense exchange between Kelley and the spirits, which Kelley was honest enough to report to Dee, argues strongly against any conscious deception on the part of the seer. The angels regarded Kelley as a kind of human telephone, nothing more, through which they could communicate with Dee. Although they respected Dee as a good man, and needed his immense scholarship and knowledge of languages and ciphers to accurately transmit their works, it was quickly apparent to them that even Dee was incapable of grasping the true magnitude of what he was ushering into the world.

The apocalypse glimpsed in the vision of St. John is a complex magical working that cannot be initiated by the angels themselves but must be called into the universe by the living Word vibrated in a vessel of flesh that wears the form of the warrior Christ. The angels of wrath cannot call themselves into being. What they could, and did, do is teach mankind how to summon them through the guardian gates of the four Watchtowers that sustain the universe.

Once Coronzon and his angels gain access through the Watchtowers, their mere presence in our world will render it unfit for human habitation by increasing the degree of chaos and disrupting the balance of the natural laws that presently provide stability and order. Coronzon will transform our universe into a suitable dwelling place for himself and his ministers, in the process destroying the human race. If we are to believe St. John the Divine, his sovereignty over our blasted universe will be of brief duration, but this will yield scant consolation to those billions who are slaughtered by war, famine, plagues, and natural disasters.

It remains to be seen how long it will take some eager Enochian magician to accurately perform the complete working of the Keys from beginning to end, and what will happen to the world in the event that this working ever takes place. Fortunately (or unfortunately, for those who consider themselves the elect of God), the working is more than the mere recitation by rote of the Enochian words. Since we are all still here, we may assume that the full Enochian Apocalypse Working (as I am inclined to call it) has never yet been accurately performed in its full perfection, not even by Aleister Crowley, who was able to part the gates a crack, but not to fling them wide open. Perhaps this performance is impossible, since so many details of Enochian magic are missing—overlooked or deliberately omitted by Dee from his records. Some of those records are lost to us. This may be a good thing for world, at least as we have come to know it.

APPENDIX B

''''''''''''''

COMMENTARIES ON TETRAGRAMMATON

The following is a collection of observations by mystics, occultists, and kabbalists both ancient and modern on the meaning of Tetragrammaton. It is interesting to compare one with another. Often it is possible to trace influences—Eliphas Levi, in the second passage quoted, has derived his inspiration from Fabre D' Olivet; Frater Achad is obviously echoing the teachings of his magical master, Aleister Crowley. There are also many errors or discrepancies, which I have let stand—for example, the assignment of the four letters to the *sephiroth* of the kabbalistic tree made by Isaac Myer is in disagreement with that of Gershom Scholem. Necessarily there is repetition, because many authors say much the same thing about the Name and indeed have little else to say. The wide variety of transliterations of the Hebrew IHVH into Latin characters takes a little getting used to, but should not prove confusing.

Moses

And God said moreover unto Moses, Thus shalt thou say unto the children of Israel, the Lord God (IHVH) of your fathers, the God of Abraham, the God of Isaac, and the God of Jacob, hath sent me unto you; this is my name for ever, and this is my memorial unto all generations. (Pentateuch [ninth century BC], Exod. 3:15, King James translation)

239

Philo Judaeus

If anyone, I do not say should blaspheme against the Lord of men and gods, but should even dare to utter his name unseasonably, let him expect the penalty of death. (*Vita Mosis* [first century], 3.2)

Flavius Josephus

Moses having now seen and heard these words that assured him of the truth of these promises of God, had no reason left him to disbelieve them: he entreated him to grant him that power when he should be in Egypt; and besought him to vouchsafe him the knowledge of his own name; and since he had heard and seen him, that he would also tell him his name, that when he offered sacrifice he might invoke him by such his name in his oblations. Whereupon God declared to him his holy name, which had never been discovered to men before; concerning which it is not lawful for me to say any more. (*Antiquities of the Jews* [first century], bk. 2, ch. 12, sec. 4 [London: George Routledge, n.d.], p. 66)

Sepher Yetzirah

He selected three letters from among the simple ones and sealed them and formed them into a Great Name, IHV, and with this He sealed the universe in six directions. (*Sepher Yetzirah* [third century], Wynn Westcott edition [New York: Weiser, 1980], p. 17)

And from the non-existent He made Something; and all forms of speech and everything that has been produced; from the empty void He made the material world, and from the inert earth He brought forth everything that hath life. He hewed, as it were, vast columns out of the intangible air, and by the power of His Name made every creature and everything that is... (ibid., pp. 18-9)

Sepher ha-Bahir

It is thus written (*Micah* 2:13), "God (YHVH) is at their head." We have a rule that every Name that is written *Yud, Heh, Vav, Heh* is specific to the Blessed Holy One and is sanctified with holiness. (*The Bahir* [twelfth century], Aryeh Kaplan translation [York Beach, Maine: Weiser, 1989], p. 25)

Moses Maimonides

It is well known that all the names of God occurring in Scripture are derived from His actions, except one, namely, the Tetragrammaton, which consists of the letters *yod, he, vau* and *he*. This name is applied exclusively to God, and is on that account called *Shem ha-meforash,* "The nomen proprium." It is the distinct and exclusive designation of the Divine Being; whilst His other names are common nouns, and are derived from actions...The derivation of the name, consisting of *yod, he, vau,* and *he,* is not positively known, the word having no additional signification. This sacred name, which, as you know, was not pronounced except in the sanctuary by the appointed priests, when they gave the sacerdotal blessing, and by the high priest on the Day of Atonement, undoubtedly denotes something which is peculiar to God, and is not found in any other being. It is possible that in the Hebrew language, of which we have now but a slight knowledge, the Tetragrammaton in the way it was pronounced, conveyed the meaning of "absolute existence." In short, the majesty of the name and the great dread of uttering it, are connected with the fact that it denotes God Himself, without including in its meaning any names of the things created by Him. (*The Guide for the Perplexed* [twelfth century], Friedlander translation [New York: Dover, 1956], pp. 89-90)

Clavicula Salomonis

O God Almighty Who art the Life of the Universe and Who rulest over the four divisions of its vast form by the strength and virtue of the Four Letters of Thy Holy Name Tetragrammaton, YOD, HE, VAU, HE... (*Key of Solomon the King* [fourteenth century], MacGregor Mathers edition, bk. 1, ch. 13, [York Beach, Maine: Weiser, 1989], p. 55)

Pico della Mirandola

The letters of the name of the evil demon who is the prince of this world are the same as those of the name of God—Tetragrammaton—and he who knows how to effect their transposition can extract one from the other. (*Kabbalistic Conclusions* [1486], as translated by A. E. Waite in *The Holy Kabbalah* [New Hyde Park, New York: University Books, 1975], p. 447)

Cornelius Agrippa

Therefore a four square is ascribed to God the Father, and also contains the mysterie of the whole Trinity, for by its single proportion, *viz.* by the first of one to one, the unity of the paternall substance is signified, from which proceeds one Son, equall to him; by the next procession, also simple, *viz.* of two to two, is signified by the second procession the Holy Ghost from both, that the Son be equall to the Father by the first procession; and the Holy Ghost be equal to both by the second procession. Hence that super-excellent, and great name of the divine Trinity in God is written with four letters, *viz. Iod, He,* and *Vau, He,* where it is the aspiration *He,* signifies the proceeding of the spirit from both: for *He* being duplicated, terminates both syllables, and the whole name, but is pronounced *Jove* as some will, whence that *Jovis* of the heathen, which the Ancients did picture with four ears, whence the number four is the fountain, and head of the whole divinity. (*Three Books of Occult Philosophy* [1531-3], bk. 2, ch. 7, English translation of 1651, p. 183)

But the true name of God is known neither to men nor to Angels, but to God alone, neither shall it be manifested (as the holy Scriptures testifie) before the will of God be fulfilled; Notwithstanding God hath other names amongst the Angels, others amongst us men; for there is no name of God amongst us (as *Moses* the Egyptian saith) which is not taken from his works, and signifieth with participation, besides the name *Tetragrammaton,* which is holy, signifying the substance of the Creator in a pure signification, in which no other thing is partaker with God the Creator; therefore it is called the separated name, which is written and not read, neither is it expressed by us, but named, and signifieth the second supernall Idiome, which is of God, and perhaps of Angels. (ibid., bk. 3, ch. 11, pp. 378-9)

Edward Kelley

And seeing that the Quaternary rests in the Ternary, it is a number which stands on the horizon of eternity, and doth exhibit everything bound with God in us, thus including God, men, and all created things, with all their mysterious powers. Adding three, you get ten, which marks the return to unity. In this arcanum in concluded all knowledge of hidden things which God, by His word, has made known to the men of His good pleasure, so that they might have a true conception of Him. ("Theatre of Terrestrial Astronomy" [sixteenth century], *The Alchemical Writings of Edward Kelly,* edited by A. E. Waite [New York: Weiser], pp. 117-8)

Robert Fludd

The Soul of the World is therefore Metatron, whose light is the Soul of the Messiah or of Tetragrammaton's virtue, in which is the light of the living God, in which is the light of the Ain Soph, beyond which there is no progression. (*Philosophia Moysaica,* 1638)

Fabre d'Olivet

This name presents first the sign which indicates life, repeated twice, and thus forming the essentially living root EE (הה). This root is never used as a noun, and is the only one which enjoys such prerogative. It is from its formation not only a verb, but an unique verb, from which all the others are merely derivations; in short, the verb הוה (ÉVÉ), to be, being. Here, as we can see, and as I have carefully explained in my Hebrew grammar, the sign of intelligible light ו (VÔ) is placed in the midst of the root of life. Moses, when using this unique verb to form the proper name of the Being of Beings, added to it the sign of potential manifestation and of eternity, י (I); he thus obtained יהוה (IEVE), in which the facultative Being is placed between a past tense without origin, and a future without limit. This admirable word thus exactly signifies the Being who is, who was and who will be. (*La Langue Hébraïque Restituée* [1810], as translated by A. P. Morton in his translation of *The Tarot of the Bohemians* by Papus [New York: Arcanum Books, 1958], pp. 18–9, footnote 1)

Adolphe Franck

The Talmud tells us that in ancient times three names were known to express the idea of God: the famous Tetragrammaton, or name of four letters, and two names foreign to the Bible, the first of which consisted of twelve letters, the other of forty-two. The first, though forbidden to the masses, circulated freely enough within the schools. "The wise men," the text says, "taught it once a week to their sons and their disciples." (*The Kabbalah* [1843] [New York: Bell Publishing, 1940], pp. 18-9)

The Absolute Being and visible nature have but one name, whose meaning is God. (ibid., p. 112)

Éliphas Lévi

A single word comprehends all things, and this word consists of four letters: it is the Tetragram of the Hebrews, the AZOT of the alchemists, the Thot of the Bohemians, or the Taro of the Kabalists. This word, expressed after so many manners, means God for the profane, man for the philosophers, and imparts to the adepts the final term of human sciences and the key of divine power; but he only can use it who understands the necessity of never revealing it. (*Transcendental Magic* [1855–6], A. E. Waite translation [New York: Weiser, 1970], pp. 16–7)

Adam is the human tetragram, summed up in the mysterious JOD, type of the kabalistic phallus. By adding to this JOD the triadic name of Eve, the name of Jehova is formed, the Divine Tetragram, which is eminently the kabalistic and magical word, יהוה, being that which the high-priest in the temple pronounced JODCHEVA. So unity, complete in the fruitfulness of the triad, forms therewith the tetrad, which is the key of all numbers, of all movements and of all forms. (ibid., p. 37)

When a man pronounces the Tetragram—say the Kabalists—the nine celestial realms sustain a shock, and then all spirits cry out one upon another: "Who is it thus disturbing the kingdom of heaven?" Then does the earth communicate unto the first sphere the sins of that rash being who takes the Eternal Name in vain, and the accusing word is transmitted from circle to circle, from star to star, and from hierarchy to hierarchy. (ibid., p. 50)

According to consecrated dogma, there are Three Persons in God, and these Three constitute one only Deity. Three and one provide the conception of four, because unity is required to explain the three. Hence, in almost all languages, the name of God consists of four letters, and in Hebrew these four are really three, one of them being repeated twice, that which expresses the Word and the creation of the Word. (ibid., p. 53)

The Kabalistic Tetragram, JODHEVA, expresses God in humanity and humanity in God. (ibid., p. 54)

Christian D. Ginsburg

He [man] is still the presence of God upon earth...and the very form of the body depicts the Tetragrammaton, the most sacred name Jehovah (יהוה). Thus the head is the form of the י, the arms and the shoulders are like the ה, the breast represents the form of the ו, whilst the two legs with the back represent the form of the second ה. (*The Kabbalah* [1863] [London: Routledge and Kegan Paul, 1970], p. 113)

There is no doubt that the tetrad (τετρακτύς) of Pythagoras is an imitation of the Hebrew Tetragrammaton, and that the worship of the decade has simply been invented in honour of the *ten Sephiroth*. The four letters composing this name represent the four fundamental constituents of the body (*i.e.,* heat, cold, dryness and humidity), the four geometrical principal points (*i.e.,* the point, the line, flat and body), the four notes of the musical scale, the four rivers in the earthly paradise, the four symbolical figures in the vision of Ezekiel, &c., &c., &c. Moreover if we look at these four letters separately we shall find that each of them has equally a recondite meaning. The first letter י, which also stands for the number *ten,* and which by its form reminds us of the mathematical point, teaches us that God is the beginning and end of all things. The number *five,* expressed by ה the second letter, shows us the union of God with nature—of God inasmuch as he is depicted by the number three, *i.e.,* the Trinity; and of visible nature, inasmuch as it is represented by Plato and Pythagoras under the dual. The number *six,* expressed by ו, the third letter, which is likewise revered in the Pythagorean school, is formed by the combination of one, two, and three, the symbol of all perfection. Moreoever the number *six* is the symbol of the cube, the bodies (*solida*), or the world. Hence it is evident that the world has in it the imprint of divine perfection. The fourth and last letter of this divine name (ה) is like the second, represents the number *five,* and here symbolizes the human and rational soul, which is the medium between heaven and earth, just as five is the centre of the decade, the symbolic expression of the totality of things. (ibid., pp. 209–10)

H. P. Blavatsky

The primordial point in a circle; the circle squaring itself from the four cardinal points becomes a quaternary, the perfect square, having at each of its four angles a letter of the mirific name, the sacred TETRAGRAM. It is the four Buddhas who came and have passed away; the Pythagorean *tetractys*—absorbed and resolved by the one eternal NO-BEING. (*Isis Unveiled* [1877] [California: Theosophy Company, 1931], vol. 1, p. 507)

We must now give some proofs of what we have stated, and demonstrate that the word Jehovah, if Masonry adheres to it, will ever remain as a substitute, never be identical with the lost mirific name. This is so well known to the kabalists, that in their careful etymology of the יהוה they show it beyond doubt to be only one of the many substitutes for the real name, and composed of the twofold name of the first androg-yne—Adam and Eve, Jod (or Yodh), Vau and He-Va—the female serpent as a symbol of Divine Intelligence proceeding from the ONE-Generative or *Creative* Spirit. Thus, Jehovah is not the sacred name at all. Had Moses given to Pharaoh the *true* "name," the latter would not have answered as he did, for the Egyptian King-Initiates knew it as well as Moses, who had learned it with them. *The* "name" was at that time the common property of the adepts of all the nations in the world, and Pharaoh certainly knew the "name" of the Highest God mentioned in the *Book of the Dead.* But instead of that, Moses (if we accept the allegory of *Exodus* literally) gives Pharaoh the name of *Yeva,* the expression or form of the Divine name used by all the *Targums* as passed by Moses. Hence Pharaoh's reply: "Who is that *Yeva* that I should obey his voice?"

"Jehovah" dates only from the Masoretic innovation. When the Rabbis, for fear that they should lose the keys to their own doctrines, then written exculsively in consonants, began to insert their vowel-points in their manuscripts, they were utterly ignorant of the true pronunciation of the NAME.

Hence, they gave it the sound of *Adonai,* and made it read *Ja-ho-vah.* Thus the latter is simply a fancy, a perversion of the Holy Name. And how could they know it? Alone, out of all their nation, the high priests had it in their possession and respectively passed it to their successors, as the Hindu Brahmaâtma does before his death. Once a year only, on the day of atonement, the high priest was allowed to pronounce it in a whisper. Passing behind the veil into the inner chamber of the sanctuary, the Holy of Holies, with trembling lips and downcast eyes he called upon the dreaded NAME. The bitter persecution of the kabalists, who received the precious syllables after deserving the favor by a whole life of sanctity, was due to a suspicion that they misused it. (ibid., vol. 2, pp. 398–9)

MacGregor Mathers

The name of the Deity, which we call Jehovah, is in Hebrew a name of four letters, IHVH; and the true pronunciation of it is known to very few. I myself know some score of different mystical pronunciations of it. The true pronunciation is a most secret arcanum, and it is a secret of secrets. "He who can rightly pronounce it, causeth heaven and earth to tremble, for it is the name which rusheth through the universe." Therefore when a devout Jew comes upon it in reading the Scripture, he either does not attempt to pronounce it, but instead makes a short pause, or else he substitutes for it the name *Adonai,* ADNI, Lord. The radical meaning of the word is "to be," and it is thus, like AHIH, *Eheieh,* a glyph of existence. It is capable of twelve transpositions, which *all* convey the meaning of "to be"; it is the only word that will bear so many transpositions without its meaning being altered. They are called the "twelve banners of the mighty name," and are said by some to rule the twelve signs of the Zodiac. These are the twelve banners:—IHVH, IHHV, IVHH, HVHI, HVIH, HHIV, VHHI, VIHH, VHIH, HIHV, HIVH, HHVI. (*The Kabbalah Unveiled* [1887] [London: Routledge and Kegan Paul, 1962], pp. 30–1)

But IHVH, the Tetragrammaton, as we shall presently see, contains all the Sephiroth with the exception of Kether, and specially signifies the Lesser Countenance, Microprosopus, the King of the qabalistical Sephirotic greatest Trinity, *and*

the Son in His human incarnation, in the Christian accepta-
tion of the Trinity.

Therefore, as the Son reveals the Father, so does IHVH, *Jehovah,* reveal AHIH, *Eheieh.*

And ADNI is the Queen "by whom alone Tetragrammaton can be grasped," whose exaltation into Binah is found in the Christian assumption of the Virgin.

The Tetragrammaton IHVH is referred to the Sephiroth, thus: the uppermost point of the letter *Yod,* I, is said to refer to *Kether;* the letter I itself to *Chokmah,* the father of Micro-prosopus; the letter H, or "the supernal *He,*" to Binah, the supernal Mother; the letter V to the next six Sephiroth, which are called the six members of Microprosopus (and six is the numerical value of V, the Hebrew *Vau*); lastly, the letter H, the "inferior *He,*" to Malkuth, the tenth Sephira, the bride of Microprosopus. (ibid., pp. 31–2)

Isaac Myer

The Hebrews...most probably designated the Primal Cause, at first by the triadic שׁדי Shaddai, the Almighty, subse-quently by the Tetragrammaton, יהוה YHVH, symbol of the Past, Present and Future, and also the equivalent for the really highest name of the Deity אהיה Eh'yeh, *i.e.,* I Am. Against the unnecessary pronunciation of יהוה the Third Commandment was made, and an Israelite always uses אדני A Do Na Y (Adonai) Lord, in place of it, hence the rendering "Lord" in the English version, whilst the lowest designation, or the Deity in Nature, the more general term Elohim, is translated, God. In the Qabbalah the Name יהוה YHVH, expresses a He and a She, two persons in one Deity, *i.e.,* the Unity of the Holy One, blessed be Hû, *i.e.,* He, and His She'keen-ah. See also the Jewish Liturgy, for Pentecost, also the daily "In the Name of Unity, of the Holy and Blessed Hû and His She'keen-ah, the Hidden and Concealed Hû, blessed be YHVH forever." Hû is said to be masculine and YaH femi-nine, together they make the יהוה אחד, *i.e.,* One YHVH. One but of a male-female nature. The She'keen-ah is always con-sidered in the Qabbalah as feminine. (*Qabbalah* [1888] [New York: Weiser, 1974], p. 175)

The letter of Kether is ' (Yod), of Binah ה (Heh), together YaH, the feminine Name. (comp. *ante,* p. 175), the third letter, that of 'Hokhmah, is ו (Vav), making together, יהו YHV of יהוה YHVH, the Tetragrammaton, and really the complete symbols of its efficaciousness. The last ה (Heh) of this Ineffable Name being always applied to the Six Lower and the last, together the seven remaining Sephiroth; and finding its resting place in the last, Malkhuth or Kingdom, the 10th Sephiroth; the Harmony of all the Sephiroth. (ibid., p. 263)

Papus

According to the ancient oral tradition of the Hebrews, or *Kabalah,* a sacred word exists, which gives to the mortal who can discover the correct way of pronouncing it, the key to all the sciences, divine and human. This word, which the common people of Israel never uttered, and which the High Priest pronounced once a year, amidst the shouts of the laity, is found at the head of every initiatory ritual; it radiates from the centre of the flaming triangle in the 33rd degree of the Scottish Rite of Freemasonry; it is displayed above the gateways of our old cathedrals; it is formed of four Hebrew letters, and reads thus, *Yod-he-vau-he,* יהוה. (*The Tarot of the Bohemians* [1889], translated by A. P. Morton, New York: Arcanum Books, 1958, pp. 17-8)

Aleister Crowley

26. IHVH. Jehovah, as the Dyad expanded, the jealous and terrible God, the lesser Countenance. The God of Nature, fecund, cruel, beautiful, relentless. (*777 and Other Qabalistic Writings* [1909] [York Beach, Maine: Weiser, 1977, p. 30)

The formation of the *Yod* is the formulation of the first creative force, of that father who is called "self-begotten," and unto whom it is said: "Thou hast formulated thy Father, and made fertile thy Mother." The adding of the *Hé* to the *Yod* is the marriage of that Father to the great co-equal Mother, who is a reflection of Nuit as He is of Hadit. Their union brings forth the son *Vau* who is the heir. Finally the daughter *Hé* is produced. She is both the twin sister and the daughter of *Vau.*

His mission is to redeem her by making her his bride; the result of this is to set her upon the throne of her mother, and

it is only she whose youthful embrace can reawaken the eld of
the All-Father. In this complex family relationship is symbolised the whole course of the Universe. (*Magick in Theory and
Practice* [1929] [New York: Dover, 1976], pp. 22–3)

P. D. Ouspensky

The world in itself, as the Kabalists hold, consists of four elements, or the four principles forming One. These four principles are represented by the four letters of the name of
Jehovah. The basic idea of the Kabala consists in the study of
the Name of God in its manifestation. Jehovah in Hebrew is
spelt by four letters, Yod, He, Vau and He—I. H. V. H. To
these four letters is given the deepest symbolical meaning.
The first letter expresses the active principle, the beginning
or first cause, motion, energy, "I"; the second letter expresses
the passive element, inertia, quietude, "not I"; the third, the
balance of opposites, "form"; and the fourth, the result or
latent energy.

The Kabalists affirm that every phenomenon and every
object consists of these four principles, i.e., that every object
and every phenomenon consists of the Name of God (The
Word),—Logos.

The study of this Name (or the four-lettered word, tetragrammaton, in Greek) and the finding of it in everything constitutes the main problem of Kabalistic philosophy.

To state it another way the Kabalists hold that these four
principles penetrate and create everything. Therefore, when
the man finds these four principles in things and phenomena
of quite different categories (where before he had not seen
similarity), he begins to see analogy between these phenomena. And, gradually, he becomes convinced that the whole
world is built according to one and the same law, on one and
the same plan. The richness and growth of his intellect consists in the widening of his faculty for finding analogies.
Therefore the study of the law of the four letters, or the name
of Jehovah presents a powerful means for widening consciousness. (*The Symbolism of the Tarot* [1913] [New York:
Dover, 1976], pp. 8–9)

Frater Achad

Now we should note that the Ineffable name יהוה is particularly attributed to the FOUR ELEMENTS, Jehovah being, as we shall see later on, the God of the Elements. Now י is FIRE, ה is Water, ו is Air and the final ה is Earth. Again we find the same symbolism, The fire of the Father, the Water of the Great Sea or Mother, coming together and forming Air, the Son, which with the previous two produces Earth, the Daughter. These again correspond with the Tarot Symbols, Wands= Fire, Cups=Water, Swords=Air and Pentacles=Earth. (*Q.B.L., or the Bride's Reception* [1922], [New York: Weiser, 1972], p. 54)

When the Qabalists tell us of the Creation of the Universe through the Father, Mother, Son and Daughter symbolized in the NAME יהוה, which is active in the SEPHIROTH, we must not think that the process ends with the production of MALKUTH, the Material World, for this is likened to the UNREDEEMED or Animal Soul in Man, viz: that which only Perceives and Feels. This "fallen one" must be RAISED TO THE THRONE OF THE MOTHER, that is to say, come to UNDERSTAND. The process of redemption is symbolised as follows, The DAUGHTER must marry the SON, she then becomes THE MOTHER who in turn arouses the active force of THE FATHER, and these twain being UNITED, all is REABSORBED into THE CROWN. (ibid., pp. 61–2)

Further 6= ו (Vau) the letter of the SON in the Ineffable Name יהוה and this SON is the result of the Union of the Father and Mother, which is in turn true numerically, since י=10 and ה=5, 10+5=15, 1+5=6=ו. (ibid., p. 71)

A. E. Waite

TETRAGRAMMATON, the so-called Ineffable or Unpronounceable Name, is the Name of Four Letters, יהוה = YHWH = YAHWEH or YAHAWEH, the Jehovah of our incorrect rendering, which Hebrew scholarship has characterized as philologically impossible. It is a *Nomen Ineffabile,* that is to say, inexpressible, because the vowels thereto belonging are now unknown, having passed out of memory after the destruction of the Temple in the year 70 A.D. There is an explanatory Talmudic tradition that the utterance of the Sacred Name was

prohibited at the death of the High Priest Simeon the Righteous. When it is said that the pointing of Adonai or Elohim is
substituted by Massoretic practice for the lost vowels, this
does not mean that there was an attempt to pronounce the
Name with their aid but that one of the alternatives was to be
used instead. It will be remembered that God is made to say
in the ZOHAR: My Name is written YHVH but is read Adonai.
(*The Holy Kabbalah* [1929] [New Hyde Park, New York: University Books, 1975], p. 617)

Israel Regardie

The Father is given the letter "Y" of this name, and the first
"H" is attributed to the Mother. From the union of the Y and
the H flow the rest of all created things. In other words, from
consciousness and its vehicle are all things formed, and every
conceivable being, god or human, divine or animal, has its
basis in the Y and the H of the divine name. (*The Tree of Life*
[1932] [New York: Weiser, 1969], pp. 47–8)

The formula of Tetragrammaton is also applied to the Four
Worlds, and the primordial four elements. To the Archetypal
World the letter "Y" is given. Hence the Archetypal World is
the Father, the all-begetter, and all-devourer of the worlds.
The "Y" also represents, in this instince, the element of Fire,
showing forth the fierce, active, spiritual nature of the Father.
The "H" primal of the Tetragrammaton is allocated to the
Creative World to which, being receptive and passive, the element of Water pertains. This plane represents the Mother
who, before the Son can be given birth, awaits the creative
energy and the influx of divine life from the Father. The Formative World is assigned to the letter "V," the Son, and the
latter, like the Father, is active, male and energetic; hence the
element Air is the attribution. Completing the divine name is
a second "H," this letter being similar to the Mother, passive
and inert, receiving whatever influences are poured into her.
"H" is called in the Book of Splendour, the King's Palace, and
the Daughter, representing the Physical World, which is the
synthesis of all the worlds. (ibid., pp. 55–6)

Paul Foster Case

A circle enclosing a cross is a mathematical symbol of the Name of Names, IHVH, because every circle corresponds numerically to the number 22, and every cross to the number 4. Thus the circle enclosing the cross represents 22 plus 4, or 26, the value of IHVH, the Unutterable Name. [*The Book of Tokens* [1934] [Los Angeles: Builders of the Adytum, 1968], pp. 94-5)

To commemorate this fourfold manifestation of Life, the Divine Names in many languages are four-lettered. This is particularly true in Hebrew, and of the Divine Names in that language the most important is the Tetragrammaton, IHVH. Each letter of this Name represents one of the four aspects of Life called "elements." I stands for FIRE; the first H for WATER; the V for AIR; and the second H for EARTH. (ibid., p. 125)

The doctrine of the fourfold activity of Spirit occurs again and again in the Qabalah, and is expressed in many ways. The Name of God, IHVH, is four-lettered, each letter corresponding to one of the four elements and to one of the four Qabalistic worlds. The letters of this name are represented by the four animals described in the Vision of Ezekiel: "They four had the face of a lion, of an eagle, of a man, and of an ox." These living creatures correspond to the four aspects of the Absolute. The lion corresponds to Life, to the element of Fire, to ATZILUTH, the archetypal world, to YOD in IHVH, and to the Sephirah CHOKMAH, Root of Fire. The eagle corresponds to Mind, to the element of Water, to BRIAH, the creative world, to the first HEH in IHVH, and to the Sephirah BINAH, the Root of Water. The man corresponds to the third aspect, Truth or Law, to the element of Air, to YETZIRAH, the formative world, to VAV in IHVH, and to the Sephirah TIPHARETH, attributed to Air. The ox or bull corresponds to the fourth aspect, Love, to the element of Earth, to ASSIAH, the material world, to the final HEH in IHVH, and to the Sephirah MALKUTH, attributed to Earth. (ibid., pp. 189–90)

The master-key to the Hebrew wisdom is the "name" translated "Lord" in the Authorized Version of the Bible, and "Jehovah" in the revised versions. It is not really a *name* at all, but rather a verbal, numerical and geometrical formula. In Roman letters corresponding to Hebrew it is spelled IHVH. (*The Tarot* [1947] [Los Angeles: Builders of the Adytum, 1990], p. 3)

E. M. Butler

A great and almost impenetrable mystery had indeed gradually grown up round the name which to us seems the most familiar of all, even though its pronunciation has shifted in our own day: Jehovah or Jahweh. Represented by the letters JHVH (Yod He Vau He), it seems at first to have been openly spoken. But a time came when, possibly owing to the mystery-mongering about divine names in Egypt and Babylonia, the Hebrew priests refrained from pronouncing it, and substituted ADONAI (Lord) when they read the sacred texts out loud. The Jewish people followed their lead; and, because of the absence of vowels from the Hebrew alphabet, the original pronunciation was finally forgotten and not rediscovered until A.D. 300 or thereabouts. It was the Kabbalists who emphasized the mystery surrounding the letters JHVH by referring to the name they represented as the "word of four letters," TETRAGRAMMATON, and this caught on like wild-fire in the magical texts. Few indeed and far between are those modern rituals in which that awe-inspiring name does not occupy the place of honour. (*Ritual Magic* [1949] [Hollywood: Newcastle Publishing, 1971], p. 40)

William Gray

Until the Left-hand limit of the Feminine Binah came into being, nothing further could be created in mind or matter. It is therefore technically true to say that the Female Principle made possible the knowledge between Good and Evil, (Daath), but it made all other knowledge possible at the same moment. Once Binah exists, so does distinction between Right and Left, Black and White, This and That etc. Once the Monad becomes the Dyad, the Triad are automatically in existence, which combine in the Tetrad, and so the Mighty Name (IHWH) is "uttered." (*The Ladder of Lights* [1968] York Beach, ME: Samuel Weiser], p. 174)

The Symbolic sonic or alphabetical Glyph YHWH is supposed to be so powerful a Name that if it were ever pronounced properly the world would be destroyed. This is literally and strictly true, because it represents the explosive force of the Primary "Bang" which accompanied the commencement of our Creation. An equivalent "Bang" or "utterance" of the Name will be heard (though not by us) when our present planet explodes into Cosmic dust at the end of its existence. YHWH will have uttered YHWH, and That will be That. (ibid., p. 194)

The concept of Original Creation was that the Divine One emerged from Ocean calling for Light with His first Breath (Ain Soph Aur and Kether) when His first perception was His own image in the water which He immediately named as YHWH. Perhaps it was an exclamation of pure shock which produced the Initial Explosion of the Universe (I.E.U.). Be that as it may, the Initial Creative Cry of "Good God!" or its equivalent brought Being into Existence out of Nothing.

In the old Qabalistic Tradition, the Divine Name was only passed on once in seven years from Master to disciple, "mouth to ear." At the Temple the High Priest alone was empowered to "speak" the Name once a year when he entered the otherwise silent Holy of Holies which no other mortal might penetrate. Doubtless it was fully realized that the Tetragram used on such occasions was only a human substitute for the "Lost Word" which if once recovered would restore Mankind to Godstatus. Possibly the sound of this conclusive Word is not unlike an atomic explosion. (ibid., p. 196)

Gershom Scholem

In a similar fashion the name YHWH denotes just one *Sefirah* (*Tiferet*) but also contains within it all the fundamental stages of emanation: the spike at the top of the *yod* represents the source of all in *Ayin,* the *yod* itself is *Ḥokhmah,* the first *he* is *Binah,* the *vav* is *Tiferet* or, because of the numerical value of the letter *vav,* the totality of the six *Sefirot* and the final *he* is *Malkhut.* Since the latter comprises the other *Sefirot* and has no independent power, it cannot be assigned a letter of its own but only that *he,* which has already appeared at the beginning of the emanation of the structure of the *Sefirot* and whose manifestation has reached its final development at the end of the process. (*Kabbalah* [1974] [Jerusalem: Keter, 1977], p. 111)

Appendix C

'''''''''''''''''''''''''''

The Hours of the Wings

Since there is such a strong correspondence between the Wings of the Winds and the twenty-four hours of the day, it is necessary to assign these angels to the individual hours they rule. The occult, or lunar, angels relate to the twelve hours of the night; the overt, or solar, angels relate to the corresponding twelve hours of the day.

In traditional magic, the period between sunrise and sunset is divided into twelve parts. These are called the hours of the day. Similarly, the period between sunset and sunrise is divided into twelve parts, called the hours of the night. Usually the hours of the day are said to be equal to each other, and the hours of the night equal to each other, although this is merely a convention based upon the old equal house system of astrology. During the summer months in the northern hemisphere each nominally equal magical "hour" of the day will contain more than sixty minutes, because in the summer the days are longer than the nights. During the winter months each "hour" will have less than sixty minutes, because in the winter the days are shorter than the nights. The inverse is true of the magical hours of the night. Only on the two days of the equinox will the magical hours and clock hours be of the same length, and even then they will not correspond exactly, since the first "hour" of a magical day begins at the moment of sunrise.

Those wishing to calculate the magical hours for a given night will need an ephemeris or almanac for the current year that gives the exact minute of sunrise and sunset for that day and local latitude. Determine how many hours and minutes lie between sunset and sunrise, convert the duration into minutes, then divide by twelve, and this will give you the number of minutes in each of the twelve magical hours of the night, which begins at the minute of sunset. Similarly, to find the magical hours of a given day, convert the span between sunrise and sunset into minutes and divide by twelve. This will yield the number of minutes in each magical hour of that day, which begins at the minute of sunrise.

We may assign the first hour of day to the overt angel of IHVH (Kethahel) in the first house of the zodiac, the house of Aries; the second hour to the overt angel of HHVI (Shiael) in the second house, the house of Taurus; and so on. The first hour of the night may be assigned to the occult angel of IHVH (Hatakiah) in the first house, the second hour to the occult angel of HHVI (Aishiah) in the second house, and so on.

The Banners and Wings of the hours of day and night are tablulated below:

	Day		**Night**
1	Kethahel	IHVH	Hatakiah
2.	Shaiel	HHVI	Aishiah
3.	Vihael	VHHI	Hiviah
4.	Daviel	HVHI	Yodiah
5.	Keliel	IVHH	Yelekiah
6.	Shahavel	HIVH	Vaheshiah
7.	Vahael	VHIH	Haviah
8.	Dabael	HHIV	Badiah
9.	Kazahel	IHHV	Hazekiah
10.	Shabuel	HIHV	Vabashiah
11.	Vivael	VIHH	Viviah
12.	Demuel	HVIH	Vamediah

APPENDIX D

❜ ❜

THE STONES ON THE BREASTPLATE

T he sources for the following table of the stones said to have been set into the breastplate of Aaron, the high priest of ancient Israel, are all based upon the Hebrew book of Exodus. As the biblical scholar W. E. Addis points out: "The meaning of the Hebrew words for the precious stones named here is in almost every case quite uncertain" (*The Documents of the Hexateuch* [*London:* David Nutt, 1898], vol. 2, p. 260, note 2). Since I was unable to find any source for these stones that I could regard as authoritative, I compiled my own list (given in Chapter XII) by making a comparative study of seven texts: (1) the authorized King James Bible; (2) the Knox Bible; 3) the eleventh edition of the *Encyclopedia Britannica; (*4) *Amulets and Superstitions* by E. A. Wallis Budge (reprinted by University Books under the title *Amulets and Talismans,* New York, 1968); (5) William Wiston's translation of the *Works of Flavius Josephus* (London: George Routledge and Sons, no date); (6) W. E. Addis' *Documents of the Hexateuch,* mentioned above; (7) *The Pentateuch and Rashi's Commentary,* translated by R. Abraham Ben Isaiah and R. Benjamin Sharfman (Brooklyn: S. S. & R. Publishing, 1949], volume 2: "Exodus"). No two of these sources agree in all respects, as can be seen in the accompanying table:

James	Knox	Brit.	Budge	Josephus	Addis	Rashi
1. Sardius	Sardius	Sard	Carnelian or Sard	Sardonyx	Carnelian	Carnelian
2. Topaz	Topaz	Topaz	Topaz or Peridot	Topaz	Topaz	Topaz
3. Carbuncle	Emerald	Emerald	Emerald	Emerald	Emerald	Smaragd
4. Emerald	Carbuncle	Carbuncle	Ruby or Carbuncle	Carbuncle	Ruby	Carbuncle
5. Sapphire	Sapphire	Sapphire	Sapphire or Lapis	Jasper	Sapphire	Sapphire
6. Diamond	Jasper	Jaspis	Jasper or Onyx	Sapphire	Jasper	Emerald
7. Ligure	Jacynth	Ligure	Jacinth	Ligure	Jacinth	Jacinth
8. Agate	Agate	Agate	Agate	Amethyst	Agate	Agate
9. Amethyst	Amethyst	Amethyst	Amethyst	Agate	Amethyst	Amethyst
10. Beryl	Chrysolite	Chrysolite	Beryl or Y. Jasper	Chrysolite	Chrysolite	Beryl
11. Onyx	Onyx	Beryl	Chrysolite	Onyx	Beryl	Onyx
12. Jasper	Beryl	Onyx	Jasper	Beryl	Onyx	Jasper

APPENDIX E

ﬧ ﬧ ﬧ ﬧ ﬧ ﬧ ﬧ ﬧ ﬧ ﬧ ﬧ ﬧ ﬧ ﬧ ﬧ ﬧ ﬧ ﬧ

TABLE OF THE BANNERS

The accompanying table shows the occult correspondences for the permutations of Tetragrammaton that have been examined in this book. They are based on the orientation of the zodiac and the elements to the four directions that occurs in the *New Magus* system of magic—south (fire), Leo; west (water), Scorpio; north (air), Aquarius; and east (earth), Taurus. It must be pointed out that this differs in minor respects from the more commonly used Golden Dawn system, where (earth) Taurus is placed in the north and (air) Aquarius in the east.

The correspondences of the Enochian names of God to the Banners are based upon my own Restored Great Table of the Watchtowers, which uses the lettering of the reformed Great Table of Raphael. I have attributed the directions of space to the quadrants as these were revealed to Dee and Kelley by the angle Ave (see Casaubon, pp. 173-7), and have placed the Watchtowers upon the quadrants in the order in which they were delivered by Ave, beginning with the east (upper left) and proceeding clockwise around the Table. This is inevitable if the table is to be laid down in the circle with its corners pointing to the four directions, as is evident was the intention from Dee's own diagram of the Enochian banners (reproduced by James, *The Enochian Magick of Dr. John Dee,* p. 119). This results in a different set of associations from those used by Dee and those used in the Golden Dawn (which differ from one another).

The twenty-four Enochian seniors are drawn from the Restored Great Table using the same alignment of the table to the four directions. The names of the seniors related to the overt Banners of each Watchtower begin with the letter in the intersection of its great cross that is on the right side. The names of the seniors related to the occult Banners of each Watchtower begin with the letter in the intersection of its great cross that is on the left side.

The senior names for the pair of cardinal Banners in each Watchtower frame the upper left quadrant of the Watchtower, which forms an undivided whole. The senior names for the pair of mutable Banners in each Watchtower frame the upper right quadrant, the addition of which results in two equal halves that are divided down the middle. The senior names for the pair of fixed Banners in each Watchtower define the lower right and lower left quadrants, resulting in four equal quarters that are divided by a cross. This very well reflects the three sigil shapes of the Banners.

Table of the Banners

No.	Banners	Wings of the Winds	Enochian God Names	Enochian Seniors	Polarity	Direction	Zodiac	Tribe of Israel	Apostles of Christ	Gem	Beast of IHVH	Letter
1.	IHVH	Kethahel	MOR	Laidrom	+	ENE	Aries	Reuben	Peter	Sard		
2.	IHVH	Hatakiah		Aczinor	–							
3.	IHHV	Kazahel	DIAL	Lzinopo	+	WNW	Sagittarius	Simeon	Philip	Topaz	Lion	Yod
4.	IHHV	Hazekiah		Alhctga	–							
5.	IVHH	Keliel	HCTGA	Liiansa	+	South	Leo	Levi	James the Lesser	Emerald		
6.	IVHH	Yelekiah		Ahmlicv	–							
7.	HVHI	Daviel	OIP	Aaetpio	+	SSE	Cancer	Judah	Andrew	Garnet		
8.	HVHI	Yodiah		Adoeoet	–							
9.	HVIH	Demuel	TEAA	Alndvod	+	NNE	Pisces	Issachar	Bartholomew	Sapphire	Eagle	First He
10.	HVIH	Vamediah		Aapdoce	–							
11.	HHIV	Dabael	PDOCE	Arinnap	+	West	Scorpio	Zebulun	Thaddeus	Jasper		
12.	HHIV	Badiah		Anodoin	–							
13.	VHIH	Vahael	MPH	Lsrahpm	+	WSW	Libra	Dan	James the Greater	Jacinth		
14.	VHIH	Haviah		Saiinou	–							
15.	VHHI	Vihael	ARSL	Laoaxrp	+	ESE	Gemini	Naphtali	Thomas	Agate	Man	Vau
16.	VHHI	Hiviah		Slgaiol	–							
17.	VIHH	Vivael	GAIOL	Ligdisa	+	North	Aquarius	Gad	Simon	Amethyst		
18.	VIHH	Viviah		Soniznt	–							
19.	HIHV	Shabuel	ORI	Habioro	+	NNW	Capricorn	Asher	John	Chrysolite		
20.	HIHV	Vabashiah		Aaozaif	–							
21.	HIVH	Shahavel	IBAH	Htmorda	+	SSW	Virgo	Joseph	Matthew	Onyx	Bull	Second He
22.	HIVH	Vaheshiah		Ahaozpi	–							
23.	HHVI	Shiael	AOZPI	Hipotga	+	East	Taurus	Benjamin	Matthias	Beryl		
24.	HHVI	Aishiah		Avtotar	–							

APPENDIX F

''''''''''''''''''''''''''

THE BANNERS ACCORDING
TO AGRIPPA

The great Renaissance magician Henry Cornelius Agrippa included a table of the twelve Banners of Tetragrammaton and their occult correspondences in his *Three Books of Occult Philosophy*. I have reproduced some of this table below for comparison with the same correspondences that appear elsewhere in this book.

Agrippa was a skilled occultist and a careful scholar. He can usually be trusted to copy his sources accurately, although he seldom bothers to tell his reader who those sources are. He probably derived his material on the Banners from Reuchlin or Pico della Mirandola, but I cannot speak with assurance on this point since I have not run across the text from which he extracted this matter. That a source exists for the relationships in Agrippa's table seems almost certain, since Agrippa displays no innovation in his book, which is merely a wide-ranging compendium of existing information about magic. All of Agrippa's considerable genius lies in the way he organizes these available materials.

I have allowed the categories reproduced from the table (which is found on pages 218–9 of the 1651 English translation of the *Occult Philosophy)* to stand as Agrippa gives them, even though he obviously did not understand the correct order for the Banners. Banners seven, eight, and nine, which are the three Banners of air, are all out of their natural positions—a fact that is indisputable once the numerical pattern of the Banners is examined. In Agrippa's list, the tribes Manasseh and Ephraim take the place of the tribes of Joseph and Levi. For a corrected version of this table, see my own annotated edition of the *Three Books of Occult Philosophy* (Llewellyn, 1993).

Banner	Sign	Month	Stone	Tribe	Apostle
IHVH	Aries	March	Sardonyx	Dan	Matthias
IHHV	Taurus	April	Carnelian	Ruben	Thaddeus
IVHH	Gemini	May	Topaz	Judah	Simon
HVHI	Cancer	June	Chalcedony	Manasseh	John
HVIH	Leo	July	Jasper	Asher	Peter
HHIV	Virgo	August	Emerald	Simeon	Andrew
VHHI	Libra	September	Beryl	Issachar	Bartholomew
VIHH	Scorpio	October	Amethyst	Benjamin	Philip
VHIH	Sagittarius	November	Hyacinth	Naphtali	James Eld.
HIHV	Capricorn	December	Chrysoprase	Gad	Thomas
HIVH	Aquarius	January	Crystal	Zebulun	Matthew
HHVI	Pisces	February	Sapphire	Ephraim	James Yng.

APPENDIX G

'''''''''''''''''''''''''

THE TWELVE APOSTLES

The order of the twelve apostles of Jesus that appears in the table of the Banners in Appendix E and elsewhere should not be regarded as cast in bronze. The correct ordering of the apostles is in considerable dispute. As is true of the ordering of the tribes of Israel in the Old Testament, they appear in different sequences in various places. The order I have given should be looked upon as a workable compromise. The only certain feature of the apostle sequence is its division into three groups of four apostles, which evidently is intended to reflect the fourfold division of Tetragrammaton.

The accompanying table illustrates the various orders of the apostles that appear in different books of the New Testament. I have favored the order given in Matthew, but have no compelling reason for so doing. Following the common practice of the Renaissance, I have substituted Matthias, the 13th apostle, for Judas. Readers who have a more emphatic opinion about the correct order of the apostles may wish to modify their relationship with the Banners, tribes, zodiac signs, and so on.

ACTS 1:13	MATTHEW 10:2-4	MARK 3:16-9	LUKE 6:14-6
Peter	Peter	Peter	Peter
James	Andrew	James Z.	Andrew
John	James Z.	John	James Z.
Andrew	John	Andrew	John
Philip	Philip	Philip	Philip
Thomas	Bartholomew	Bartholomew	Bartholomew
Bartholomew	Thomas	Matthew	Matthew
Matthew	Matthew	Thomas	Thomas
James A.	James A.	James A.	James A.
Simon	Thaddeus	Thaddeus	Simon
Thaddeus	Simon	Simon	Thaddeus
(Matthias)	Judas	Judas	Judas

APPENDIX H

❟❟❟❟❟❟❟❟❟❟❟❟❟❟❟❟❟❟❟❟❟

NUMERICAL BREAKDOWN
OF THE BANNERS

Whether the twelve Banners of Tetragrammaton should be assigned to the signs of the zodiac successively in the natural order of the signs (IHVH—Aries; IHHV—Taurus; IVHH—Gemini) or in four sets of elemental trines (IHVH—Aries; IHHV—Sagittarius; IVHH—Leo) is a question every occultist must decide independently. It was the common practice to assign the Banners to the signs successively among the kabbalists and magicians of the Renaissance. If nothing else, it has simplicity to recommend it.

However, it is no longer possible to dispute the true order of the Banners, which I revealed in *The New Magus* through a simple process of numerical substitution. The traditional order of the Banners is that given by the great German magician Cornelius Agrippa in his *Three Books of Occult Philosophy* (1533): IHVH, IHHV, IVHH; HVHI, HVIH, HHIV; VHHI, VIHH, VHIH; HIHV, HIVH, HHVI. This order was reproduced in the influential work of Francis Barrett, *The Magus* (London 1801), and probably from this latter source found its way into the magical system of the Golden Dawn through the work of its founding member, S. L. MacGregor Mathers.

Mathers reproduces this ordering of the Banners in his influential translation of part of Knorr von Rosenroth's *Kabbalah Denudata* (see *The Kabbalah Unveiled* [London: Routledge & Kegan Paul, 1962], p. 31). Mathers' book was first published in 1887, a year before the establishment of the

Isis-Urania Temple of the Hermetic Order of the Golden Dawn. In fact, it
had circulated in manuscript a year before its publication—Mathers had
shown it with obvious pride to Madame Blavatsky, the founder of the Theo-
sophical Society, in 1886.

As is so often the case in magic, five centuries of magicians adhered to
this order without ever questioning it. When I came to write *The New
Magus* around 1984, I decided to analyze the order of the Banners using the
simple expedient of substituting numbers for the letters. I made *Yod* equal
1, the first *He* equal 2, *Vau* equal 3, and the second *He* equal 4. It was no
surprise when a numerical pattern emerged; what was surprising was the
obvious anomaly in that pattern. The numbers very clearly revealed the
important distinction between the first and second He, which was hidden by
the duplicate Hebrew letter in each Banner.

Writing out the Banners in the traditional ordering of Agrippa and
Mathers, and converting the Hebrew letters to numbers, the following
numerical pattern resulted:

IHVH	1234	VHHI	3421
IHHV	1243	VIHH	3124
IVHH	1342	VHIH	3412
HVHI	2341	HIHV	4123
HVIH	2314	HIVH	4132
HHIV	2413	HHVI	4231

Although all twelve Banners are represented in this list, it is clear from
the numbers that the three Banners that begin with V are out of their correct sequence. By using the numbers as a reference, it is not a difficult task
to restore the Banners beginning with V to their proper ordering:

IHVH	1234	VHIH	3412
IHHV	1243	VHHI	3421
IVHH	1342	VIHH	3124
HVHI	2341	HIHV	4123
HVIH	2314	HIVH	4132
HHIV	2413	HHVI	4231

The pattern of the substituted numbers is so clear as to permit no dispute. It is quite possible that the ordering of the Banners that occurs in
Agrippa's *Occult Philosophy* was originally deliberate, an attempt to protect
the Name from misuse. Agrippa did not originate this order of the Banners,
but copied it from some older source. If the error was deliberate camouflage,
it worked far better than its deviser had any reason to expect, enjoying the

status among many occultists as the correct order of the Banners for five centuries. There is no reason to believe that Mathers or any other member of the original Golden Dawn had the slightest suspicion that it was incorrect.

In recent years several important texts of the Kabbalah have become available in English translation. From these I have learned that the correct sequence of the Banners (or Seals) was known to Hebrew Kabbalists during the Middle Ages. It appears in the *Sha'are Orah* (Gates of Light) of Rabbi Joseph Gikatilla, a book written around the beginning of the fourteenth century, and first published at Mantua in 1561. It also occurs in the *Pardes Rimonim* of Moses Cordevero, which was written in 1548.

Had these works been available to me during the writing of *The New Magus**, I might have saved myself considerable labor over the permutations of the Name, but perhaps would not have understood so clearly the reason for the correct sequence of the Banners, and why all other sequences are incorrect.

**New Millennium Magic*, an updated and expanded version of *The New Magus*, will be available in May 1996 from Llewellyn Worldwide, Ltd.

Appendix I

‚ ‚

TABLE OF THE HEBREW ALPHABET

Letter	Value	Name	Meaning	Transliteration	Kind
א	1	Aleph	Ox	A	Mother
ב	2	Beth	House	B	Double
ג	3	Gimel	Camel	G, Gh	Double
ד	4	Daleth	Door	D, Dh	Double
ה	5	He	Window	H	Single
ו	6	Vau	Nail	O, U, V	Single
ז	7	Zayin	Sword	Z	Single
ח	8	Cheth	Fence	Ch	Single
ט	9	Teth	Snake	T	Single
י	10	Yod	Hand	I, J, Y	Single
כ, ך	20, 500	Kaph	Fist	K, Kh	Double
ל	30	Lamed	Ox-goad	L	Single
מ, ם	40, 600	Mem	Water	M	Mother
נ, ן	50, 700	Nun	Fish	N	Single
ס	60	Samekh	Prop	S	Single
ע	70	Ayin	Eye	Aa, Ngh	Single
פ, ף	80, 800	Pe	Mouth	P, Ph	Double
צ, ץ	90, 900	Tzaddi	Hook	Tz	Single
ק	100	Qoph	Ear	Q	Single
ר	200	Resh	Head	R	Double
ש	300	Shin	Tooth	S, Sh	Mother
ת	400	Tau	Cross	T, Th	Double

Appendix J

TABLE OF THE ENOCHIAN ALPHABET

Letter	Value	Name	Transliteration
Ᵹ	1	Pa	B
ß	2	Veh	C/K
ꞇ	3	Ged	G/J
ꭓ	4	Gal	D
⨍	5	Or	F
⅄	6	Un	A
ꓶ	7	Graph	E
ℰ	8	Tal	M
ꭏ	9	Gon	I/Y
ꓧ	10	Na	H
Ϲ	20	Ur	L
∩	30	Mals	P
⊔	40	Ger	Q
Ⅎ	50	Drux	N
Γ	60	Pal	X
∟	70	Med	O
ℰ	80	Don	R
Ρ	90	Ceph	Z
ꓘ	100	Van	U/V/W
⅂	200	Fam	S
∕	300	Gisg	T

GENERAL INDEX

Aaron (high priest), 14, 73, 77, 79, 81-83, 85, 90, 92, 153, 156, 194, 259

Abba (Supernal Father), 8, 28, 120

Abraham (patriarch), 3, 72, 239, 259

Abyss (Bottomless Pit), 93, 148, 206-207, 213, 220

Achad, Frater (Charles Stansfeld Jones), xiv, 217, 239, 251

Acts, Book of, 166

Adam, Greater (Heavenly), 99

Adam, Lesser (Earthly), 38, 100, 119, 233, 244, 246

Addis, W. E. (writer), 259-260

Adonai (name of God), 2, 4, 40, 247-248, 252, 254

Adonai ha-Aretz (name of God), 40

Adonai Tzabaoth (name of God), 40

Aeons, 232

Aethers, thirty Enochian, 173, 180, 183-184, 191, 200, 208, 221, 230-232

Agate (stone), 79, 81, 137-138, 260, 263

Agrippa, Cornelius (writer), 38-39, 48, 50, 56, 61, 63, 80, 242, 265-266, 269-270

Ahasuerus, King (biblical), 203-204

Aima (Supernal Mother), 8, 28, 120

Ain (Nothingness), 10-11, 100, 108, 243, 255

Ain Soph (Limitless Void), 10-11, 100, 108, 243, 255

Ain Soph Aur (Infinite Light), 100, 108, 255

Alchemical Writings of Edward Kelly, The (ed. Waite), 243

Alchemy, 15-16, 93, 184, 201

Altar(s), 14, 67-75, 108-118, 154-161

Amethyst (stone), 74, 79, 81, 139-140, 260, 263, 266

Amina (Solomon's concubine), 93

Amulets, 32, 35, 90, 259

Amulets and Talismans (Budge), 106-107

Anael (angel of Venus), 149

Ancient Ones—see Elders, 149, 156-157, 192

Angels, 7-8, 35, 48-49, 60-66, 70, 73, 91, 93-95, 97-105, 111-152, 154-155, 163-166, 169-171, 173-175, 178-185, 189-192,

195-196, 198, 201-202, 205-206, 208-211, 218-228, 232-237, 242, 253-254, 257-258

Angels (Spirits), Enochian, xv-xvi, 35, 64-66, 163-164, 166-167, 169-184, 186-187, 190-193, 196-204, 206-233, 235-237

Angels, fallen, 93, 119, 198, 213-214

Angels, four, 91, 112-113, 115-116, 118, 149, 155, 161, 179-180, 192

Angels, four fallen, 213-214

Antiquities of the Jews (Josephus), 240

Aphrodite (goddess), 148

Apocalypse, 61, 186-187, 189, 210-211, 216, 220-221, 223, 225, 229, 233, 237

Apollo (god), 148, 205

Apostles, twelve, 48, 74, 154, 267

Archons (Rulers), 234-235

Ark of the Covenant, 68, 71, 225

Armageddon—see Apocalypse, 187, 211, 233

Ash tree, 222

Ashmodai (king of the demons), 90, 92-94

Assiah (Physical World of the Kabbalah), 13, 100, 253

Astrology, 17, 57, 81, 99, 103, 194, 232, 257

Atropos (a Fate), 226

Atziluth (Archetypal World of the Kabbalah), 100, 253

Augustine, Saint (writer), 233

Aurora (goddess), 203

Ave (Enochian angel), 164, 170-171, 173, 179-180, 182, 196, 221, 236, 261

Azael (fallen angel), 93

Ba'alai Shem (Masters of the Name), 1-2, 37-39, 41-42, 63, 241

Babalon (Crowley's Scarlet Woman), 216

Babylon the Great (biblical), 73, 178, 206, 210, 216, 225, 234

Bahir, The (ed. Kaplan), 63, 240

Balance, 41, 84, 190, 222, 237, 250

Banishing, 31-33, 51-53, 61, 66, 109, 112, 114, 120, 123-146

Banner angels, 60-66, 98, 102, 111, 114, 120, 153

Banners (of IHVH), 1-4, 7-8, 10, 12-14, 16-18, 20, 22-24, 31-35, 40-41, 44-45, 48, 50, 59-61, 63, 65-68, 71, 73, 78-85, 92, 95, 97-106, 110-115, 117, 119-146, 149, 151, 153-154, 156-157, 165-166, 179-180, 182-183, 194-197, 203, 222-224, 239, 247-249, 253-254, 258, 261-263, 265-267, 269-271

Banners, Enochian—see Ensigns, Enochian

Baptism, ritual, 70, 111, 113-116

Barbelo (Great Mother), 186, 234

Barrett, Francis (writer), 269

Bathsheba (mother of Solomon), 88, 92

Beast, Great, 44, 187, 200, 216

Beast, mark of the, 209, 211

Beasts, four, 60-62, 64-65, 74, 88, 112, 119, 149, 183, 191, 197, 204, 208, 220, 223

Beasts, twelve, 74, 88

Beryl (stone), 74, 79, 81, 145-146, 260, 263, 266

Binah (2nd Sephirah), 8-12, 40-41, 83, 99, 120, 248-249, 253-255

Binary numbers, 25-26, 28

Binding, occult, 70, 94

Blavatsky, Helena Petrovna (writer), 246, 270

Blessing of Aaron, 194

Blessing of Jacob, 81

Blessings, six, 70

Book of Secrets, The, 106

Book of the Miracles of R. Loew (Rosenburg), 40

Book of Thoth, The (Crowley), 17, 25

Book of Tokens, The (Case), 253

Brass vessel(s) of Solomon, 73

Breastplate of Aaron, 14, 73, 77, 79, 81-83, 85, 90, 92, 153, 156, 194, 259

Briah (Creative World of the Kabbalah), 253

Budge, E. A. Wallis (writer), 90, 182, 259-260

Burning bush, 2

Burton, Richard F. (writer), 89, 91

Butler, E. M. (writer), 254

Cakes, twelve, 73

Calls, Enochian—see Keys, Enochian

Carbuncle (stone), 79, 81, 260

Carnelian (stone), 78, 260, 266

Carpet, Solomon's flying, 87-88

Casaubon, Meric (writer), 164-166, 168, 170-173, 181-183, 186, 189, 192, 196, 208, 214, 217, 222, 225, 237, 261

Case, Paul Foster (writer), 253

Cassiel (angel of Saturn), 149

Chalcedony (stone), 74, 78-79, 266

Change (Wilhelm), 27

Channels, Sephirothic, 9, 212

Chariot of God, 88

Chesed, 8-9, 12, 40, 100, 108, 150-151, 204

Chokmah, 8-10, 12, 40-41, 83, 99, 120, 248, 253

Christ, Jesus, 2, 4, 47-50, 53, 55-57, 60, 62, 65-66, 74, 99-100, 106, 119, 148-155, 158-160, 183, 190-193, 197-198, 200, 202, 206-208, 210-212, 215-216, 222-225, 227-229, 232, 235, 237, 263, 267

Christ-form, assuming the, 147, 149-155, 157, 159-161, 198, 232, 248

Chrysolite (stone), 74, 79, 81, 141-142, 260, 263

Chrysoprase (stone), 266

Circle, magic, 32, 93, 108-110, 112-113, 115-118, 122, 147, 155-157, 161, 168, 198

Circle, squaring the, 15-16

Circles, stone, 69, 72

City of God, The (Augustine), 233

Cleansing prayer, 107-108, 111, 116, 118, 155

Cleansing, ritual, 108, 110-111, 154, 160, 203

Clement of Alexandria, 4

Clock in the Piazza San Marco, 196-197, 223

Clock, cosmic, 189, 194, 196-197, 224

Clotho (a Fate), 226

Commanding voice, 45-46

Complete Enochian Dictionary, The (Laycock), 164, 189, 214

Conclusions, Kabbalistic (Pico), 241

Contagion, principle of, 106

Coronzon (the Death-Dragon), 181, 186-187, 206-208, 233, 237

Cross, 5, 23-24, 31-32, 55-59, 71, 110-112, 115-116, 118, 155, 157-159, 164, 167, 172-173, 181-182, 191, 194, 196, 212, 224, 253, 262

Cross, Kabbalistic, 106-108, 111, 116, 118, 155

Crosses of the Watchtowers, 164, 181-182, 191, 196, 262

Crowley, Aleister (writer), 17, 25, 28, 44, 147, 187, 200, 216-217, 237, 239, 249

Cube, 13-14, 73, 83, 245

Culpeper's Complete Herbal, 89

Culpeper, Nicholas (writer), 89

Current, 200, 257

Curses, six, 70

Curses, twelve, 68-69

Cutting of the shoots, 100

Daath (quasi-Sephirah), 254

De arte cabalistica (Reuchlin), 48

De harmonia mundi (Giorgi), 48

De heptarchia mystica (Dee), 226

De verbo mirifico (Reuchlin), 48

Death, house of, 205-206, 216-217

Death-Dragon—see Coronzon

Decans (astrological), 92

Dee, John (writer), 44, 55-66, 95, 99-100, 163-173, 178, 180-182, 184-186, 189, 194-197, 200, 203, 207-208, 210-212, 214-215, 217, 219-220, 223-226, 228, 232, 236-237, 261

Demons (Devils), 2, 17, 48-50, 66, 87-90, 92-93, 119, 140, 148, 170, 179, 187, 190, 205-206, 213-214, 220, 241, 246

Denning, Melita and Osborne Phillips, 189

Deuteronomy, Book Of, 68-70, 80

Devil, the—see Satan

Diamond (stone), 90, 94-95, 110, 207, 209-210, 260

Dictionary of Phrase and Fable (Brewer), 82

Dictionary of the Bible (McKenzie), 71

Din (5th Sephirah, alternate name), 10, 100, 191, 222, 225

Dionysus (god), 43

Directions of space, xiv, 3, 7-8, 17, 35, 105, 112, 116, 122, 156, 168, 170-171, 181, 197, 227, 261

Dispositors, sixteen, 179-181

Divination, 28, 77, 82-85

Divination, Hebrew, 10, 62, 253-254

DNA, 20

Documents of the Hexateuch, The (Addis), 259

Dragon, alchemical, 168

Dragon, Great (Coronzon), 186, 205-206, 208, 233

Dragon, red, 208

Dream of the Rood (Cynwulf), 212

Druids, 43, 213

Eagle, 60, 88, 93, 105, 113, 149, 208, 216, 253, 263

Earth (planet/goddess), 8, 14, 17, 37-38, 57-58, 64-65, 74, 91, 99-100, 152, 158-159, 170, 179-182, 187, 193-194, 196-202, 204-213, 215-216, 218, 221-222, 224-230, 232-236, 244, 246-247

Ebal, Mount (biblical), 68-71

Ecclesiastes, Book Of, 92

Eden, Garden of, 233-234

Eheieh (name of God), 40, 247-248

El (name of God), 40

El Chai (name of God), 40

Elders of Solomon, seventy-two, 88

Elders, twenty-four, 35, 60, 149-151, 180-181, 183, 192-193, 207, 214, 218, 222, 262-263

Elements, 16-17, 25, 38-39, 41, 50-52, 56-60, 64-65, 78, 80, 94, 118, 164-166, 168, 170, 184, 195, 250-253, 261

Elijah (prophet), 71

Elizabeth I, Queen, 164, 173

Elohim (name of God), 2, 40, 248, 252

Elohim Gibor, 40

Elohim Tzabaoth, 40

Emerald (stone), 20, 60, 74, 79, 81, 127-128, 260, 263, 266

Emerald Tablet, 20

Enochian diaries, 163, 165, 210

Enochian Magick of Dr. John Dee, The (James), 182, 186

Enochian language, 164, 182, 216

Enochian magic, 66, 163-164, 173, 178-179, 187, 196, 199, 210, 221, 231, 237

Ensigns (Banners), Enochian, 171, 179-182, 194-195, 198-199, 261

Entropy, 235

Ephod—see Breastplate of Aaron, 48, 77-78, 153

Epiphanius, 4

Esther, Book Of, 203

Euclid, 55

Evangelists, four, 14

Eve, 244, 246

Evocation, 186, 198, 210, 231

Exodus, Book Of, 2, 63, 77, 79-80, 82, 88, 246, 259

Exorcism, 52, 89

Exorcists, Jewish, 89, 148

Ezekiel (prophet), 48, 150, 220, 245, 253

First-born males, 72

Fivefold Name—see Pentagrammaton

Flame, altar, 111

Flames, Burning (angels), 64-65, 191-192, 203, 229

Fludd, Robert (writer), 243

Franck, Adolphe (writer), 243

Freemasonry, 4, 249

Gabriel (angel), 105, 112-114, 149

Garnet (stone), 79, 129-130, 263

Gates To the Old City (Patai), 40, 42, 88, 90

Gates, twelve, 48, 73, 153

Geburah (5th Sephirah), 8-9, 12, 40, 105, 108, 150-151, 222, 225, 227

Gedulah (4th Sephirah, alternate name), 106, 108

Genesis, Book Of, 37, 39, 80, 201, 208

Geomancy (Earth divination), 28-29

Gerizim, Mount (biblical), 69-71

Gilgal (stone circle), 69

Ginsburg, Christian D. (writer), 63, 88, 245

Giorgi, Francesco (writer), 48, 56

Gnomes (Earth elementals), 51

Gnosis, 56, 103, 235-236

Gnosticism, 3, 184, 186, 189, 232, 234-236

God-forms, 147, 149

Gods of the Egyptians, The (Budge), 182

Golden Dawn, Hermetic Order of the, 4, 164, 187, 270

Golden Dawn, The (Regardie),44, 147, 165, 189

Golem, 39-42

Gray, William (writer), 254

Griffin, T. Wynne (writer), 196

Guardians of the quarters—see Angels, four

Guide for the Perplexed, The (Maimonides), 241

Gurdjieff, G. J. (mystic)

Hadit, 249

Headband, black, 161

Headband, white, 160-161

Hebrew letters, 1, 4, 10, 14, 39, 47, 50-53, 56, 62, 97-98, 104, 117, 156, 212, 249, 270

Helena (First Thought), 234

Helix, double, 19-20, 22

Heptagram, 50, 53

Herb, magic, 94

Hermaphrodite Christ, 152

Hermes, serpent staff of, 20-23

Hexagram, 86, 89, 94

Hexagrams (I Ching), 27

Hieroglyphic Monad, The (Dee), xv, 55-59, 61-63, 65-66, 99, 194, 224

High priest, Hebrew, 259

History of the Occult (Griffon), 196

Hod (8th Sephirah), 8-9, 12, 40, 227

Holy Kabbalah, The (Waite), 225, 241, 252

Holy water—see Water, consecrated

Horeb, Mount (biblical), 2-3

Horns, altar, 71, 74

Horus, eyes of, 182, 232

Hours, twenty-four, 35, 59, 168, 197, 223, 257

Houses, astrological, 194

Hyacinth (stone), 204-206, 208, 266

Hyacinth pillars, 204, 206, 208

Hyacinthus, 205

I Ching, 27

IAO, 3

IHShVH (name of God), 47-48, 50-54, 57, 65-66, 109, 115, 117-118, 152, 160-161, 166

IHV (name of God), 3, 17, 240

IHVShH (name of God), 50-52, 66, 109-110, 115, 117-118, 152, 160-161, 166

Instruments, ritual, 106, 108

Intelligences, 35, 52

Intelligences, Banner, 34

Intelligences, celestial, 38, 42

Invocation, 32, 52, 107, 112, 118, 148, 155, 160

Irenaeus (writer), 234

Isaac (patriarch), 3, 72, 239, 248

Isaiah (prophet), 62-63, 150, 208, 259

Isis Unveiled (Blavatsky), 246

Jacinth (stone), 74, 79, 81, 135-136, 213, 260, 263

Jacob (patriarch), 3, 71, 80-81, 84-85, 236, 239

James, Geoffrey (writer), 95, 166, 184, 189, 203, 214, 226

Jasper (stone), 60, 74, 79, 81, 133-134, 260, 263, 266

Jehovah (name of God), 3-4, 49, 245-251, 253-254

Jerada (wife of Solomon), 94

Jeremiah (prophet), 73, 150

Jerusalem, new, 73, 153, 229-230, 233

Jesus—see Christ

Jewels, Solomon's four, 91-92, 94

Jewels, twelve—see Stones, twelve

Jinn (spirits), 88-89, 92, 150

Job (biblical), 104, 141, 226, 228

John the Apostle, 37, 141-142

John the Divine, Saint, 14, 66, 153-154, 237

Jordan River, 67-72, 194

Joshua (biblical), 67-72, 82, 194

Jove (god), 3, 242

Judaeus—see Philo Judaeus

Jung, Carl (writer), 15-16, 93

Jupiter (planet), 17, 50-51, 58, 99, 149, 194

Kabbalah (Scholem), 3, 100, 108

Kabbalah Denudata (Rosenroth), 269

Kabbalah Unveiled, The (Mathers), 4, 247, 269

Kabbalah, 3-4, 7-8, 39, 41-42, 44, 47-48, 56, 62-63, 74, 80, 88, 99-100, 108, 120, 200, 208, 212, 217, 222, 225, 241, 244-245, 247, 252, 255, 269, 271

Kabbalah, The (Ginsburg), 63, 88

Kabbalists, Christian, xiv, 47-48, 50, 56, 65, 152

Kaplan, Aryeh (writer), 63, 80, 86, 240

Karma, 74, 235

Keats, John (poet), 230

Kedushah, 62-63

Kelley, Edward (seer and alchemist), 163-168, 170-171, 173, 178, 181-182, 184-186, 243

Kerubic Squares, 196

Kether (1st Sephirah), 8-12, 40-41, 44, 108, 247-249, 255

Key of Solomon the King, The (ed. Mathers), 89, 241

Keys, Enochian, xv-xvi, 64, 66, 164, 182-187, 189-237

Kings of the Watchtowers, 179, 181-182, 191, 216

Kings, First Book Of, 14, 71, 74, 90

Knox, Ronald (writer), 259-260

Koran, The, 87

Kundalini, 200

Ladder of Lights, The (Gray), 8, 254

Lamps, seven, 60, 99, 149, 200

Lapis lazuli (stone), 79, 260

LAShTAL, 200, 217

Law of Moses, 68

Laycock, Donald C. (writer), 164, 189, 214, 217, 226

Lesser Key of Solomon, The, 89

Levi, Eliphas (Alphonse Louis Constant), 69-70, 80-81, 85, 127-128, 239, 263, 266

Leviticus, Book Of, 82

Ligure (stone), 79, 260

Little Book of Protection, 92

Living creatures, four—see Beasts, four

Loew, Rabbi (Kabbalist), 39-42

Lucifer, 148, 181, 233

Luke (Evangelist), 14, 268

Macrocosm, 12, 37, 85

Madimi (Enochian spirit), 186, 191, 193, 207, 215, 236-237

Magic mirror, 90

Magick in Theory and Practice (Crowley), 250

Magus, The (Barrett), 17, 50, 65, 105, 122, 234, 261, 269-271

Maimonides, Moses (writer), 3, 241

Malbush (garment), 10

Malkuth (10th Sephirah), 8-10, 12, 40, 108, 248, 251, 253

Mandalas, 16, 170-171

Mann, A. T. (writer), 103

Mansions of the Moon, 204, 218

Mantras, 42-43

Mark (Evangelist), 14, 61, 73, 104, 209, 211, 221, 226, 268

Mark of God, 73, 221, 226

Mars (planet), 17, 50-51, 58, 95, 99, 148-149, 194

Masters of the Name—see Ba'alai Shem

Mathers, George Samuel Liddell (Mac-Gregor), 4, 147, 165, 241, 247, 269-271

Matthew (Evangelist), 14, 143-144, 263, 266-268

Maximilian II, German Emperor, 55

McKenzie, John L. (writer), 71

Meditation and the Bible (Kaplan), 80, 86

Meditation, 39, 41, 86, 103, 159-160

Mercury (planet), 17, 50-51, 55, 99-100, 149, 193-194

Messiah, 8, 53, 99-100, 108, 117-118, 149-152, 158-160, 190, 196, 198, 200-202, 204, 207, 226, 232-233, 243

Metatron (angel), 94, 149-150, 243
Michael (angel), 94-95, 105, 112, 114-115, 148-149, 181, 205, 233
Microcosm, 12, 37-38, 85
Microprosopus (Son), 193, 247-248
Microprosopus, Bride of (Daughter), 193, 229, 248-249, 251
Millstones, 207, 209, 213
Mistletoe, 213
Mithridates, Flavius (kabbalist), 48
Monad, Hieroglyphic, xvii, 55-59, 65-66, 194, 197
Moon, 17, 50-51, 56-59, 66, 81, 84, 98-104, 116-118, 120, 124, 126, 128, 130, 132, 134, 136, 138, 140, 142, 144, 146, 149, 182, 186, 190-191, 193-194, 196-197, 202, 204-205, 218, 224, 229, 232, 236
Mortlake, 163, 184
Moses, 2-3, 5, 48, 67-69, 73, 77, 82, 87, 90, 150, 154, 194, 225, 234, 239-243, 246, 271
Moss, 207, 209
Mother letters, Hebrew, 41
Mother of Madimi, 186, 191, 193
Myer, Isaac (writer), 239, 248
Mysteria Magica (Denning and Phillips), 189

Nalvage (Enochian angel), 164, 173, 181-182, 186, 211, 217, 219, 225, 236
Names of power—see Words of power, 39, 44, 53, 92, 115, 155, 161, 196
Nebuchardrezzar, King (biblical), 73
Netzach (7th Sephirah), 8-9, 12, 40
New Magus, The (Tyson), 17, 50, 105, 122, 261, 269-271
New Millennium Magic (Tyson)—see *New Magus, The* (Tyson)
Nigredo (alchemical), 93
Nuit, 249

O.T.O. (Ordo Templi Orientis), 169, 172, 200
Oak, 211-213
Occult Philosophy, Three Books of (Agrippa), 38, 49, 61, 80, 242, 265-266, 269
Odysseus, 226

Olive tree, 200
Olives, Mount of, 199-200
OM, 43
Onyx (stone), 72, 78-81, 83-84, 86, 143-144, 260, 263
Onyx shoulder stones, 84, 86
Oracle, 39, 42, 77, 82-86
Osiris, aeon of, 25
Ouspensky, P. D. (writer), 19, 250
Oxen, twelve, 73

Papus (Gerard Encausse), 243, 249
Paradise—see Eden, Garden of, 15, 245
Patai, Raphael (writer), 40, 42, 88, 90
Paths, kabbalistic—see Channels
Paul (apostle), 4, 63, 148, 245, 247, 253, 269
Pearce, Alfred J. (astrologer), 81
Penelope (wife of Odysseus), 226
Pentagram, 50-52, 89-90, 92, 94, 152, 158-159, 165-166
Pentagrammaton, 47, 54, 56-57, 65, 115, 117-118, 166
Pentateuch and Rashi's Commentary, 82, 259
Peridot (stone), 79, 260
Permutations of IHVH—see Banners
Peter (apostle), 49, 123-124, 263, 266, 268
Philo Judaeus (writer), 1-2, 83, 240
Philosopher's stone, 16, 185
Philosophia Moysaica (Fludd), 243
Pico della Mirandola (writer), 47-48, 56, 241, 265
Pillars, twelve, 73
Plagues, biblical, 206, 208, 237
Planets, 17, 49-50, 53, 56, 58, 92, 94, 99, 101, 103, 149, 151, 165, 232
Portae Lucis (Ricius), 48
Possession, 4, 53, 147, 152, 165, 184, 187, 209, 247
Precession of the equinoxes, 224
Priests, Hebrew, 44, 254
Prima materia (alchemical), 93
Prima, Diane de (writer), 56
Princes of the Watchtowers, 216
Principles, three—see Qualities, astrological
Projection, ritual, 109-110, 112
Pronunciation of IHVH, 1, 4, 48, 123-124, 247

Prophets, biblical, 49, 62, 71, 73, 82, 85, 88, 126, 150, 152, 208, 210, 212, 214-215, 220, 234

Prose Edda, The (Sturluson), 219

Psalms, Book Of, 106

Psychology and Alchemy (Jung), 15-16, 93

Ptah (god), 232

Purification—see Cleansing, 1, 38-39, 52, 103, 106, 108, 111, 154, 203-204, 209

Pythagoras (philosopher), 14, 19, 245

Q. B. L., or The Bride's Reception (Achad), 251

Qualities, astrological, 17, 57-58, 122

Quarters, four—see Directions

Queen of Heaven, 186, 197, 234

Ra (god), 172, 177, 232

Raphael (angel), 40, 88, 101, 105, 112, 114, 149, 166-171, 173-174, 178, 181, 195-196, 261

Raphael's Ephemeris, 101

Rashi (writer), 82-83, 90, 259-260

Regardie, Israel (writer), 44, 147, 165-166, 189, 252

Reuchlin, Johannes (writer), 48, 50, 56, 63, 265

Revelation, Book Of, 62, 153, 212

Ricius, Paulus (Kabbalist), 48

Ring of Solomon, 87, 89, 91-95

Ring, exorcism, 89

Rings, Banner, 97-104, 105-118

Rings for the Finger (Kuntz), 90, 100-102, 109, 117

Rod of iron, 151, 208

Rosenburg, Judah (writer), 42

Rosenroth, Knorr von (writer), 269

Round Art, The (Mann), 103

Ruach ha-Qadesh, 86

Ruby (stone), 79, 152, 260

Runes, 212

Sachiel (angel of Jupiter), 149

Sacrifice, 68, 71-73, 86, 100, 140, 240

Salamanders (Fire elementals), 51

Samael (angel of Mars), 149

Samuel, First Book Of, 4, 56, 254

Sapphire (stone), 74, 79, 81, 88, 90, 94, 131-132, 205, 260, 263, 266

Sapphire, Solomon's, 88

Sard (stone), 78, 81, 123-124, 260, 263

Sardis (biblical), 153

Satan, 179, 186, 205-206, 208, 215-216, 233

Saturn (planet), 17, 50-51, 99, 149, 194

Saul (king of Israel), 82, 164

Saul, Barnabas (seer), 164

Scepter, golden, 159

Scholem, Gershom (writer), 3, 100, 108, 239, 255

Scorpions, 211, 213-214, 220

Sea, molten, 73

Seal, Solomon's, 89, 91, 93

Seniors—see Elders

Sepher Yetzirah (Book of Formation), 3, 7-8, 17, 240

Sephiroth, 8-12, 35, 40-41, 74, 83, 90, 99, 106, 108, 150, 152, 181, 190, 200, 205, 212-213, 227, 239, 245, 247-249, 251

Sermon on the Mount, 200

Serpent(s), 20-21, 88, 202, 205, 208, 213-214, 217, 234, 246

777 and Other Qabalistic Writings (Crowley), 257-258

Shaddai (name of God), 3, 40, 48, 248

Shakta—see Shiva

Shakti, 43

Shamir, 90, 92, 94

Shao Yung Sequence, 27-28

Shem ha-Mephoresh, 1, 63

Shemittah (cosmic cycle), 11-12

Shield of Solomon, 90, 92

Shiva, 43

Sickle(s), 193-194, 209, 213, 223

Sigils, Banner, 32, 34-35, 120-122

Signs—see Zodiac

Simeon the Righteous (high priest), 252

Simon Magus, 234

Simon the Gnostic, 234

Solomon, King, 13

Sophia, 234-235

Soter (Savior), 235

Soul of the World, 200, 213, 215, 225, 233-235, 243

Spheres, heavenly, 8, 232

Spiral, 22, 45, 109-110, 117, 152, 154, 182

Spirits of the Earth, 35, 50-51, 100, 171, 200

Spirits, 17, 31, 34-35, 39, 44, 51-53, 60-61, 64, 70-71, 87-89, 91-94, 99, 114-115, 119, 130, 134, 148-149, 156, 159, 164, 171-178, 182, 184, 190-191, 196, 198-204, 206-207, 218-219, 221, 231-232, 236-237, 244

Spirits, Banner, 17, 32, 34-35, 114, 130

Spirits, Enochian—see Angels, Enochian

Spirits, evil, 52, 89, 93-94, 134

Spirits, planetary, 35, 99

Spirits, seven fiery—see Lamps, seven

Square, 13-16, 24-25, 31, 71, 73-74, 95, 97, 106, 108, 139, 145-146, 154, 164-166, 178, 197, 242, 246

Standards, Enochian—see Ensigns, Enochian

Stones, twelve, 67-75, 82, 86, 92, 153

Sturluson, Snorri (writer), 219

Sun, 17, 42, 50-51, 56-59, 66, 81, 84, 88, 95, 98-104, 110, 117-118, 120, 123, 125, 127, 129, 131, 133, 135, 137, 139, 141, 143, 149-150, 168, 182, 186, 190-191, 193-194, 196-197, 204, 219, 224, 229, 232

Swallowing Solomon's ring, 92-93

Sword(s), two-edged, 150-151, 207-208

Sword, 5, 95, 148, 150-151, 155, 159, 190, 207-208, 222

Swords (Enochian angels), 16, 191, 207, 219-220, 251

Sylphs (Air elementals), 51

Symbolism of the Tarot, The (Ouspensky), 197, 250-251

Synchronicity, 66

Table, Great, 164, 166-174, 178, 184-185, 195-196, 198, 202, 220, 223, 261-262

Table, Restored Great, 170-172, 174

Table, Revised Great, 88, 164-166, 181

Tablet of Union, 164, 166, 183-184

Talbot, Edward—see Kelley, Edward

Talismans, 32, 90, 259

Talmud, The, 87, 90, 92, 243

Tarot Of the Bohemians, The (Papus), 243, 249

Tarot, 16, 25, 165, 197, 243, 249-251, 254

Telocvovim (Him-that-is-fallen), 181

Tetractys, 14, 19, 246

Tetragram, 30-31, 34, 156, 244-246, 255

Tetrahedron, 23-24, 31

Tew (god), 50, 148

Textbook of Astrology, The (Pearce), 81

Thaddeus (apostle), 133-134, 263, 266, 268

Thaddeus (Jesuit priest), 39

Theatre of Terrestrial Astronomy (Kelley), 243

Thelema, cult of, 200

Theodoret, 4

Thoth (god), 148, 244

Thoth, The Book of (Crowley), 17, 25

Thousand Nights and a Night, Book of the (Burton), 87, 89, 91

Throne of God, 62, 74-75, 99, 112, 114-115, 149-150, 156-157, 200, 209, 212

Throne of Solomon, 74

Thummim—see Urim and Thummim

Tiphareth (6th Sephirah), 8-10, 12, 40, 108, 150-151, 181, 253

Topaz (stone), 74, 79, 81, 125-126, 260, 263, 266

Transcendental Magic (Levi), 244

Tree of Knowledge, 100

Tree of Life, The (Regardie), 74, 100, 213, 252

Tree, Sephirothic, 8, 10, 12, 40, 212, 222

Tribes, twelve, 67, 71, 73-74, 78, 80, 83, 92, 194, 203

True and Faithful Relation, A (ed. Casaubon), 164, 168, 179-180, 189, 210-211, 215, 221, 223, 236

Tziruph, 56

Undines (Water elementals), 51

Uriel (angel), 105, 112-115, 149, 226

Urim and Thummim, 80, 82-86, 156, 194, 224

Uzza (fallen angel), 93

Venus (planet), 17, 50-51, 99, 149, 194, 205

Vespasian (Roman emperor), 89

Vials of wrath, 208

Vibrating names, 5, 7, 37-39, 41-45, 50, 52-54, 109-110, 112, 114, 117, 182

Virgins, house of, 202-203, 217

Vision, Kelley's Enochian, 168, 170, 178, 181-182, 192, 194, 196, 210, 216, 223

Vita Mosis (Philo), 240

Vortex, occult, 41, 51-53, 109, 113, 116, 118, 155, 160, 182

Waite, Arthur Edward (writer), 241, 243-244, 251

Watchtowers, Enochian, 66, 163-175, 177-179, 181-183, 185-187, 191-192, 195-196, 199-200, 202, 204, 206, 223, 236-237, 261

Water of Life, 16, 74

Water, consecrated, 106, 108, 111-112, 114, 154, 158

Westcott, W. Wynn (writer), 8, 165, 240

Wilhelm, Hellmut (writer), 27

Will, 12, 15, 22, 25, 28, 34, 37, 39, 44-46, 49-50, 52, 54, 56, 59, 63, 65, 73, 78, 80, 82, 86, 94, 97-98, 103-106, 108-111, 114-118, 120-122, 124, 134, 146, 148-149, 152-154, 156-158, 160, 166, 170-171, 180-181, 186-187, 189, 195-198, 202, 206, 209-210, 212, 215-216, 222, 225, 227-229, 232-237, 242-243, 246-247, 252, 255, 257-258

Winds, 3, 35, 64-66, 87-88, 91, 97-99, 105, 111, 113, 119-121, 149, 154, 179, 181, 183, 191-192, 257, 263

Wings of the Winds (angels), 35, 64-66, 97-99, 119-146, 149, 179, 181, 183, 191-192, 257

Woden (god), 50, 219

Words (names) of power, 40-45, 51, 53, 92, 95, 115, 118, 147, 155, 161, 192

Wormwood, 207, 209

Yah (name of God), 40, 248-249

Yaldabaoth, 184, 234-235

Yeheshuah—see IHShVH

Yehovashah—see IHVShH

Yesod (9th Sephirah), 8-9, 12, 40

Yetzirah (Formative World of the Kabbalah), 3, 7-8, 17, 240, 253

Yin-Yang, 26-27

Zechariah, Book of, 200

Zimzum (contraction), 10

Zodiac, 17-18, 26, 34-35, 38, 41, 49, 56-57, 59, 61, 79-81, 85, 92, 94, 98-103, 106, 120-122, 149, 165-166, 193-197, 208, 224, 247, 258, 261, 263, 267, 269

Zohar, The (Book of Splendor), 8, 89, 93, 252

ORDER LLEWELLYN BOOKS TODAY!

Llewellyn publishes hundreds of books on your favorite subjects! To get these exciting books, including the ones on the following pages, check your local bookstore or order them directly from Llewellyn.

Order Online:

Visit our website at www.llewellyn.com, select your books, and order them on our secure server.

Order by Phone:

- Call toll-free within the U.S. at 1-877-NEW-WRLD (1-877-639-9753). Call toll-free within Canada at 1-866-NEW-WRLD (1-866-639-9753)
- We accept VISA, MasterCard, and American Express

Order by Mail:

Send the full price of your order (MN residents add 7% sales tax) in U.S. funds, plus postage & handling to:

Llewellyn Worldwide
P.O. Box 64383, Dept. 0-7387-0528-4
St. Paul, MN 55164-0383, U.S.A.

Postage & Handling:

Standard (U.S., Mexico, & Canada). If your order is:
Up to $25.00, add $3.50
$25.01 - $48.99, add $4.00
$49.00 and over, FREE STANDARD SHIPPING
(Continental U.S. orders ship UPS. AK, HI, PR, & P.O. Boxes ship USPS 1st class. Mex. & Can. ship PMB.)

International Orders:

Surface Mail: For orders of $20.00 or less, add $5 plus $1 per item ordered. For orders of $20.01 and over, add $6 plus $1 per item ordered.

Air Mail:

Books: Postage & Handling is equal to the total retail price of all books in the order.
Non-book items: Add $5 for each item.

Orders are processed within 2 business days. Please allow for normal shipping time.
Postage and handling rates subject to change.

Familiar Spirits
A Practical Guide for Witches & Magicians

DONALD TYSON

For centuries, familiars have assumed many forms: the heavenly lover of the shaman, the wise imp of the witch, and the elemental companion of the theurgist. Their function, always, is to help the magician.

Many beginners find it difficult or impossible to make the initial link with a spirit. Renowned occultist Donald Tyson wrote *Familiar Spirits* in response to repeated requests for an effective technique that does not require expertise in formal ritual, astrology, or the Kabbalah. Here he unveils his unique system for generating spirit sigils based on a set of symbols called power glyphs. Familiars made with this method become like magical children, doing everything in their power to fulfill your goals.

0-7387-0421-0
312 pp., 6 x 9, illus. $14.95

To order, call 1-877-NEW-WRLD
Prices subject to change without notice

The Magician's Workbook
Practicing the Rituals of the Western Tradition

DONALD TYSON

Contains everything that beginners need to start their esoteric training! *The Magician's Workbook* has a single purpose: to present a graded and integrated series of practical exercises designed to teach the essentials of ritual magic.

It contains no history or theory—just forty exercises that anyone can do without prior training, special tools, or costly materials. The content ranges from simple mental exercises to complete rituals that form templates for future work in Western magic.

These exercises do not merely teach—they transform. When practiced regularly, they cause changes in the body, brain, perceptions, emotions, and the will—changes necessary for the successful working of magic in any of its ancient or modern traditions.

0-7387-0000-2
352 pp., 7 ½ x 9 ⅛, illus. $17.95

To order, call 1-877-NEW-WRLD
Prices subject to change without notice

Sexual Alchemy
Magical Intercourse with Spirits

DONALD TYSON

Sexual Alchemy is a system of ritual magic that allows you to initiate and sustain satisfying erotic relationships with loving spirits who are the active agents of the Goddess, the creative mother of the universe.

At the heart of sexual alchemy lies the most potent and jealously guarded of all occult mysteries—the method for using the forces liberated by the union with spiritual beings for self-empowerment and personal transformation.

Erotic unions with gods, angels, and demons have occurred throughout human history in all cultures, but the methods have been suppressed and lost, save for references and fragments in ancient alchemical and magical texts.

Sexual Alchemy is the first book exclusively devoted to a detailed examination of sex between human beings and spirits, and the uniquely transformed products of the human body that such unions generate. Most other books on sex magic focus on the Tantra of India and Tibet, or the Western magical practice of auto-eroticism.

1-56718-741-2
 408 pp., 7 ½ x 9 ⅛, 17 illus.   **$19.95**

To order, call 1-877-NEW-WRLD
Prices subject to change without notice

Scrying for Beginners
Tapping into the Supersensory Powers of Your Subconscious

DONALD TYSON

Scrying for Beginners is for anyone who longs to sit down before the mirror or crystal and lift the rolling grey clouds that obscure their depths. Scrying is a psychological technique to deliberately acquire information by extrasensory means through the unconscious mind. For the first time, all forms of scrying are treated in one easy-to-read, practical book. They include such familiar methods as crystal gazing, pendulums, black mirrors, Ouija™ boards, dowsing rods, aura reading, psychometry, automatic writing, and automatic speaking. Also treated are ancient techniques not widely known today, such as Babylonian oil scrying, fire gazing, Egyptian lamp scrying, water scrying, wind scrying, ink scrying, shell-hearing, and oracular dreaming.

1-56718-746-3
320 pp., 5 ⁹⁄₁₆ x 8, illus.   **$12.95**

To order, call 1-877-NEW-WRLD
Prices subject to change without notice

Enochian Magic for Beginners
The Original System for Angel Magick

DONALD TYSON

The most remarkable artifact in the entire history of spirit communication is the legacy of the Enochian angels, who presented themselves to the famed Elizabethan mathematician Dr. John Dee through his seer, the infamous alchemist Edward Kelley, between the years 1582–1589. Enochian Magic is a method for summoning and commanding angelic beings and demons, although the angels gave Dee strict instructions never to use the magick for evoking evil spirits. Now, *Enochian Magic for Beginners* provides this system in its complete and original form.

Newcomers to Enochian Magic will not find a clearer or more comprehensive overview. Experienced Enochian scholars will be pleasantly surprised by how many gaps in the communications have finally been filled. Donald Tyson gives all of the essential magical teachings of the angels along with the neccessary symbols, sigils and letter squares required to put these teachings into practice. More importantly, he explains how these sigils and squares were derived and what they signify.

1-56718-747-1
408 pp., 5 ³⁄₁₆ x 8, softcover $14.95

To order, call 1-877-NEW-WRLD
Prices subject to change without notice

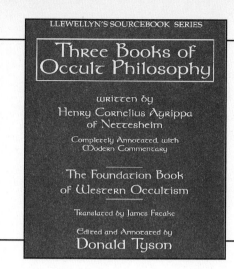

LLEWELLYN'S SOURCEBOOK SERIES

Three Books of
Occult Philosophy

written by
Henry Cornelius Agrippa
of Nettesheim

Completely Annotated, with
Modern Commentary

The Foundation Book
of Western Occultism

Translated by James Freake

Edited and Annotated by
Donald Tyson

The Three Books of Occult Philosophy

Completely Annotated, with Modern Commentary—The Foundation Book of Western Occultism

HENRY CORNELIUS AGRIPPA, EDITED AND ANNOTATED BY DONALD TYSON

Agrippa's *Three Books of Occult Philosophy* is the single most important text in the history of Western occultism. Occultists have drawn upon it for five centuries, although they rarely give it credit. First published in Latin in 1531 and translated into English in 1651, it has never been reprinted in its entirety since. Photocopies are hard to find and very expensive. Now, for the first time in 500 years, *Three Books of Occult Philosophy* will be presented as Agrippa intended. There were many errors in the original translation, but occult author Donald Tyson has made the corrections and has clarified the more obscure material with copious notes.

This is a necessary reference tool not only for all magicians, but also for scholars of the Renaissance, Neoplatonism, the Western Kabbalah, the history of ideas and sciences and the occult tradition. It is as practical today as it was 500 years ago.

0-87542-832-0
1,024 pp., 7 x 10 $39.95

To order, call 1-877-NEW-WRLD
Prices subject to change without notice

Ritual Magic
What It Is & How To Do It

DONALD TYSON

For thousands of years men and women have practiced it despite the severe repression of sovereigns and priests. Now, Ritual Magic takes you into the heart of that entrancing, astonishing, and at times mystifying secret garden of magic.

What is this ancient power? Where does it come from? How does it work? Is it mere myth and delusion, or can it truly move mountains and make the dead speak . . . bring rains from a clear sky and calm the seas . . . turn the outcome of great battles and call down the moon from heaven? Which part of the claims made for magic are true in the most literal sense, and which are poetic exaggerations that must be interpreted symbolically? How can magic be used to improve your life?

This book answers these and many other questions in a clear and direct manner. Its purpose is to separate the wheat from the chaff and make sense of the non-sense. It explains what the occult revival is all about, reveals the foundations of practical ritual magic, showing how modern occultism grew from a single root into a number of clearly defined esoteric schools and Pagan sects.

0-87542-835-5
288 pp., 6 x 9, illus. $12.95

To order, call 1-877-NEW-WRLD
Prices subject to change without notice

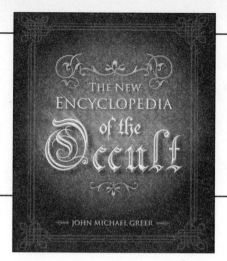

The New Encyclopedia Of The Occult

John Michael Greer

From "Aarab Zereq" to "Zos Kia Cultus," it's the most complete occult reference work on the market. With this one text, you will gain a thorough overview of the history and current state of the occult from a variety of North American and western European traditions. Its pages offer the essential knowledge you need to make sense of the occult, along with references for further reading if you want to learn more.

You will find the whole range of occult tradition, lore, history, philosophy, and practice in the Western world. *The New Encyclopedia of the Occult* includes magic, alchemy, astrology, divination, Tarot, palmistry, geomancy, magical orders such as the Golden Dawn and Rosicrucians, Wiccan, Thelema, Theosophy, modern Paganism, and biographies of important occultists.

1-56718-336-0
608 pp., 8 x 10 $29.95

To order, call 1-877-NEW-WRLD
Prices subject to change without notice

Magic Of Qabalah
Visions of the Tree of Life

KALA TROBE

This introduction to the Golden Dawn system of Qabalah covers the usual ground in an unusual way. It uses creative visualizations and analysis of mythologies and tarot symbolism to bring the reader into a direct, personal experience of this universal system. Use the exercises for specific purposes as diverse as physical/spiritual courage (Geburah), integration (Binah), and magickal foundation building (Malkuth).

The introduction provides a condensed history of the Qabalah, along with a quick trip up the Tree of Life to familiarize the novice with the system, plus information on its metaphysical context and use of tarot attributions.

Ten chapters follow, one for each Sephirah, containing an exploration of its traits and contemporary application, a brief description of the Path by which one might mentally arrive at the desired destination, and information on the God names, angels, and symbols. Each chapter culminates in a guided creative visualization.

0-7387-0002-9
336 pp., 6 x 9 $14.95

To order, call 1-877-NEW-WRLD
Prices subject to change without notice

Simplified Qabala Magic

TED ANDREWS

The mystical Qabala is one of the most esoteric yet practical systems for expanding your consciousness and unfolding your spiritual gifts. Within its Tree of Life lies a map to the wisdom of the ancients, the powers of the universe and to ourselves. As the earliest form of Jewish mysticism, it is especially suited to the rational Western mind.

The Qabala has traditionally been presented as mysterious and complex. *Simplified Qabala Magic* offers a basic understanding of what the Qabala is and how it operates. It provides techniques for utilizing the forces within the system to bring peace, healing, power, love, and magic into your life.

- Presents the basics of the Qabala from a non-denominational background
- Provides sufficient working knowledge of the Tree of Life without intimidating, unnecessary detail
- Includes easy-to-follow meditative techniques
- The perfect introduction for those who wish to pursue the complex study of ceremonial magick
- Introduces the Qabalistic Cross and the Middle Pillar exercises for strength and protection, along with the basics of Pathworking

0-7387-0394-X
5 ³⁄₁₆ x 8, 240 pp., appendix, bibliog., index $9.95

To order, call 1-877-NEW-WRLD
Prices subject to change without notice

The Essential Golden Dawn
An Introduction to High Magic

CHIC CICERO AND
SANDRA TABATHA CICERO

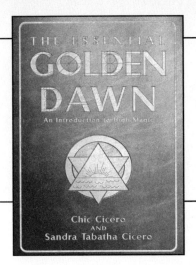

Is the Golden Dawn system for you?

Today the Golden Dawn is one of the most sought-after and respected systems of magic in the world. Over a century old, it's considered the capstone of the Western Esoteric Tradition. Yet many of the available books on the subject are too complex or overwhelming for readers just beginning to explore alternative spiritual paths.

The Essential Golden Dawn is for those who simply want to find out what the Golden Dawn is and what it has to offer. It answers questions such as: What is Hermeticism? How does magic work? Who started the Golden Dawn? What are its philosophies and principles? It helps readers determine whether this system is for them, and then it guides them into further exploration as well as basic ritual work.

0-7387-0310-9
360 pp., 6 x 9 $16.95

To order, call 1-877-NEW-WRLD
Prices subject to change without notice